Additional Praise for *The Body of Money*

"In our world today, money is the only thing I know of that touches every aspect of what it means to be human. Despite all the writings about the subject of money, incredibly, no one, has spoken to the subject and importance of our physical relationship with money, until now. It's long past due if we are to affect real sustainable change in people's lives."

—Ted Klontz, Ph.D., Associate Professor of
Practice Creighton University, Heider College of Business,
Founder of the Financial Psychology Institute®,
Co-Author of seven psychology of money related books

"Gayle Colman's insightful book brings sanity and depth to the often insane and superficial world of money. In her tapestry of wisdom and practical advice, Gayle skillfully teaches the reader how to integrate our body, mind, and heart into our personal finance. I highly recommend this book to all of those who want to dive deeper into the mysteries of money."

—Dustin DiPerna, Adjunct Professor Stanford University;
Author of *Streams of Wisdom*

"Gayle Colman is a pioneer in integrating mind, heart, and body to personal finance. She teaches that advisors "can only take clients as far as we've gone ourselves," and she can take people far. Once again, she is leading the way with this experiential exploration of the connection of our bodies and emotions to our financial behavior. "

—Rick Kahler, MS, CFP, CFT,
Co-Author of *The Financial Wisdom of Ebeneezer Scrooge*.

"Gayle Colman's new book is a breakthrough in an area where many people need a breakthrough. Gayle's special domain is how to integrate mind AND body, so that we come to the subject of money with a whole-person perspective. For those who think a book about money might be dull, Gayle Colman's book is anything but! I urge you to read it and put her breakthrough tools to work for you."

—Gay Hendricks, Ph.D., Author of *The Big Leap*

"*The Body of Money* gives us what we didn't think to ask for but desperately need: A way to break the industrialized, intellectualized shell around finance so that we can integrate money into our actual, real lives. Gayle Colman deftly and lyrically transforms money from something to be 'smart' about to a tool for greater insight and wisdom, and in so doing, returns us to our own power and agency."

—Terri Trespicio, Author of *Unfollow Your
Passion: How to Create a Life that Matters to You*

The BODY of MONEY

The BODY of MONEY

A Self-Help Guide to Creating Sustainable Wealth through Innate Intelligence

Gayle Colman

WILEY

Published by John Wiley & Sons, Inc., Hoboken, New Jersey.
Published simultaneously in Canada.

For general information on our other products and services or for technical support, please contact our Customer Care Department within the United States at (800) 762-2974, outside the United States at (317) 572-3993 or fax (317) 572-4002.

Wiley also publishes its books in a variety of electronic formats. Some content that appears in print may not be available in electronic formats. For more information about Wiley products, visit our web site at www.wiley.com.

Library of Congress Cataloging-in-Publication Data is Available:

ISBN 9781394166558 (Hardback)
ISBN 9781394166633 (ePDF)
ISBN 9781394166640 (epub)

COVER DESIGN: PAUL McCARTHY
COVER ART: © GETTY IMAGES | BAAC3NES

SKY10039735_120822

To
all the explorers
who courageously blaze
a trail for others to follow,

and

for the precious
loves in my life ~
Rich, Katelyn, and Knight.
You fill my vessel with
love, joy, and magic.

Contents

Preface

*T*he *Body of Money* captures our attention to bring us face to face with Somatic Finance®, which we have been avoiding for centuries. Ostensibly two separate human experiences now stand side by side, walk hand in hand, leading you forward through the work of Somatic Finance®.

Somatic Finance. These two words together turn heads and squish foreheads. In over a decade of using these words together in conversation, writing, coaching, and teaching, the response is similar, "What does that mean? I've never heard of that before."

Somatic is straightforward. From the Greek, it means "relating to the body."

Finance is many things, but generally it means "relating to money."

But together?

Somatically oriented folks ask, What does finance have to do with the body?

Financially oriented folks don't ask. They state, "The rational intellectual brain is the *only* place for money."

When you read the words *Somatic Finance,* what do you notice in your body?

Do you feel tension in your upper back?

Is there a sudden fluttering in your belly?

Is your head shaking, lips pursing, nah!

Is a knot arising on the side of your neck or a throb in your right temple?

Do you find yourself dismissing sensations almost as soon as they arise? Only to be replaced by the thought that money must be figured out, it is not easy; or: *I must listen to someone more knowledgeable—my parent, a grandparent, an advisor, or someone; who knows?*

Even as your body offers a few clues and sensations, do you cling to a belief that a subject so complicated as money really needs more than the body; it needs knowledge?

You're so right.

My friends, our body and brain have never been separate. Even on the subject of money.

Finance needs our body along with our brain.

Finance in our modern world is limited. We've managed to get by, and some might say create a few messes, with knowledge, concepts, and ideas—driven from fear, uncertainty, and doubt. While some have thrived, many steep in a field of panicked adrenaline. Including the body when working with money offers us opportunities and a new way of being, a new way forward.

Somatic Finance gives access to the best decision-making tools to meet new realities from wholeness—with integrity and keener insights—including love, compassion, generosity, and creativity for the good of all humanity.

Simply stated, Somatic Finance connects the brilliance of our brain, the integrity of our belly, with the generosity of the heart.

Our body is, and always has been, present and alive, but we have severed it from our awareness in deference to limiting stories, ideas, and beliefs about money.

The Seed of Somatic Finance

Throughout the early 2000s, I asked my financial planning colleagues when we were going to bring the wisdom of the body into matters of money. Money and the body had been my focus for over three decades, like two streams running side by side. I'd wondered for years when these water flows would merge. Wouldn't it be great to access our body intelligence to improve our money relationship? I'd spoken about it. I'd written about it. I'd trained in it. But nothing moved.

Then the words Somatic Finance flashed into my awareness. Seriously, it was like something pried my skull open and permanently planted a seed.

Once planted in my mind, the Somatic Finance seed nourished herself with tears before sprouting in the heart. Not long after the words arrived, I was flying home to Boston sitting next to my dear friend Anna. She asked me a simple question.

"Gayle, what's your work in the world?"

After my three sentence well-articulated (sort of) elongated elevator speech, she said, with her hands and words, "That's floating everywhere and says nothing."

I remember her facial expression. It said, bullshit and WTF? I tried again.

"I don't know what this is exactly," I replied, "but the phrase *Somatic Finance* swarms my mind. It excites me and terrifies me." I spoke with my eyes lowered.

I looked up and she blurted, "That's landing! Right here!" pointing to my heart.

I burst into tears. Somatic Finance began to sprout with my tears of recognition that something so vital and important to life was being activated in my being. I did not ask to have this move me. But it did. So much so that I never let go.

The sprouted Somatic Finance seed didn't let go of me either.

Over more than a decade, Somatic Finance and I rooted together, penetrating deep into rich soil, forming invisible connections like trees and fungi beneath the earth. We grew up together reaching toward the sky as a solid trunk, building a vertical foundation for branches and shoots to follow.

As I built my own muscles through training in integral coaching, breath and bodywork, apprenticing for years in conscious living and leadership, somatic meditation, and serving in leadership roles in my profession, I brought those two streams of money and body together, being my first student. On my journey, my confidence and skills evolved, and I started offering Somatic Finance practices for my Integral Wealth Coaching clients and weaving somatic awareness with my financial planning clients. I created MoneyMoves®, a deck of cards and a friendly curriculum to help people engage money with less fear and more trust. Years of workshops, field play, writing, blogging, deep and wide conversations, exploration, and training filled my life and work. This work stirred my passion to write seriously. The book you're holding now is the result.

While the seed of Somatic Finance planted in me as a working adult in my mind, a different seed planted in my heart as a child began to crack as a junior in college reviewing insurance policies in Dr. O'Toole's risk management class at Auburn University.

As my mind drew in the concepts and information about homeowners, liability, automobile, health, and life insurance, I was keenly aware of the practical need for knowledge in regular financial decisions—for everyone! This question churned: what are my friends going to do with their liberal arts degrees? They know nothing about these financial matters.

I was concerned about people who did not receive this basic training until I spoke with my aunt visiting us from the West Coast during a spring break. When I answered her question about my career pursuits and told her that I wanted to help people make wise financial decisions, citing my recent class experience, she said, "Gayle, you want to be a financial planner." Great! I was delighted to know the name for my career interests.

My quest to land my first job after college was launched. It took me from the west coast of Florida up to Boston. Not knowing a soul, but certain that my destiny lay in a strong financial center, I packed my car and drove north, to my father's chagrin and parting words, "You're going to freeze your fanny off." I did drive north. And I can assure you my father's fears were unfounded.

I found my first real job with a small boutique financial planning firm. Two years with this firm in the early 80s, when limited partnerships and tax write-offs were the rage, was sufficient time to learn the foundation of financial planning, earn my CFP® designation, and the limitations of "eating what you kill."

We can do better.

Leaving this firm, I worked for another two years in corporate management in downtown Boston in the tax and financial planning division. Soon I realized our work was educating brokers with sufficient facts for them to appear competent to their clients when their primary motivation was selling the investment flavor of the day. After these forays into financial planning, developing relationship skills serving both the client and the broker with competing goals, and running a department, I said, we can do better. My partner and I started our own firm; that was 35 years ago.

Now, the seeds of Somatic Finance have matured within me, growing roots formed and deepened from a clear motivation to do better. And you bring your seeds with you. How do we want to grow together?

Let me declare my motivation now.

My motivation is a heart offering that fosters more roots and shoots cascading and circling and nurturing mycelium connections between and among forest dwellers. You, as a seedling, sprouting your own roots and shoots are reading and practicing and embodying with a collective force to survive, thrive, and prosper with a thing called money, which ostensibly makes the world go round.

I welcome you with open arms, Heart, Head, and Belly.

Two sections comprise the book, along with a special companion site with practice resources and guides for your experience. Access these extra treasures as fuel for your progress. In this book, the "Landscape" section defines the territory of Somatic Finance and will feed your brain with information and tease your body with Tiny Practices.

The "Fruition" section weaves the landscape section and your engaged practices together as nutrients—sun and rain—for your integration and deeper motivation.

Between Landscape and Fruition is a gentle pause, a few transition pages that offer calm abiding, a place for you to rest, digest, and be with your experience.

The book includes my stories and the stories of the thousands of people I've worked with who share similar money stories. In the companion site you'll find resources, references, and lots of goodies I've gathered and created along the way meant to support you. I speak from my direct experiences having engaged in these activities myself and with others over the past three decades. Some material will resonate, and some of it will not. Follow your gut, literally, when you engage in the practices. As a precious teacher reminded me often, "You are your own boss," which means, you choose your actions, and we cocreate together.

Now, let's get going.

What sensations do you notice in your body?

Introduction

Consider the subtleness of the sea; how its most dreaded creatures glide under water, unapparent for the most part, and treacherously hidden beneath the loveliest tints of azure..... Consider all this; and then turn to this green, gentle, and most docile earth; consider them both, the sea and the land; and do you not find a strange analogy to something in yourself?

—Herman Melville

The depth of the ocean has long been a wild mystery to us on land. Black and cold, a place where Western imagination conjures ravaging terrors, Melville's "dreaded creatures," a treacherous unknown that is utterly separate from the "gentle, green, and most docile earth."

Money produces a similar view. Terrifying and uncontainable, a source of evil, a corruptor of people's souls, an untamable force making the world go round. We must hunt it and control it with our precious intellect. It may destroy us. It is not human. Worse yet, it can make us feel less than human, regardless of how much we have, or have not.

But Melville, writing *Moby-Dick*, did not understand the real life of whales, or the sea. On the sides of these saltwater giants he captured a horrifying portrait of our most savage fears, cleaving the ocean and the land, sea creature and man, into adversaries.

We know better now. Whales are not monsters. They are majestic stewards of the ocean's health, feeding the phytoplankton that sequester carbon and make our oxygen. Their massive bodies are inseparable from our own. The sea and the land aren't warring but interdependent, in a constant conversation of weather and animals, electromagnetism and gravity.

Now is the time to know the mysteries of money, too. Our experienced and inherited fearful, greedy, multigenerational stories about it have sustained suffering far too long. It's time to strip away money veils and reveal a new way. Money is not a monster. So let's stop assigning it godlike power. Money is not separate from our humanity. It can, in fact, boost our human potential.

Our gateway is the other "dreaded creature" of our lives, the other thing we fear, control, battle, misunderstand, and sometimes hate with the intensity of Ahab:

Our bodies.

Somatic Finance® is the practical, whole-body method for integrating body intelligence with the mind in all matters of finance, reclaiming a world gone mad over money. Whatever money situation you face—debt management, wedding planning, auto insurance renewal, business investment, salary negotiation, a date to retire, or even choosing vegetables for your next meal—Somatic Finance® pairs the knowledge sourced from your brain with viscerally felt senses of your body, supercharging your ability to create and navigate a life with money.

No modern-day society has applied the intelligence of the body to matters of modern finance. To the contrary, we seek to manage money—some might say control—with rigorous thinking, robust research, highly iterated plans, complicated tools, and books upon books of judgment and advice. Money remains the exclusive domain of the brain.

The brain is not sufficient. The very best thinking and research and tools have not dented our culture's destructive money patterns, from individual debt to global climate-destroying corporate profit.

The mind is not enough, yet body intelligence has barely been perceived as a source of any kind of wisdom, much less invaluable money wisdom. Even the widespread, mainstream popularity of mindfulness, which sometimes includes body awareness, and money psychology or behavioral finance find acceptance because they give us an advantage in managing our minds.

These mind-based territories are not enough.

Our bodies possess potent, reliable, and proven intelligence to change our monstrous lives with money. Our body calms the shores so we can know better, do better, and be better regarding money.

Who Is This Book For?

You probably don't know me, but I know you—or at least a little about you. I've been working in the field of finance with clients like you for just shy of 40 years. Here's what I know about you.

You have a body. By body I mean you have a human form that keeps you alive as you move, breathe, sleep, eat, bathe. In this body you inhabit you have a head that houses a brain. Your brain forms lots of concepts and ideas into thoughts, stories, beliefs, and conclusions. Some of these concepts and ideas focus on money.

How am I doing so far?

Regularly, meaning at least once a week but more likely daily, you think about money and maybe take action with money. Sometimes dealing with money is positive. Sometimes dealing with money is negative.

You have lots of feelings about money.

You have lots of beliefs about money.

You wonder how money is used by others, organizations, governments, society, cultures.

You likely question our money systems, economics, global trade, capitalism, consumerism, all of the "isms."

You may have favorable experiences with financial professionals, or you may have experienced a colossal disaster. You may lack trust and doubt the integrity of all financial institutions and the people who run them.

Money has probably made you uncomfortable (at the very least) or given you great challenges (or even dire hardship) at some point in your life. Your family of origin perpetuated unhealthy ancestral money habits.

Are some of these statements true for you? If so, this is normal, not a problem, and thus workable.

You believe we can do better, you can do better with money, and you have tried, made some great progress—but we can still do better. And you may not know how or where to begin. You may have worked with many tools and optimized them. Strategies, seminars, self-help programs have supported your struggles. You may have hired different kinds of professionals—coaches, financial planners, therapists, teachers—to assist you on your journey. Well done!

You know that money doesn't buy happiness, you know that you have limiting beliefs and behaviors that cause you harm, doubt, and confusion and less-than-helpful money decisions. The feelings you experience around money range from contentment to joy to despair to shame, anger, fear, terror, and a bit more anxiety. These emotions recycle, and as the world changes, money seems to produce more complexity and more intensity—life with money is not getting easier.

You might hold more than one PhD or have dropped out of college. But you have engaged in some personal development over the years formally and informally. You may be a part of several communities (spiritual, vocational, philanthropic), and you may engage in practices such as meditation, yoga, contemplative prayer, running, tai chi. You read. You write. You dialogue. You think, deeply and often.

Are you still with me?

You are a gorgeous, worthy, bright human being with a generous heart, creative ideas, and gifts to share with others. With a little clarity, a little insight, a few tools, and a warm embrace, you know your capacity to fully claim your gifts; to do good, heal the past, and serve others is possible. You believe others want this and can do this too.

You believe we all have a right to be here, to work, love, explore, and create, just by being human. You value sufficient financial rewards for what you generate in this world. You recognize we are all different in our capacity to generate, but our different capacities do not translate to inequality.

All humans want safety, connection, and dignity.

All humans deserve these basic human nutrients.

You want the world to be a better place—for you, for your family, for others—to live, to create, to sustain life, for the planet to heal, for our species to survive.

If only money wasn't so hard.

You probably have not considered how money and our bodies can cocreate toward this reality of a better world. This book, the teachings, practices, and stories will assist you on your journey for a healthier relationship with money and a better world.

My motivation for writing this book is a heart offering to:

- Illuminate new ways of integrating money with our life;
- Demonstrate the possibility of friendly and meaningful money habits;
- Share a living and vibrant landscape for growing up, waking up, and cleaning up money ways—ours, others, and all;
- Open your awareness—including body, mind, and heart;
- Encourage body practices enabling all of the above to happen; and
- Be a catalyst for shape-shifting the polluted and outdated financial systems, processes, and institutions, which no longer work for us in the modern world.

If you are willing to explore with openness, curiosity and a blurt, "Well, goodness, I never considered," please continue to read and claim your openness to learning. Being open will serve you and supercharge the offerings in this book and your life.

If you are skeptical, not so sure, very doubtful, well, you can explore too—but recognize your doubt. Doubt is an extra burden, like a heavy backpack and prickly barnacles, pointing to the opportunity to build new muscles. Eventually, your doubt will shed and pristine clarity and discernment will take its place. You won't need the backpack or barnacles anymore.

When motivation is present, clear, and determined, right action follows.

Let's keep going.

Why, How, What

As a reader of this book and the leader of your money life, I offer you these three simple words to ignite potent reading. Simon Sinek coined these as a "golden circle"—a model for inspirational leadership. Customizing for you, consider these your first practice.[1]

Asking *why* you are reading sets a beautiful tone and foundation for your reading experience.

Asking *how* you are reading energizes your action with vitality.

Asking *what* you are reading focuses your attention on importance and priority.

What's Your Why?

Why gives our life motivation that precedes action. When we know what the meaning of our lives are, we feel motivated. When we have purpose, we want to act.

Why answers the deepest longing we are able to hold for ourselves.

Why is an eternal flame that never burns out.

Why is sourced from the heart.

Why wants your attention.

In Somatic Finance, our *why* gives us genuine resourceful fuel for *how* we engage our money and *what* we do with our money.

Here is a **Tiny Practice** to use your soma, or body, to support your discovery of *why* you are reading this book. I will remind you of this centering practice throughout this book. Please engage any time you're prompted or spontaneously inspired.

Pause reading.

Breathe and bring your attention into your body. Watch your breath move in and out of your body. Don't try to change it, just follow it.

Open your heart while feeling your connection to the ground under your feet and under your seat. Relax and release any felt tension through your feet and seat.

Now ask, "What is my heart's longing?"

Drop your attention down to your heart center.

Feel your heart space. (Place your hand over your heart if access is difficult.)

Allow your heart to speak.

This question accesses your *why*. The answer may be your *why* right now or for your life.

For example, if I asked what my heart is longing for, and stories arose that emotionally move me on issues around wildlife abuse, my heart might ache. (In fact, it does ache.) How I engage money and what I do with money would be affected by the very real somatic message my heart delivers. **My *why* around money would be tethered to the health of wildlife, and my money actions would follow with clarity. I might establish a monthly donation to a wildlife cause.**

In short, our *why* is the juice that sources our authentic joy. (Joy juice! Can't you see it on the shelf of the local grocery store?)

Now answer your *why* below, in writing. A word, a short phrase, or one sentence will do.

Pause.

Breathe.

Open.

Now ask, "What is my heart's longing?"

My **why** is: _____

Awesome. Well done. You rock. Thank you!

Now let's explore your how.

What's Your How?

In Somatic Finance we claim our *why* and we choose our *how*, over and over and over.

How will you be in this book?

How will you read?

How will you engage this material?

How matters.

In "the *how*" is where you experience the world, life, others, reading a book.

Choose your *how* each time you pick up this book.

You can go slow. You can go fast. You can skip around. You can stay linear. You can schedule. You can be spontaneous. How you choose to engage this material is totally up to you, with one strong suggestion: of every choice possible, choose to be open to learning— regardless of how the content lands.

Big choice.

Openness to learning is a powerful *how* steeped in authentic embodied curiosity. True curiosity is open to receiving whatever arises, which means we might feel delight in the good times and we might feel scared in the bad times, in the wobbles, and in the trenches. But we remain open. We will review learning this way in more detail. For now, just get more curious.

What is your how, right now?

Are you open and curious?

Are you closed and skeptical?

Now let's explore your *what*.

What's Your What?

What is the object of your affection, your attention, your focus.

What is the organizing question that allows you to prioritize importance, right now.

Lots of issues and possibilities are important.

But *what* is important now?

Where do you focus your attention, held in your deeper motivation (**why**) and with a way of engaging (**how**) that will be most beneficial? What reveals itself naturally from a clear why and how. What always presents itself in the here and now.

What has your attention?

Pause.

Breathe.

Open.

Now, let's get going, for real.

Note

1. Source: "How Great Leaders Inspire Action" (2010). TEDxPuget Sound talk by Simon Sinek. Fair use.

Part I

Landscape

Part IA

Introduction

Chapter 1
Diving In

The kindest and most effective way to learn is in a state of openness and well-being where we feel relaxed in our body.

And along with being relaxed in our body, our mind wants relaxation too! This is why we begin to explore the landscape of Somatic Finance through the head center—anxious minds settle when they have information. Somatic Finance focuses on three body centers: the Head, the Heart, and the Belly. We start with our head center because cognition (reading, thinking, analyzing) is our most familiar way of settling in. Once we understand something, we relax. Our body settles, and we are able to receive something new.

Next we move down to the belly center, which tends to our comfort and ability to feel safe. Then we move upward into the heart center. Here we learn how the heart expands us outward, making connections.

We will explore how each center relates to finance individually and as a culture. We'll look at the neuroscience research that underpins somatic finance. And we'll cover essential ideas about how to approach the practice of somatic finance. I will share stories from my lifelong practice of personal development and from my 30 years practicing as a Certified Financial Planner®, working with thousands of clients. (Names have been changed to protect privacy.)

Along the way, "Tiny Practices" will help you practice being in and with your body sensations as you learn. Don't be alarmed if you feel like you don't get these immediately. They are like a handshake; we're just getting to know each other with a gentle hello.

When I express the kindest and most effective way to learn is in a state of openness and relaxation, you might want to understand more about that. A relaxed body may be very clear. But are there other ways to be open? Yes. Being open, curious, free of analysis, and releasing thoughts such as, "I need to get this right" assists you in receiving new ideas and enjoying the process of learning. Including the body in the web of intelligence, particularly around finance, can rattle us. Many people become distressed and close down, and learning slows if not stops.

So what does it feel like to be open? To relax into learning?

To me, openness feels fun, vibrant, alive, and the meaning of possibilities. When I know there is no possible way to "do it wrong" or urgent need to "get it right," my body automatically relaxes and my exploration holds that view. My body jumps in with joy—a full-bodied relaxed-ready experience. I learned about openness to learning in my first training with Kathlyn Hendricks, world-renowned author and speaker in the field of body intelligence and conscious loving. A full day into the training, she stated that we learn best when we are having fun. I did a *whaaaaat?*

Up until that point I was not having a lot of fun. I was trying hard to get it right, figure it out, and "help" my partner to get it right too. When I tasted the play of fun in this learning environment, I knew the richness in her words, which came alive in my experience, and they would go on to support me for decades as I continued my personal and professional development. Can you imagine or have you consistently experienced fun with money? Another *whaaaaaat?* I offer them to you for your reading and practice journey as you learn, play, and grow.

On the flip side, learning anything is hard when you're in a rigid closed state. It becomes difficult, if not impossible, to be aware of the emotions, sensations, thoughts, and energy coursing through our body. Without somatic awareness, we cannot learn new ways.

In fact, this is when we typically close further and pull our body in tight.

Learning anything new and innovative around money is even harder. A lot of us exist in closed states around money. They take shape physically, mentally, and emotionally, looking like:

1. **Physical instincts**—fighting, fleeing, freezing, fainting;
2. **Mental anxiety**—a mind of stories, beliefs, confusion, doubt-circling 24/7;
3. **Emotional panic**—a constant hit of adrenaline, sourced from fear.

Let me share a few client stories with you. They may help you identify your own closed states identified above—and what they feel like in the body. Let this knowledge settle you a bit. And if it's hard to take a step forward, just stand in one place feeling your feet firmly on the ground, your head reaching tall, your spine elongated, and chest lifted. Breathe. You will learn that sometimes before we can open we need to locate ourselves first.

Sam and Sandy (Fear and Anger)

Sam and his spouse were clients for many years before they embarked on a six-digit home renovation project. They hired all the qualified building professionals to ensure there would be no money surprises. The cost of the project escalated to three times the budget. Sam was angry, and Sandy was terrified. They argued. He blamed her for not paying attention to the cost overruns. She sat paralyzed with fear. In this meeting, my partner noted the costs and where capital could be sourced to fund the overrun. He pointed to the fact that their finances would be fine. He skillfully scrambled to put it all together using financial reports, spreadsheets, and account statements.

In this tense dynamic, I turned to my partner and asked him what was going on for him. What did he notice in his body? He said he felt agitated, and he noticed nausea in his belly. He went on to say, "Their arguing triggered my fear response." He wanted to stop their arguing and believed the way to stop the arguing was to fix the problem.

"What do you notice in your body?" I asked Sandy. She responded that she felt sick to her stomach and was very scared about the cost overruns. She did not know what to do and how to discuss the matter with Sam.

When I asked Sam what he noticed in his body, he replied, "I feel nothing." He said he was terrified about their finances and their lifestyle and long-term retirement. He was steeped in fear and constricted.

In those closed fearful and angry states, nothing new was going to happen.

Ellen and Dov (Sadness)

Ellen and Dov, another couple we enjoyed working with for many years, remained in a stuck, somber place when we discussed money, saving, and how to allocate their resources. Their earnings were sufficient to pay their bills and make partial contributions to their retirement plans. Some years they were able to save more than others. Dov did not pay close attention to their savings. So in times when his earnings were higher than normal, he was unaware that his wife would give away any "extra earnings" to family and friends.

Ellen held an unconscious belief that if you were well-off financially, meaning if you had a surplus of funds, it was best to give that money away. Because rich people became sick and died. The somberness masking her fear of her spouse's death if he became too successful caused her to give away their surpluses that could have supported them in their future retirement.

In this fearful, sad state nothing new was going to happen.

Fred (Doubt and Confusion)

We worked with Fred, a man in his mid-thirties intent on understanding finances using his brilliant mind solely by reading books. He explained he was mired in confusion about money and was convinced that there was something he was missing. Teaching him the fundamentals of finance still perplexed him even though his intelligence was never in question. To satisfy Fred's thirst for knowledge, we offered him many books to read coming from different perspectives; he remained fixed on a view that he needed to know more and his confusion was unmovable.

We suspected his doubt and confusion was a mask for his fear and his unwillingness to get curious and open to learning about money in new ways. Sometimes we hold on to beliefs, family stories, and well-worn patterns because they are familiar; being familiar is more comfortable than the unknown.

In the closed, confused, and constrained state, nothing new was going to happen.

Get willing to be open. Choose to be open to learning. Write in the margins of this book, "I choose to relax and open to learning." Dog-ear the page so you can find it again. It's allowed. It's your book. If not, grab your notebook or journal and write your intentions.

When you feel closed, because there are times you will feel scared and closed, acknowledge you are closed and recommit to open. Then open again, one breath at a time.

Chapter 2
The Head

The head is the first of three areas of the body that contribute to the development of Somatic Finance. Even though the head is the last physical development of the human embryo, we begin with our head center because the most familiar and comforting way of settling into new information is through our intellect.

To start, please orient yourself with the picture of the human brain, this intricate system that lives below the top of our skull, behind our eyes, above our throat. The visual gives us a strong reference point to deepen our understanding of how the head contributes to our experience of money.

Our brains are made of three major parts, together called the *triune brain*:

- The primitive brain, our brainstem—its main function: surviving;
- The emotional brain, our limbic system—its main function: feeling;
- The rational brain, our neocortex—its main function: thinking.

These three areas are the source of two ways we learn about and interpret our world: intuition and knowledge.

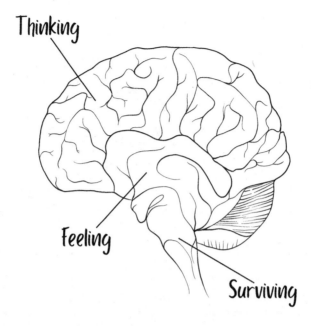

Thinking

Feeling

Surviving

Figure 2.1   Illustration of Human Brain.

Intuition is connected to the brainstem and limbic system, in the primitive and emotional brain, while knowledge is sourced in our neocortex, our rational brain. Intuition allows us to pay attention to and interpret emotional and physical sensation as valuable information about our money-related experience. Knowledge, on the other hand, covers measurements, metrics, and numbers. Knowledge includes the facts and figures related to money and finance. It is knowledge that permeates economics and calculates facts and demands answers.

Together, the triune brain helps us operate from a place of wisdom—the unity of knowledge and intuition. Wisdom allows us to see clearly what is possible or what is unlikely in regard to our money. It helps us make decisions based in reality. Our brains are built for both intuition and knowledge; we are made for wisdom.

As we move forward, it may be helpful to think of knowledge as the "right brain" and intuition as the "left brain." If you're familiar with this shorthand, and it helps for understanding, please use it.

The Obsession with Knowledge

Despite the fact that the emotional brain and the primitive brain are essential components of our understanding, 99.9% of the financial world operates exclusively on knowledge, the specialty of the neocortex. We review our options and make decisions based upon AOP, AP, BEP, CAGR, CFCT, DSO, EAR, EPS, FV, GFCF, IRR, LTV, MWC, NOI, OCF, P & L, P/E, PPP, RER, WC, FYF . . . to name a few acronyms of knowledge measurements in money business.

Relying on knowledge alone excludes intuition. Without intuition, knowledge about money puts us at risk for fear, doubt, confusion, and greed. As you wrap your head around the letters and what they might mean, what's happening inside you? How do you feel in your belly and in your chest? Does your feeling point to confusion? Or maybe excitement?

Over the past several decades, finance researchers have recognized and tried to rectify this dysfunctional, lopsided, painful relationship many of us have with money. Behavioral finance and the psychology of money emerged as important new fields of study in the mid-1990s, and both try to understand the emotional side of money. How do our feelings affect our money decisions?

But, and this troubles me, both fields exclusively use the application of cognitive intelligence to try to understand why money is so fraught and painful. These fields use the capacity for knowledge to solve the problem of relying on knowledge alone to understand money. Talk about irony! You cannot reconcile behavioral and psychological issues with knowledge alone. These practices don't simplify, clarify, or resolve problems of greed, fear, helplessness, or confusion around money; they create the emotional equivalent of more dust bunnies. Cognitive fields of study do not make people freer.

Repeating use of the neocortex, or knowledge brain, for information, interpretation, and answers around money means that we simply rehash and reconfigure the same old and painful territory. More knowledge about knowledge goes nowhere. We need intuition to get somewhere new.

Understanding Intuition

Intuition can be a troubling word in finance. Who wants to trust their money to something as weird and unmeasured as *intuition*?

And yet intuition is connected to the other two-thirds of our brains. When we rely on knowledge alone to understand our money, we leave much of our massive, sense-making brain and its sophisticated, comprehensive, and finely calibrated nervous system off the table.

Intuition, in the frame of Somatic Finance®, is the ability to sense and interpret the emotional and physical sensations of your experiences. When you integrate your capacity for intuition with your ability to gather and assess knowledge, you bring far more of your brain and body, your nervous system, online. You open up the potential to be vastly more intelligent about your experiences— particularly your experiences with money.

In my work, I have largely seen and felt what I call "brain polarity," where we favor one capacity over the other. Finance, as we've all experienced, favors rigid analytical knowledge and disparages "head in the clouds" intuition. The irony is that letting rigid knowledge dominate one's experience of money puts your head in the clouds (or the sand) because you aren't living in the full reality of the current moment, informed by thinking *and* feeling.

It's also delusional to think that our physical and emotional experiences don't affect our thinking or our knowledge about money. Our bodies are not, in fact, disconnected from our heads. We simply ignore the information and wisdom of the soma at our peril. Intuition is vital to our happiness. It's vital to our evolution.

Intuition is vital to our life with money. Neither extremely rigid thinking nor feeling floaty "head in the clouds" avoidance produces a favorable financial result. Ever. Developing a healthy balance between our two capacities allows us to remain in steady connection with a clear strategic path (knowledge) while navigating change (intuition).

Countering Bias

Unfortunately, the distrust of intuition, of "feelings," is in the bedrock of our money culture. To counter this detrimental bias, I find it helpful to turn to the work of Dr. Jill Bolte-Taylor, Harvard-trained neuroanatomist and author of *My Stroke of Insight*.[1]

In 1996, Dr. Bolte-Taylor suffered a massive stroke that incapacitated her *thinking* brain, the center that searches for measurements, facts, and answers. Her *feeling* brain dominated. She did not experience emotions or sensations cognitively, as thoughts; she felt them. Joy was a feeling in her body; peace was a feeling in her body.

As she recovered and her thinking capacity returned, she was able to maintain this awareness of the body's presence in every single experience. She now knew in her body what she had known intellectually through her neuroanatomical research, that the brain constantly gathers information from the body and integrates it with cognitive thought to sense, understand, organize, and respond to the world.

For those of us who love more information, here's more on brain anatomy. Let's geek out, learning how the integration of intuition and knowledge works in the brain.

Our emotions are generated by cells in the limbic system, explains Dr. Bolte-Taylor. Physical sensations such as touch involve the postcentral gyrus of the cerebral cortex. This emotional and physical information combines to form our sense of intuition. Then, when we compare or reconcile our intuition and cognitive learning, "this insightful awareness involves a higher cognition grounded in the right hemisphere of the cerebral cortex," she writes in chapter two of *My Stroke of Insight*.[2]

Dr. Bolte-Taylor experienced the intuitive capacity of the brain and body with stunning intensity. She was also able to see and describe her experience cognitively. With unprecedented clarity she saw how intuition and knowledge work together as intimate partners to navigate us through every single experience. And because her thinking brain did not have its previous white-knuckle grip on her overall awareness, as it does for most of us, she was able to see how emotions and sensations have a natural catch and release rhythm.

Intuition and Knowledge as a Path to Growth

When a new emotion arose, Dr. Bolte-Taylor could feel the emotion flood her body and then release. She learned, she writes in chapter thirteen, that she had the power "to choose whether to hook into a feeling and prolong its presence in my body, or just let it quickly flow right out of me."[3]

This experience of "flow" has important implications for our work in Somatic Finance. We have feelings about money. We always will. Our central repeating pattern—feel feelings, attach thoughts, stories, beliefs, reify a cognitive conclusion—remain at play. This is the body-brain closed circuit—looping money, feeling, and thought into a never-ending tight knot.

This circuit keeps that feeling about money—say, fear or frustration—stuck regardless of reality. We lose the ability to fully feel and release emotion and shift our thinking based on expanded intuitive and cognitive information. We are locked in, blind and void of wisdom, the foundation of money suffering.

Yet money suffering—in greed, selfishness, fear, confusion, scarcity—is not inevitable or intractable. As Dr. Bolte-Taylor recovered, and maintained her understanding and felt experience of intuition and knowledge working together, she came to a beautiful question:

Could I value money without hooking into the neurological lops of lack, greed and selfishness?[4]

When I read that line, my heart went, *Wow!* and my thoughts said, *Yes!* I recognized my *Wow* because I felt a shimmer and warmth arise in my chest. My *Yes* rose (spine lifting) from my intellectual knowledge regarding money, greed, and the power of perception. (Yes, I experienced an integration of my intuition and knowledge as I considered Dr. Bolte-Taylor's question!)

My intuition and knowledge aligned around the truth that we can value money without lack, greed, or selfishness. Why? Because we do not control our money experiences; we control how we choose to perceive them. We make better choices. How do we do that? By drawing on the full monitoring, assessing, and organizing power of the head: body-based intuition and cognitive knowledge. What's more, we do not need to endure a brain hemorrhage, like Dr. Bolte-Taylor, to feel our physical and emotional sensations and integrate our intuition with our knowledge. We need only to choose to inhabit the world of our soma, our place of power, sovereignty, grace, and full perception. That is the work of Somatic Finance, and what you will learn to do in this book and begin to embody as you practice.

Intuition and Knowledge in Practice

Remember our couple Sam and Sandy, during home renovations? He was angry, and she was scared. The conversation between them was vitally important to help them unify intuition and knowledge, to help them see a bigger perspective, and to enable an action that served their situation.

If we had stayed with knowledge alone and intensified his anger over not knowing the numbers, we would have gone nowhere. If we had stayed paralyzed with her churning fear of his anger, we would have gone nowhere. Even if we just talked about their feelings, at best each would have said, *I feel angry, I feel scared*. We still would have gone nowhere.

With gentle coaching, Sandy was able to call up her cognitive knowledge and assess the situation at hand, less clouded with fear. (As you'll learn to do in the Practice Guidebooks, she did this by becoming fully aware of and then consciously softening the fear sensation in her body, that stomach churn.) She was more able to relate to Sam. Sam, on the other hand, stayed locked in his drive for more hard facts and figures, trying to figure out an answer. He was not able, at that time, to use his body as a source of information or a tool to free himself from his stuck anger.

I share this not to point fingers—I'm not saying, "She did it right, and he did it wrong!" No. Unifying intuition and knowledge, welcoming body intelligence in our development requires practice and time. Seeing where people get stuck and where they can move forward helps us see our own path. Witnessing these stories ultimately helps us make our own choices toward freedom.

With Sandy and Sam, I followed my intuition to ask about sensations in their body. They each responded as best they could to step closer to wisdom: the unity of knowledge and intuition.

Tapping into Safety, Connection, and Dignity

Something else happens when we unify the gifts of the head and connect with the soma. As somatic intelligence researcher Amanda Blake writes:

> *Your entire distributed nervous system evolved to take care of safety, connection, and respect via sensation and motion. In other words, your brain—and by extension your entire body—is your social and emotional sense organ.*[5]

You'll notice that Blake includes the words "safety," "connection," and "respect" in her definition of the work of the brain and nervous system. When you bring the capacity of the head online, with all three areas of the triune brain in play, you activate profound, positive feelings that forever alter your experience of money. I have articulated this dynamic through years of experience and study; you will see it in action throughout the book and learn how to practice it in the Somatic Finance Practice Guidebooks.

A Bit More for the Academic about the Triune Brain

- The primitive brain, our brainstem, activates fear—where we want a sense of *safety*.
- The emotional brain, our limbic system, activates longing—where we want a sense of *connection*.

- The rational brain, our neocortex, activates drive—where we want a sense of *respect*.

The triune brain comprises the brainstem, the limbic system, and the neocortex. The brainstem, often referred to as the primitive brain and the home of the amygdala, is our instinctual response to threat for survival. It is said to move ten times faster than the cerebral cortex.

The limbic system progressed as the "emotional brain" with the evolution of mammals and their unique capacity to give live birth to offspring. Communication and feelings between mother and baby require communication through the senses: vocalization, facial expression, caring touch, smell, and taste for meaningful and nurturing connection.

The neocortex came online when social groups became more complex than a simple family structure. Individuals needed roles, positions, structures, processes, and organization to navigate the complexity of living together in groups. The idea of a unique, dignified self to fulfill a purpose within a group emerged developmentally, as the thinking brain and culture developed.

The integration of safety, connection, and respect is what I call *integrated dignity*—our beautiful right to be here and human. When our brains are fully activated, tapping into both intuition and knowledge, connected to the body, money can no longer lock us into fear, doubt, regret, and scarcity. Money, the idea of it and the use of it, is liberated into a much larger potential. With head gifts in play, we can experience authentic joy—even in the world of money.

Take a moment to consider the devastating consequences of knowledge-only behavior around money, in your own life, in the life of your community, in the life of the country, in the life of our world and planet. Can you think of times that relying on the head alone has led to poor outcomes at best and deep suffering at the worst? (It's worth noting that the opposite happens too: relying solely on emotional triggers and reacting impulsively—selling in a down market, for example.)

Forgoing a current joyful experience focusing on a future (or potential) fear would be a knowledge-only move. For example, postponing a family camping trip to work and earn income to save for retirement. What happens in this situation when a parent becomes terminally ill the following year? Let me emphasize that often final money decisions in our work with clients may not be the best financial decision, but they are the optimal decision, which considers our deepest why.

Some of you might be confused. Making an irrational money decision based on fear or another emotional trigger is a problem. In these intense states we are asked to calm down and "get our sh*t together." It is true. It would be helpful to focus, clarify, and decide, but our fear is telling us to listen beyond the constructs of our rational brain. How helpful is it to hear that you should focus, get clear, and decide, when you are paralyzed in fear?

We can't stay in that paradigm of knowledge only. Including the totality of our head gifts and sourcing additional wisdom from the body is our complete path to liberation.

From that wiser place, we can see that financial growth doesn't always mean more money and property. Success doesn't always mean a higher salary and multiple degrees. We can see, feel, and even accept the impermanent nature of the physical form and our material wealth. From that wiser place, we can act differently. The money issues that used to trigger anger, fear, or sadness might no longer grab us because our body wisdom helps connect us to more meaning, more joy, more truth. Our *why* begins to permeate and then saturate our life. Our conduct is resonant with our deepest truths of what matters most—when intuition, knowledge, and the soma are working as one.

"Imagine," Dr. Bolte-Taylor writes, "the compassionate world we could create if we set our minds to it."[6]

Tiny Practice

Here's a tiny practice to offer you a simple and easy experience of your body awareness.

Pause for a moment.

Put your right hand on this book. Put your left hand on your Heart.
Breathe feeling under your left palm.

What do you notice inside your Body?
Are thoughts circling?
Are sensations churning?
Are emotions bubbling?

Beautiful. Let them flow. Let them go.

Appreciate

With a healthy balance, the head expresses:

Clarity;
Luminosity;
Knowledge; and
Vision.

Recognize

With an unhealthy balance, the head constricts:

Intuition;
Connection;
Creativity; and
Confidence.

Reflection

In the Practice Guidebooks, you utilize what you learn about your "head way"—what you currently optimize and where you are called to grow, regarding your head skills. Consider the following questions to get a sense of your present head way.

Do you lean on facts and figures about money with enthusiasm?
Or do you react with negative feelings about money by putting your head in the sand?
Do you feel like you can't hold on to numbers or you might hold too tight?
Do metrics and measurements make you panicky or instill you with clarity and ease?
Do you wonder why some people have intense feelings about money?
In general, does money knowledge create more clarity or confusion?

Writing from the Voice of the Head

The voice from the Head says, "Greetings."

"I am the ultimate experience of awareness. But the only way to gain awareness is through a journey. I learn to speak last, when I normally speak first, because my job is to surrender to the freedom of the Belly and the connections of the Heart. When I practice letting go, my awareness opens further. When you experience life from my way, there is no doubt, there is only sweet surrender.

"But let's start at the beginning. Most of your problems arise because you come to me first, ignoring the intelligence of your belly and heart. I love that you rely on me for information and direction. Money issues have a unique way of bypassing the body. Relying on me makes me feel good and powerful and in control. I have many ideas about how to keep you safe, to help you take the right action, to figure it out, to decide, to plan and vision and forecast, to create the tools to get the job done.

"The information I have answers your questions. If I don't have the information you need, I will respond with an answer anyway, typically including fear, anger, confusion, blame, regret, grief, shame. I'm going to give you an answer even if it is limited because that is my job. I have a lot of responses. Some might be helpful. Many are not. But I do my job well, focusing, narrowing the scope, and responding quickly. My job is really hard, and I might fatigue easily when money is involved.

"Unless you pay attention to the belly and the heart, I will continue to ignore them. It is what I do. It is the only response I can offer when my view is partial. My view is always partial if there is no belly and no heart.

"By myself, I am not aware if the synapses firing in the primitive brain (amygdala) are due to a current emergency (there is a fire blazing, and I need to get out of the building) or I am reliving an unresolved memory. I cannot resolve any old material without **somatic awareness** (metacognitive awareness of the physical body) and **somatic practice**. Somatic awareness and somatic practice co-occur; you'll learn more in the forthcoming chapters. Somatic practice is an intentionally designed practice for development, which requires somatic awareness. All practices (running, tai chi, yoga, writing, breathing—any physical movement) can be a somatic practice. Somatic awareness and practice are well-defined and used in many disciplines, including somatic meditation, martial arts, breathwork, dance, and movement, among many more. For now, understand that without body wisdom we can only respond and react to *limited* information that flows in our neural pathways. Some of the information looks the same. And the response is usually the same. Everything looks like a nail to our hammer.

"But when I listen to the belly and the heart, fresh current reality seeps up my spine into the prefrontal cortex and limbic system—and I relate to the information better. There is more space in the belly to feel the energy of fear and let that energy move through the vibrations and pulses. There is more softness in the heart to feel the energy of sadness and let that energy flow through the letting go.

"When I recognize the wisdom of the belly and heart, they give me a way to integrate all of my experiences deeper, and insight arises. A bright connection to wholeness comes online that strengthens each time the belly and the heart are included. I no longer feel the burden of needing to know it all. In fact, I begin to relax with the belly, and I begin to open with the heart. I sense the interconnectedness of our strengths and the unique wisdom we offer together, as awareness expands.

"In practices, I will teach you to trust so that with each experience your awareness expands more and more.

I look forward to knowing you better as we read this book."

Yum. Gayle here.

Did hearing the voice of your Head center spark a crush?

What are your Belly, Heart, and Head saying now?

Notes

1. Source: Bolte-Taylor, Jill. (2008). *My Stroke of Insight: A Brain Scientist's Personal Journey*. New York: Viking. Fair use.

2. Ibid.

3. Ibid.

4. Ibid.

5. Source: "Body=Brain," Online Course (2015, 2018). Created and taught by Amanda Blake, MD. https://embright.org/body-brain. Fair Use.

6. Source: Bolte-Taylor, Jill. (2008). *My Stroke of Insight: A Brain Scientist's Personal Journey*. New York: Viking. P. 138. Fair use.

Chapter 3
The Belly

Before we begin, let's appreciate our head center. Thank you for giving attention to your brilliant brain. It works really hard to assess and organize and plan. It works even harder around money. You might feel some sadness or weariness around the effort of the head. We attend to that fatigue by dropping down into our belly.

The belly is our anchor to wholeness, to our pristine integrity, to our authentic confidence, to the vast unceasing awareness that is calm like the ocean floor.

Tiny Practice

Pause for just a second, another tiny practice.
Place your dominant hand on your Belly. Feel.
Feel underneath your hand the potential of your Belly as vast and calm, right now.
Nothing more, nothing less. Just feel.
It's simple.

Being familiar with the ocean, maybe you have experienced the waves on top of the water and the murky debris in the middle that arise with the moving tides. We regularly swim in these waves and fragments, both figuratively and literally. But rarely do we plunge to the bottom of the ocean where still waters hold vast mysteries of life. (Unless you are an oceanographer or deep-sea diver.)

Calm waters caress our bellies too. When we are confused, anxious, full of doubt, deep in our belly center is an endless source of confidence and wholeness. We just need to pay attention. We need to see when our energy becomes distracted by the moving events in the world that create and propagate fear. Then we need to feel. Feel the belly center. Feel safe.

There will always be moving, murky events in the financial world. Just like there is moving debris in water. These events present an opportunity to experience "what is." The daily bell on Wall Street, for example, offers a consistent opportunity to feel okay or scared, depending on the positive (the market went up) or negative (the market went down) results of the market's measure.

In the midst of all this disturbing motion, whether it triggers us to feel good or bad, we look for harbors where we can feel whole, confident, safe. Some of us look to our financial statements, or our savings, or our income, or the noise on the TV, or any external money measure.

This mindset and behavior are the core trouble spots in our money journey. A sense of safety is not sourced anywhere but inside ourselves. This state of internal calm manifests *sufficiency*, an important concept and practice in Somatic Finance. In sufficiency, we gain access to our enough-ness, our okay-ness. In sufficiency, we let go of the external illusion that our bank account will keep us safe. In sufficiency, we understand the market is going to do what it does. Just like the ocean debris does what it does. Whatever is happening, we viscerally know we are still okay. Our somatic belly practice gives us access to sufficiency.

You will learn and experience more about this kind of sufficiency as you engage in practice. For now, let the potential of sufficiency be the still calm waters of the ocean floor. Sufficiency is just this, the ability to recognize in this nano-moment that we are okay. Such recognition serves us well on this journey.

Sufficiency in Emotional Turmoil

In the last century, our country has weathered numerous market declines, defined as a recession, depression, or crisis, that created emotional turmoil. Let's tour the last 100 years.

History of Market Declines

1918–1919	Post–World War I Recession
1920–1921	Depression
1923–1924	Recession
1926–1927	Recession
1929–1933	**Great Depression**
1937–1938	Second part of Great Depression
1945	End of war decline in government spending; shift from wartime to peacetime
1949	A 1.7% fall in GDP followed a period of monetary tightening
1953	Fed forced a recession post Korean War to respond to inflation fears and bubbles
1958	Ike Recession, the most significant recession post WW2; yet, 8 months later the market completely recovered; volatility, always present, intensifies fear
1963	DJIA sank 2.89% and closed 30 minutes after assassination of John F. Kennedy
1969–1970	Reaction to federal government regulating banks' higher interest rates
1973–1975	**OPEC Embargo**
1980	Fed chairman lifted interest rates to double digits to fight inflation
1982	**Latin America Sovereign Debt Crisis**
1980s	Savings & Loan Crisis
1987	**Stock Market Crash—Black Monday**
1989	Junk Bond Crash

(continued)

(continued)

1994	Tequila Crisis (yes, this was a thing. Worms were on strike)
1997–1998	Asia Crisis
2000–2001	**Dot Com Bubble; September 11th**
2007–2008	**Global Financial Crisis**
2020	**Covid-19**
2022	**Ukraine Invasion**

In every one of these market plunges, most notably in the bolded ones, fear escalated off the charts, sometimes to insanity and suicide. Even people who had no money invested in the stock market felt fear—it was an inescapable field of despair. Yet, while there is concern during these periods of market depression, there is also an opportunity to develop a broader view, a more skillful and true view that includes our body wisdom.

I recall a client conversation during the 2007–2008 market crisis. This particular market was a stellar wake-up call for me; I was very concerned for our collective mental stability. I was upset that the pervasive way of attending to economic meltdowns was fierce grasping. But I was also holding the view that we needed this experience to wake us up out of our unconscious slumber that we have any control over economic and life events. Something in our culture was not working well. We are unable to swim in unknown waters and feel okay. We needed a *Moonstruck* "snap out of it" slap in our face. In the conversation I said it was a wake-up call. My client said, "Did it need to be so harsh?" My reply, "It seems so."

The big lie rarely spoken is this: the number shown on your bank account, your investment statement, your brokerage report, your pay stub, your retirement plan distribution, your Social Security statement, or any other numeric prediction is an illusion. The number or dollars shown represent your belief—based on a guess, at a particular moment, about your financial wealth. As we experience all of the time, at any time, this number can and does move. It can drop precipitously—as in the periods depicted—or the number can increase, as we experience regularly.

The myriad factors that influence the true value shown on your reports cannot be easily calculated with the mind. We need sophisticated technology, algorithms, calculations, safe withdrawal rates, and beyond to determine how interest rates, inflation, IRRs, growth, beta values, and an infinite number of measurements affect our ability to live sufficiently.

But the embodied experience of sufficiency is very different, more stable and independent of complicated financial instruments. Embodied sufficiency is the absolute, no doubt recognition that in this moment I am okay, regardless of external forces or measurements. Sufficiency may just be this breath, and the next breath, in the face of a fire blazing. We abide here, not in the past or in the future. Sufficiency in this context is an embodied way of being, which means we are not thinking about sufficiency. It is the embodied truth.

Safety is measured by our direct felt experience in life. How am I experiencing life, right now? Can I measure my okay-ness, my safety, and my sufficiency right now? And where is that authentic measurement taken? One guess. Our belly. Our belly caresses the vagus nerve (the tenth cranial nerve that interfaces with parasympathetic control of the heart, lungs, and digestive tract) and sends a signal to our brain to be calm. There are no emergencies right now. Amygdala, please sit tight.

Our current practices around money do not, by and large, include the body, much less a specific area like the belly. Instead, we seek sufficiency in those complicated financial instruments mentioned earlier and in how we talk about money. Consider the familiar words that we use to make money feel secure and amplify fear: "guaranteed," "safe withdrawal," "permanent," "retirement," "plan," "normal," and "forecast." These may be the worst money words as they often generate unstable ground. The broader conversation and the reliable practices to support the navigation of this unstable ground are missing. The ground remains unstable because when we hear these words, we attach a meaning to them, and our safety gets glued to our meaningful story.

Unless these words are accompanied with a skillful conversation, how the issue relates directly to us, and more specifically how it relates to what matters most to us (remember your **why**?) and where

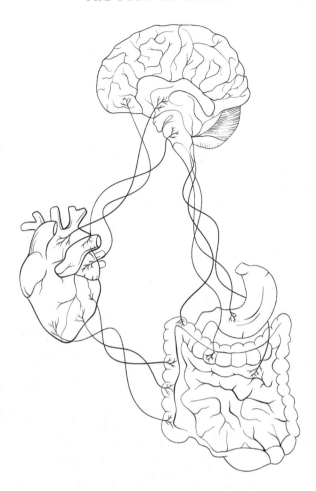

Figure 3.1   Belly Illustration.

there are limitations, they create a false reference point for our safety. Unless these conversations are accompanied by true connection to our body wisdom and somatic practices to grow with our body wisdom, the conversations fade over time—until the next market meltdown. Conversations can become a useless repeating pattern.

Let's look closer at some of these bad words. By holding them up to a clear light, we see how they cannot provide a stable sense of protection and security that the belly can.

Guaranteed

Aren't we all familiar with the old adage, there are no guarantees in life except death and taxes?

All of our physical systems (nervous, respiratory, endocrine, cardiovascular, musculoskeletal, and more) are guaranteed to stop functioning at some point to end our life as we know it now. If you are a legal resident of the United States, you are required to pay taxes. Taxes are an integral part of the operating system of this country. (We could get rid of the taxes. Perhaps there will be a time taxes are not guaranteed. But, death, as I describe above, is a guarantee.)

So why would the word "guarantee" in any kind of financial instrument be valid? We are going to die. No one gets off this "little blue dot," a la Carl Sagan, alive in this physical body.

Are there any other guarantees, truly?

This is an important question to ponder, more than once or twice.

Given the uncertainty in life, and particularly the uncertainty in our financial systems, there is no way, in my opinion, that any use of the word "guarantee" can be of service. None. Nada. Nichts.

I once heard a disturbing story about a client who wanted to be certain of her income during retirement. A planner created a financial plan that clearly indicated her finances were satisfactory given her set of circumstances. The planner could not effectively communicate these findings to his client. So, just to "be sure," this planner liquidated a large sum of savings from an ERISA plan (a tax-deferred account that benefited from tax-deferred accumulated savings) into a *guaranteed* annuity. Now, with this new guaranteed annuity, the client will feel better about her retirement. Her belly won't ache.

Until it does. Because it will.

The problem is that this woman sought a solution outside of her own being to help her feel secure and safe—when the only direction to feel whole and confident is in and down—in her body, down in the belly. The source of what she was really looking for regarding her retirement—her wholeness, her integrity, her truth, her safety—was right in her belly.

Unfortunately, this client will not feel safe in retirement with her annuity. She will pay unnecessary taxes on the liquidation of her tax-deferred assets, and her annuity will pay a fixed amount for the duration of her life. Perhaps. It depends. The fixed amount of income offers a perceived guarantee that the funds will arrive each month. However, any number of situations could arise that would prevent that income from arriving in a way that sustains her perceived safety. Three possibilities are: (1) the financial institution (the insurance company) that owns the annuity could fail, (2) the underlying securities that constitute the annuity (if it is a variable annuity) could falter, and therefore the income would drop based on the stock market performance, (3) the annuity income doesn't keep up with inflation so that the cost of living on her fixed income is insufficient to keep up with a desired lifestyle.

The missing element of safety for this woman is the universal truth that no matter what happens with this annuity, whether it performs as planned or whether it doesn't, she will feel scared. She will not feel safe at some point in her life. In fact, she (and all of us inhabiting a human body) will not feel safe many times. She may blame money for her lack of feeling safe, as our culture constantly misplaces blame on money.

When we follow money blame, that blame grows to the greedy institutions, organizations, corporations, billionaires, trillionaires, and Godzillionaires who have caused and perpetuated global misery. While there is partial truth to my statement, why would you ever outsource your authority to them?

Many years ago the Dali Lama was asked if he was angry with the Chinese for taking over his country. In his infinite wisdom, he replied, "The Chinese government has taken my land, my people, my heritage, why would I ever give them my mind?" May we all benefit from the essence of his teaching.

Rather than searching for guarantees, fighting her fear, or blaming money, this woman's best option is to welcome the fear like a long lost friend, with openness, courage, and skill. This practice, grounded in the belly, sources a reliable sense of safety.

Meeting fear with skill can look like asking ourselves, What is missing? Am I still here, just as I was before? Whether the numbers on my reports change, go up, go down, I am still here, whole and complete—right here in my belly. Nothing that really matters to me has changed.

Whenever the markets shift and create confusion, fear, or doubt, wake down into your body by accessing your belly. Our belly helps us to feel complete, here, and confident. This, my friends, is the way of life, making the best choice possible—even if the choice is about paying off lingering credit card debt or maximizing retirement plan savings, even if the choice is about which kind of treatment to receive for our cancer diagnosis, even if the choice is about downsizing to pay for college or taking out a second mortgage, even if the choice is about hiring a mediator to salvage our relationship or filing for divorce, even if the choice is about making repairs on the aging roof or taking that long desired vacation.

Help yourself access your body wisdom by letting go of these lingering language barriers of hope. Eliminate "guaranteed" from your vocabulary when describing any kind of money situation. Period. Then move inside and tend to the vibration of fear—give your fear the attention it craves. When we give attention to a craving, the craving stops, transforms, and disappears.

Remember the antidote to money fear: find your body, find your belly.

Retirement

Retirement (can I retire, or will I be able to retire) is one of the top, if not the top, financial issue professionals are asked to verify for their clients. It is an old outdated word made popular in an era when life expectancy was age 65, pre-industrial age, and our physical bodies were worn out and no longer able to physically work. We wanted and needed to retire. It was less a matter of can I *afford* to retire and more about my physical asset, my body, being no longer able to work. But the idea of retirement made its imprint in our psyche.

Now we expect a period in our life when we stop working and access leisure. Instead of reflecting deeper about what matters to us, our **why**, we short-circuit our journey with a future goal of not working/leisure that we imagine is desirable. It's my belief, and experience, that true well-being and satisfaction is what we seek; and this longing is achievable right now, not at some illusive time in the future. We need to *experience our wealth*, as noted by Jake Northrup, a rising star in financial planning and a mentee of our firm as he began his financial planning career. But, let me emphasize, the only place to experience wealth is in our body.

The irony of retirement and when work ceases is that in this transition rather than a welcome rest, intense feelings of fear arise because one of our most potent and long-lasting identities disappears. There are known studies of depression and suicide, particularly among men, when we stop working.

Instead of asking about retirement, let's access and experience the creative fire and juice of our belly to engage a full vibrant life right now.

During a fundraising event to support a building project, my teacher exclaimed, post liquidation of his six-figure retirement plan, "I'm never going to retire; what do I need a retirement plan for?" Now, I am not suggesting you liquidate all of your retirement plan savings. I am suggesting that you begin to investigate what retirement really means to you—beyond your money—toward what matters most to you in this life. A sound retirement plan is not what really makes you feel safe. Gaining access to the always here, present, stability of your wholeness is the gateway.

It is the development of our belly center that gives us roots through the earth into the ocean floor. Our belly truth is unwavering. It fosters creativity and freedom. The belly allows for confidence, strength, vitality, and stability to soar in retirement or whatever you choose to name the period in your life post working a fulltime job.

Plan

A plan is a thing that allows for interaction between people in order to relate to questions, situations, and objectives. A plan is a map, of sorts. But it is not the territory. Way too often the distinction is missed.

A financial plan is a narrower plan that focuses primarily on finances and anything related to finances—which is kind of everything—and that's the paradox of financial planning.

Why does the concept of a *plan* irk me so?

I am irked by the meaning we attach to the word "plan," as if a financial plan could ever be a rock-solid guide to how to live my life. Our attachment to a plan creates confusion, a false sense of security, hope, and sometimes a complete disaster. The truth is, a plan is only as good as the conversations that follow.

What is a financial plan, really? It's a printed (or electronic) set of numbers and reports that spit out data that was spit in—in a different form—in order to make sense of financial complexity. A financial plan is a way to simplify data in a format to be understood.

That's it. That's all a financial plan is.

In our firm, when we create financial plans, we consider it one phase of our work to engage in meaningful conversation with our clients. One of the initial statements we express is, "These are wrong." Nothing stops attachment better than stating right up front, "These are wrong."

Next question: Then why are we looking at them?

Financial plans offer us scaffolding for meaningful conversations. These conversations allow us to explore, learn, grow, navigate, contemplate, reflect, and integrate the factors involved in our financial lives and eventually make unique choices that serve us.

With the financial plan at hand, we *dynamically steer*, using a technical term borrowed from Agile Technology. Love dynamic steering. Life is a constant movement machine. The best way to be in movement is dynamically. So when we use the plan effectively, we are not attached to the numbers depicting a robust Monte Carlo analysis of a 99.99% probability of success. We are rewarded with choices guided by what matters most to us and positive financial potentials.

Financial planning thrives as a living process that moves. Grounded in the belly, we are able to be curious and motivated to make decisions that will allow for skillful investment in such deeply held goals as:

- Our (or our children's) education;
- A family reunion camping in the Grand Canyon;
- Repairs on our home;
- Funding a retirement plan aligned with our values;
- Giving to causes that feed our planet;

- Health care that optimizes physical vitality;
- Building the business of our dreams;
- Relationship nourishment;
- Minimizing taxes;
- Executing loving estate documents;
- Utilizing debt for financing;
- Engaging our creative expression for beauty and joy;
- And whatever calls our heart to engage life to the fullest.

Skillful investment choices happen with more consistency when we work with a financial plan and embodiment. The word "embodiment," and the importance of it within Somatic Finance, will be covered multiple times in our time together—both on the page and in practice off the page. For now, please note the dynamics of growth in this illustration:

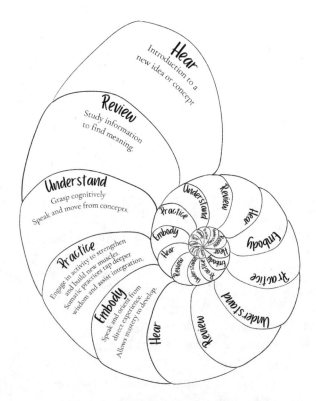

Figure 3.2   Illustration of Learning to Knowing to Embodiment.

Learning to Knowing to Embodiment

Most people's experience with a financial plan remains in the first three moves of hearing, reviewing, and understanding. Without recognizing the imperative of building new muscles that include somatic intelligence, we rarely touch move 4: Practice, or move 5: Embodiment. Reliably we have seen in our firm that limiting financial planning to understanding has moderate value. Benefit arrives with practice and embodiment, which we explore in more depth in the Practice Guidebooks.

To the point. . . Don't get attached to a plan. Get attached to exploring and learning with somatic awareness and grounding in the security of the belly.

Normal

The only phrase worse than the word "normal" is "back to normal." Back to normal is cousin to future-fearing. While fearing the future is an attempt to control what is coming, "back to normal" is a safety move that says, *I want what I know.* "What I know" is what I had, in the past. "What I had" is preferential to current reality. It's blatantly admitting an inability to *be here now.* (Rock on, Ram Dass).

There was never a normal in the first place, so what are we trying to get back to? That's funny! I'm making myself laugh. Seriously. I'm smiling—laugh is located underneath my jaw and chest and giggling eyes.

I just looked up the definition of normal:

Adjective: conforming to a standard; usual, typical, or expected.
Noun: the usual, average, or typical state or condition.

We can see the lure of normal. If something is standard or typical, then we can relax. We can breathe deeper because we know (cognitively) what to expect. This illusory knowing meets the scared space in our body that needs attention.

The good news is we have access to a consistent, reliable, always-right-here source of pure knowing—in our body. Our body is the ultimate gateway to and landscape of relaxation. Our body is always being used to relax our cognitive knowing—we just are not aware of it. The same vagus nerve action described earlier comes online, and we relax.

What if we bypassed the repeating inferior pattern of cognitive knowing and went straight to the body with our awareness? Yes. That's what we are up to. Get ready to crank up your practice to experience these words yourself.

And don't forget, numbers on the page and events in the world will move. Normal will slip away or shift when we're not looking. You might have an emotional and/or cognitive reaction to this uncertainty. Your belly and body are right here, always. Let's access a direct experience of safety through our body intelligence, an unspeakable kind of calm abiding that never goes away. Yes, we may feel the jolts and pops of uncertainty. But the core truth of our sufficiency is a breath away, a breath right into our belly center.

To be clear, we're not going to get rid of the words "guaranteed," "retirement," "plan," or "normal." That's okay! They help us communicate about life and financial issues. I don't want to exclude them. I want to include our somatic wisdom. Let's grow. Let's expand our skill base, optimizing our human potential. Including our body intelligence will make us better as financial planners providing services and as people handling their finances. It's that simple.

We'll get there with practice. But for now, pause and give attention to your belly center. Roll your hips forward and back giving rise to more movement and space in your belly center. Allow your breath to deepen down a few fingers below your belly button. Notice the calm that cascades after several nourishing breaths.

You rock too, just like Ram Dass.

Tiny Practice

Try it.
Try this tiny practice right now.

Place your hands one on top of the other on your belly center.
Breathe deep into your belly center.
Feel your unchanging presence right in the belly.
Your experience in the belly is whole and complete; nothing is missing, ever.

Appreciate

With a healthy balance, the belly expresses:

Stability;
Confidence;
Creativity;
Power.

Recognize

With an unhealthy balance, our belly constricts:

Connection;
Generosity;
Clarity;
Vision.

Reflection

In the Practice Guidebooks, you will learn about your "belly way"—what you currently optimize and where you are called to grow your belly skills. Consider the following questions to get a sense of your present belly way.

Do you move forward confidently with numbers or pause with caution and doubt?
Do you react to strong negative feelings about money by taking lots of risk?
Do you feel queasy inside when financial decisions arise?
Or do you face and follow through nonchalantly and relaxed with action?

Do you react negatively when other people have strong feelings about money?

In general, does money give you a sense of power and confidence or fear and doubt, or do you wobble back and forth depending on the situation?

Writing from the Voice of the Belly

The voice from the belly says, "Hello. I am the experience of ultimate freedom. When you experience life from my way, there is vast space—wide open pristine infinity. I offer you the vast open mystery—life's grand invitation.

"One aching desire we all have is freedom. Some say money means freedom. Freedom is this vast open mystery—a blank canvas, an open book, a clear path. Ironically, when given the freedom we deeply long for, we often get scared, shrink, and retreat from the openness. We want what we don't have, and when we get it, we run away. Does this sound familiar to you?"

The belly goes on: "Gayle's firm adopted an organizing structure called Holacracy back in 2011 that clearly defines work through roles and accountabilities. It seems like job titles and descriptions, but it is much more nuanced and refined. Each member of the firm takes on roles and accountabilities with full authority over their work. This engagement means every member of the firm has equal voice and authority to perform his or her work. Structured meetings are held to process work, create policies, and strategize support systems on behalf of the company aim.

"After practicing this structure for a couple of years, a young intern joined the firm with the intention to become a full-time employee. Most people desire full authority over their work with no micromanagement. She was no different. All people like freedom to do work and to do it well. But interestingly, Gayle discovered over the years that some, like this intern who did not join the firm, experience the freedom to make choices on that blank canvas as unnerving. This terrified intern was not willing to claim her authority that required her to rest in the unknown while making decisions.

"She wanted authority but when given the freedom to make choices, she wavered. She wanted others to make decisions for her to execute. This money dichotomy happens frequently.

"Money gives people the freedom to do what they want, when they want, with whom they want. Yes?

"No. Money does not give you freedom. I, your belly, give you freedom when you are willing to enter into the open space skillfully, with practice, and ground your freedom in that space. I offer you freedom with confidence, strength, and creativity.

"It might be hard to imagine. Actually, imagination will not get you there—only direct practice in paying attention to me will offer the authentic experience of true freedom. You might see the irony and issue now. Your concepts of freedom and ways to reach freedom block you from actually experiencing freedom.

"I offer you the way. In practice, I will teach you to relax tension knotted all over your body and tension swirling in myriad thoughts. Relaxation allows you to soften. Relaxation allows you to go deeper and receive body wisdom that is only available when you surrender.

"In practice, I look forward to engaging with you."

Oh, thank you my belly friend. I appreciate you! Now, let's take our sassy belly strength and meet the jewel of our heart.

Chapter 4
The Heart

*As more of humanity practices heart-based living it will qualify the
"rite of passage" into the next level of consciousness.*
*Using our heart's intuitive guidance will become common sense—
practical intelligence.*

—Doc Childre, founder of HeartMath[1]

After learning about the way of the head center and touching
the way of the belly center, you may be feeling the strength
of your ground and clarity in these centers. Or you may feel
out of sorts and not seen because your natural strength is accessed
in the heart center. Our insights teach us how being out of balance
in our centers can cause discomfort.

Now more than ever, we need money to move through the
heart. This statement may seem bizarre to some, perhaps interesting to others. If you are curious, or deeply touched, consider making a declaration with me to abide in the heart. I believe our world
is strengthened by those of us who carry the torch to move from and
through the heart. In fewer words, together we are stronger just by
being in the heart and, as Doc Childre expresses in the quote above,
"by using our heart's intuitive guidance."

The heart is vast and complex, and in some ways I hardly know
where to begin. Where do I start to help us understand the landscape of the most important somatic practice and radical development in modern culture? The heart is a powerful and complex

connection for all of life. The heart generously coaxes the lower body to meet the upper body. In Somatic Finance the heart connects the brilliance of the head and the power of the belly to meet financial decisions with wholeness rather than partial perspectives.

Let's Begin with a Tiny Practice

Sitting or standing, be still.

Feel your feet flat on the floor and rooted in the earth.

Lift your chest, elongate your spine, and bring your attention to your heart center.

Begin to breathe gently into the center of your heart.

Begin with the front, add the back of your heart, the bottom of your heart, the top of your heart, the left side and the right side.

After touching the six directions, allow each in-breath to intensify your connection and each out-breath to expand your heart space.

Note: it is common to feel physical pain with this practice; it is also common to feel numb or nothing at all. Whether painful or nothing, release effort, release critical thoughts, and simply offer kind attention to your heart space. Returning again and again with genuine intentional practice opens your heart when it is ready.

Now ask, what would it be like if all money moves came through the heart center?

Discovering the Heart

If you asked me a decade ago if I was open and felt deeply, I would have said without a shred of doubt, absolutely. I am sensitive and feel deeply. I always sense situations, and I am well attuned to others and myself. I am easily moved to tears and connect with ease.

My family codes movies with a "Gayle tear model" on a one- to five-tear scale.

I realized my sensitivity was not as deep and finely tuned when I was introduced to a spiritual practice that called me to open my heart, even more authentically, by shedding debris—somatically. A familiar Buddhist practice named Tonglen means giving and receiving. It is practiced to develop compassion and the ability to be present for our own suffering and the suffering of others. Tonglen is a beautiful practice, and I confess that before understanding the power of heart soma, my experience with Tonglen was quite conceptual. It came from my mind, well-meaning but hardly fruitful.

All generosity comes from the heart. All generosity comes from motivation, something that moves us to respond to something outside of ourselves. Our heart is a natural connector to all of life and generosity is the expression of these connections.

When I began to practice somatic heart-opening exercises, called bodhicitta, or "enlightenment mind" (the mind that strives toward awakening and compassion for the benefit of all sentient beings), a whole new experience emerged. At first, I was stunned by the physical pain I felt in my chest. The burning fire sensation coupled with ice pick jabs made me believe I was doing it wrong and/ or having an early heart attack. But no, this experience was normal. (Ahem, one of my favorite words.) Our heart physically hurts, even mimicking heart emergencies, when it is armored to protect us from emotional pain. With heart practices, offered in the Practice Guidebooks, the heart naturally releases obstacles and protections to reveal even more of our true essence.

You don't need a spiritual practice to access your heart. You might be curious and perhaps called to a spiritual path, but it's not necessary. You do need courage, curiosity, and willingness combined with a warrior attitude to access your heart. Breaking down the barriers of the heart is "heart work," and it hurts. Understanding that it hurts is not to dissuade you. Maybe your experience will prove differently because each of us has a unique "heart imprint" to access directly with practice.

The immediate question arising, after reading that heart practices are not a tickle adventure or cuddly hug, might be, why even consider including the heart in our work with finances? Because we can't not. We must engage the heart directly. Our minds are no longer sufficient to meet the realities of our expanding world. We need and require the wisdom that the heart brings to each situation. The veils that cover our heart center create delusion, confusion, and doubt. As you recall from the chapter on the head, wisdom is the unity of knowledge and intuition. The connection from the heart to the brain is a supercharged highway. Our intuition could be described as our heart wisdom beaming solar systems online.

The field of heart studies at HeartMath describes current scientific findings that are essential to our evolution and to the evolution of finance. The electromagnetic field generated by the heart is sixty times larger than the electromagnetic field generated by the brain. The magnetic component of the heart field is five thousand times as strong as the brain's magnetic field. Yes, that's right, 5,000 times. HeartMath also tells us the electromagnetic field of the heart permeates every cell of the body.

Let's just say, the heart is the mother lode of wisdom and compassion. Actually, she's always been in charge, and now we are asked to recognize such and wake up to this reality. You have heard of Einstein's famous quote, that you cannot solve a problem in the same plane it was created. The heart brain is a problem-solving engine. Access to the heart and brain, through developmental practices, gives us a direct link to this engine. The heart knows everything is possible, even when the head tries to prove otherwise. The brain can solve problems and bring intention into being. But it is the open connection between the heart and head that allows new solutions to manifest.

Your next question might be, Where does any of this relate to money?

The Heart Center and Money

Let me distill the necessity of our heart wisdom through my financial planning work and developmental training. Individual and collective well-being is cultivated through clarity, alignment, and right action. These three ingredients weave together in financial planning. Clarity arrives through unconditional presence (Somatic Heart practice in action), as we connect authentically with others, listening generously. In money conversations, listening with our heart expands our understanding of what is being said to a deeper level of clarity. Alignment with language, facts, and our *why* supports discernment of the best financial choices for each situation. With clarity and alignment, right action is not only possible but impeccably implemented. These are not simple words. They reflect a consistent practice empowered by integrity we can all enjoy. We feel through the heart and align with another's truth to support the right action—right action that illuminates what matters most, leading with potential and best choices.

If this description of finances and financial planning is unfamiliar, it's because you haven't experienced it yet! That's another reason I wrote this book, for you and others who long for something different.

Here we are with another anatomy illustration! Look it over, and then take a moment. Close your eyes (or at least one) and imagine strings of reliable connections from the brain to the heart and the heart to the brain. Each string has a job to do, such as slow down or speed up our heartbeats, depending on what is happening in the moment to optimize your life. Imagine the connections—the *many* connections neurologically, biochemically, biophysically, and energetically—in your mind, between the heart and head. Place a hand on the back of your head and a hand on your heart. Take a moment to give attention to your brilliant brain and your precious heart connections.

Gratitude and awe arise with these statements: Wow, the head tells us what's going on. The heart opens us to the situations, moments, and new information, reported by the head, that ask for our attention. Reasoned by the head and secured by the belly, our heart guides us to action in alignment with our *why*. The heart guides our *why* in action, where we get to feel our meaning come to life.

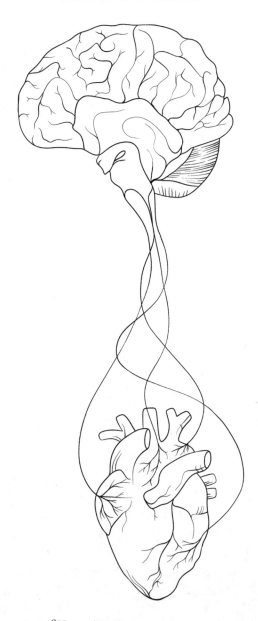

Figure 4.1   Illustration of Heart Anatomy.

You can get by in life with just your head and belly, being smart and feeling secure. But if you want to be fully alive in your whole human experience and the experience for all beings, open your heart. You'll find it is on fire, giving energy to all of *life*.

Two Stories of Generosity

As a child, my father gave me 25 cents a week for allowance. This gift was offered for being a part of the family, doing my weekly chores, and I suspect it was his way to eliminate repeated requests for money from me and my siblings to buy candy. But it was also my beginning of learning about money and his way of generosity. Growing into an adult, I would come to learn about many forms of generosity and that all generosity arises from motivation and is bound by connection.

My quarters were either saved in my pink ceramic pig piggy bank, spent on candy, or given away. Luden's cherry cough drops ("sugar medicine"), Sweet Tarts, and Pixy Stix were my favorite. Giving to my siblings or my mother's quarter change purse were my two "charities." As the youngest child in my birth family, I welcomed the attention of my older siblings and treasured the opportunity to play games with them. So when they offered me their friendship for my money or candy, I felt that the question was a no-brainer.

My values of connection over stuff or candy were well at play even at a very young age. "If you give me your money, I'll be your friend," was my earliest money memory when asked the question thirty years later in a financial workshop. In my innocence, generosity was easily expressed because connection is priceless especially to a child who knows little about money. Children's hearts are pure, and when they are able to remain in a childlike state of chronic wonder, their hearts lead and easily connect with the world. Where is your childlike wonder now?

I also gave quarters to my mother's "quarter change purse." At an even younger age, I found my mother's red cloth change purse in the drawer of the bedside table. She stated to me one time that's where quarters go. Periodically I would add quarters because, well, that's where quarters went. Later in life I would learn that my mother saved her quarters to purchase a new nightgown. Nightgowns were not part of the family budget; saving quarters until her change purse became heavy was her nightgown replacement practice.

My spouse and I had the good fortune to travel to Tibet with our spiritual teachers and friends to witness the fruition of humanitarian projects created by the organization.[2] As well, we enjoyed the native culture, deep immersion in study, and a few extraordinary ceremonies. It was during one such ceremony where thousands of villagers arrived to celebrate. Many generous gifts were bestowed on our precious teacher. But none so generous as from the crippled widow, a wandering nomad, who was carried slowly to the front of the room by two strong sherpas. When in front of our teacher, she carefully, with reverence and gratitude, placed a tarnished round coin in front of him. We were told this coin represented all of her savings. She gave it all away. I think it is near impossible for us in the west to imagine giving all of our money away.

Being introduced to the heart, and a taste of the heart's impact on our money lives, and the jewel of generosity, you might want to understand more and begin practice. But allow this initiation to be sufficient; there is so much more to share. Ultimately there is just this moment, just love, just wisdom. No inside. No outside. No here. No there. In this space, money reflects love, manifesting generosity. Who knew?

Appreciate

With a healthy balance, the heart expresses:

Connection;
Generosity;
Love; and
Empathy.

Recognize

In an unhealthy balance, the heart constricts:

Discernment;
Confidence;
Knowledge; and
Resilience.

Reflection

In the Practice Guidebooks, you will learn about your "heart way"—
what you currently optimize and where you are called to grow your
heart skills. Consider the following questions to get a sense of your
present heart way.

*Are you open to learning more about the heart center or feeling
trepidation?*
Does generosity feel natural, or do you feel a sense of lack?
*Are you able to relate your heart to money and financial
matters?*
Or do you feel confusion bringing the heart center in our conversation?
*How do your strengths (or limitations) in your Head and Belly relate
to your Heart?*
*In general, does money feel integrated in your life, or do you keep
money and relationships and planning separate?*

Now that we have explored our somatic landscape of the Head,
Belly, and Heart, it's time to learn how we behave when the three
centers are in play. Get ready to meet the financial archetypes of the
Academic, the Philanthropist, and the Capitalist, to recognize your
natural strengths and your areas of potential growth.

If this writing does not yet make sense cognitively, trust that it
may make more sense in practice. If one center proves more of a
struggle to work with than another, that struggle may simply point
to your direction for study and strengthening. This body center may
be your place to play in practice.

Writing from the Voice of the Heart

The voice from the heart says "Welcome!

"I am the ultimate experience of connection. When you experience life from my way, you are never alone. You share a rich fullness of interconnection to everything and everyone; I offer you inseparability.

"When it comes to money, one deep-seated fear is intimacy. You long and pine away for connection, being seen, deeply loved and wanted. Yet the vulnerability of being raw, ripe, and stripped naked with another makes you scramble for the hills to duck and cover.

"Herein lies the irony of me. You know, by heart, that the richest human pleasures come in the form of your connections—to others, situations, meaning, life. This intimacy is terrifying. Yet the only way for you to be authentically connected is when you are vulnerable, transparent, and open.

"Money is intimate and calls you on your contradictions. Because so often you declare your wants and then you cover up. You are not willing to bare it all. For example, you might say that you want to practice conscious spending, but you sabotage every opportunity to get real and face your spending reality. The intimacy, the truth, is too much to behold.

"In the middle of writing, years ago, Gayle attended an invitation-only retreat with thought leaders and activists from all over the world. She didn't know anyone except the organizer of the event. A new friend she met who was very interested in her work with Somatic Finance asked about Gayle's book, this book you are reading. Gayle's new friend said, 'I need it. When will it be finished?' Her direct question startled Gayle, and she offered a cautious answer. 'The book is writing itself, so I am flowing with what arises and meeting the book's schedule.' Gayle's new friend responded, 'I'm calling bullshit. I don't care whether you go past the publish date or not. Just give me a date.' Inside, Gayle laughed. Outside, Gayle appreciated her directness.

"Moments later Gayle declared a publishing date, giving way to the intimacy of that truth. Gayle needed to open to the powerful intimate connection with Somatic Finance and her fear of publicity. You must be willing to stay naked, transparent, real, raw, and vulnerable from every angle.

"Money does the same thing. Money reveals everything good, true, and beautiful, as well as bad, false, and ugly about you. That is why opening your heart to these connections can be so painful, or scary. You face all of the demons hidden in your closet.

"But I am the only way to and through. I reveal the ultimate truth of reality—your life connections with or without money create your life worth living.

"Money reflects your choices. Money reflects your word. Money reflects your motivation. Money is a powerful reflection, and this mirror is starkly revealing.

"I offer you the way through practice. I teach you to open and reveal so that eventually there is no vulnerability—pure love and generosity abide.

I look forward to connecting with you in practice."

Notes

1. Source: *A Deeper View of Intuition* (2019). Published by HeartMath.org. Fair use. https://www.heartmath.org/articles-of-the-heart/a-deeper-view-of-intuition.
2. The Pointing Out the Great Way Foundation, which has since split into two different entities/organizations. The Mustang Bon Foundation is the current foundation.

Chapter 5

The Trilogy of Archetypes: the Academic, the Philanthropist, the Capitalist

Sometimes money is so enmeshed in our psyche that we struggle to see it as the object that it is. The use of metaphors, in financial archetypes, shifts our way with money from subject to object, where we can observe it, learn new ideas, appreciate how we are, and grow in the ways that will serve us. We get to see with friendly exploration our way of being with money. We start to see what our way opens up for us and what our way closes down.

In this chapter, I introduce you to each archetype to learn how this particular way of being relates to money. In short, the Academic aligns with the head. The Philanthropist aligns with the heart. The Capitalist aligns with the belly.

Each of these archetypes opens up and closes down ways to relate to money. What I mean by "opens up" is that the strength of the archetype accesses something vital to be present. Conversely, "closes down" means that too much or too little of this archetype gets us stuck. We need all three archetypes to be energized and able to respond together in each situation.

As you read, you may find that you identify strongly with an archetype (picture yourself nodding and saying, "Yep, yep, yep") and feel confused by another (shaking your head, saying, "Huh?"). This is natural. Resonance is a signal that this archetype is your way; confusion is a signal that it is not.

Keep reading, even when confusion hits. We require all three archetypes to be online in order to operate at our best with our money. You can't rest on your laurels, and you can't brush off the unfamiliar. Let the feisty resistance sit down and snuggle with open, friendly curiosity to beautifully begin your journey into Somatic Finance. Let's dive into these ways and see what we discover about the archetypes and about ourselves.

The Academic

Mr. Duffy lived a short distance from his body.

—James Joyce[1]

The Academic, the archetype of the head way, lives in knowledge. The more knowledge and information, the better! Money systems are tailor-made for the Academic, and Academic nerds thrive in finance, because finance is skewed toward information, data, metrics, and science. (Yes, I confess; I am a financial nerd.) Academics love the many mental constructs of money—financial answers, products, strategies, laws, policies, and numbers. Yes, lots of numbers!

The Academic has impressive strengths in finance: exquisite structure, planning, strategy, clarity, perspective, details, and vision. Who doesn't want knowledge-based scaffolding to navigate the complexities of our very confusing financial systems? We need clarity, vision, organization, and structure.

But as you learned when you studied the head, many folks believe that knowledge and information are the be-all and end-all of finance, a limited view. As you may have experienced in your navigation of financial systems, a strictly academic approach can quickly become disheartening, frustrating, and even antagonistic.

Conjure up a money meeting. Picture a financial professional at the head of the table glibly gliding through the agenda and related papers and electronic screen. Around the table is a family, two parents and three adult children. The financial professional, an embodied way of the Academic, proceeds through the meeting without regard to any other way. Here are the numbers. Here is the plan. Here is the structure. The daughter and father who approach finances as the way of the Capitalist quickly become bored and frustrated by the mother and one brother who approach finances as the way of the Philanthropist. The mother and brother are confused and dejected; they don't understand the concepts and the decisions made. Their voices are lost in the conversation. Everyone becomes hostile. The financial professional and second brother see the finances clearly and why the plan works well. They do not understand the father and daughter's impatience and can't relate to the emotion of the others.

Most conversations about money are a flavor of the above meeting. It is more common than you might want to believe.

To be clear, the desire, need, or proclivity for information is not a problem. There is *nothing* wrong with the Academic. It is just a partial view and approach and will limit optimal results in how you relate to and use money.

In my Somatic Finance training programs, we explore the three archetypes with two questions:

What does this type express or create (allow for)?
What does this type constrict or limit (close down)?

Participants easily see the benefits of the Academic. It allows for exploration, curiosity, organization, new ideas, inspired communication, options, knowledge, next actions, and more. Our rational strategic mind gets cranked, jazzed, and fired up! "This is my job," the prefrontal cortex shouts.

Yet participants just as easily see that having too much of the Academic closes down other essential skills that can address the confusion, frustration, and hostility of dealing with money. These are skills such as connecting and relating to why and how these ideas matter and skills such as strength and creativity answering how these actions can reliably meet the objectives with confidence and care.

For some of us, our first impulse is *not* to research and get more information. Instead, we *feel* into the situation with our heart or belly. So when we encounter the Academic, the ruling archetype of financial systems, we feel shut down and marginalized. We don't know where to go. We distrust the systems and even more so, the professionals who work in the systems, because they don't speak our archetypal language and they don't meet us where we need to be met. For financial professionals, moving solely as an Academic closes down trust, connection, intimacy, generous listening, empathy, intuition, and more with the people who come to you for help.

Tiny Practice

Pause.
Feel your body's presence in this moment.
Are you seated and feeling the connection to the chair?
Get centered in your body by noticing your breath, inside your body.
Play with me here.
Take a moment now to notice the thoughts and feelings that may be arising.
I notice that I feel angry. My jaw is tense. What do you feel?
Let's move beyond the thoughts or feelings.
Feel the sensations in your body, as I move through mine.

As I write these words for you, my eyes are stinging. My belly is a bit funky. And my heart is a twinge achy. Sad might best describe what is underneath my anger. And most fascinating to me is that I work, swim, dance, fly in the field of finance. I *know* this world and yet I, too, feel the anger, frustration, and distrust. I feel the deeper truth of sadness under that protective shield. And under this sadness is an even deeper truth. As I stay with the sensations in my body, I sense that perhaps fear is also present. And going even deeper, allowing the truths to soften and give more space, I see that these feelings are tied to old stories and partial beliefs.

As we move through this swirl of feelings, thoughts, and sensations, we are utilizing our unique wisdom of the body.

Pause again.
Come back into your body. What feelings and sensations are present right now?
What are you experiencing?
Ask yourself:
What am I discovering?
Are any insights arising?
Is my body offering me new information or experience?
(If you skip this activity, you get a demerit. Five demerits and the book blows up. Don't say you were not warned. Goofy? Yes. And it makes me laugh.)

If your Tiny Practice produced a few new discoveries, or deeper insights, my guess is you might feel wobbly, a little confused, more curious, and willing to appreciate the importance of the way of the Academic, while recognizing that view is not enough in isolation. There is another archetype that complements the Academic.

Let's meet the way of the Philanthropist.

The Philanthropist

Aloha—the practice of giving without the expectation of anything in return.

At first blush, you might wonder how anything could be a problem about the archetype of the Philanthropist, aligned with the heart. I mean, who doesn't want to be perceived as a giver?

Those who move in the way of the Philanthropist are generous, sometimes to a fault. The strong, sometimes buried, beliefs held are "Giving is much better than receiving" and "Others need more than me." Tending to the other takes precedence over self-interest.

One might mistake the Philanthropist as someone who embodies a wide open heart—recognizing the needs of others, caring and tending to others. The Philanthropist archetype seems to come from a space of altruism. To a great extent this view is true. Our heart must be at least a bit awake to see beyond ourselves. The way of the Philanthropist allows for generosity, connection, love, and empathy. These heart capacities are essential for our human existence to cocreate, collaborate, compete, and cooperate. The heart is the moonbeam of connection.

Without the heart, which powers the Philanthropist, our web of interconnectedness of all beings would be void. There is not enough white space to convey the essential importance of the heart. Take a deep breath of WOW.

However, something interesting happens when we have an unhealthy skewing for the way of the Philanthropist. Our heart is open **and** closed. There is an unconscious protective shield that prevents the way of the Philanthropist from receiving—and one cannot authentically, purely, and cleanly give without also being able to receive.

In courses, class participants say. . .

Whaaaaat?

Giving from a partial heart means that the essence and joy of giving is tethered to unworthiness, not-enough-ness, should haves, guilt, shame, regret, doubt, and more. One of my cherished late meditation teachers, Dr. Daniel P. Brown, has described it in countless retreats and classes as "the pride of lowliness."[2]

It will come as no surprise that more women than men locate themselves as the way of the Philanthropist. (Not that men do not give. I can feel that dander getting up!) It is only that the feminine operating system is universal care. Feminine energy is vast, holding a wide berth and perspective. As we take in more of the present, and we see suffering, our heart gets activated, and we respond. This is a natural way of connection with others. We feel the pain of others and want to help. Wanting to help is authentic, and giving can be helpful, but included in the giving is also the subtle energy of lowliness.

When we operate primarily from the way of the Philanthropist, we deplete our self-reliance. Capacities such as discernment, confidence, knowledge, resilience, perspective, and more are missing. We give until nothing is left. Then we wonder what happened when our money is tight, or worse, gone—because we have been so nice giving to all of those in need. Not including ourselves in "all of those in need" creates a big problem.

Tiny Practice

Pause. (Remember the demerits for not playing.)
Locate your bottom on your chair.
Feel the connection to the surface.
Feel the earth and gravity supporting your body.
Allow your spine to rise.
Stretch your chest and heart wide.
Let the top of your head kiss the sky.
State out loud, audible so the cat (dog, hamster, bird) can hear: *"I matter too."*
Repeat this statement several times.
Bring your attention to your heart center.
Let your breath gently stroke your heart.
Keeping your attention at your heart center and gently breathing into this space, state out loud, *I matter too.*
Stay here repeating this phrase until you feel a shift in your heart space.
  Breathe.

If you are having a response to this Tiny Practice, my dear friend, stay with me. Common responses (and my response in this moment of writing) are welled-up pools of tears in the eyes, a fur-ball in the throat, and a padded blanket on the chest. If a story arises with these sensations, let it come and go. That story is a tender cloud moving through the sky. If thoughts of silliness, doubt, judgment, confusion rise (as in, *What the heck does THIS have to do with money?*), let them go. They are more clouds floating, moving, and releasing. Behind all clouds is a sun always shining unconditionally and indiscriminately, just like the rays of our heart.

The importance of giving cannot be understated. But being able to receive—wholeheartedly—along with giving is the superior practice, the embodied practice. We cannot balance these energies and skillfully respond with generosity if we lose ourselves. We matter too.

Let me introduce you to the Capitalist, who helps us matter, too, with a healthy sense of self and agency.

The Capitalist

Capital as such is not evil; it is its wrong use that is evil.
Capital in some form or other will always be needed.
                                                    —Mahatma Gandhi[3]

The way of the Capitalist is the most challenging to describe. You see, the Capitalist very often elicits a reaction of immediate repulsion. Some do not want to be seen as treading the way of the Capitalist. The reaction against the Capitalist can be surprisingly visceral. People see capital as negative: no connection, care, flexibility, collaboration.

Curiosity and determination caused me to research the etymology of the word "capital" for positive connotations. There weren't many. Colleagues urged me to find another word due to negative reactivity. Undeterred, I recognized a view that fully expressed the essence of the Capitalist and what it allows for.

Listening to *Revisionist History*, a Malcolm Gladwell podcast, I discovered what I was seeking and knew to be true. Gladwell presented capital and capitalism in the form of human capital and the unique skills individuals possess to grow and generate something, anything.[4] Capital is nothing more and nothing less than power and energy and the manifestation of our creative expression.

In our financial advising work, we often discuss human capital, emphasizing that human capital, the capacity of our body and person, is our most precious asset. The vessel from which we live life is our precious container for reaping the joys and fulfillment we all seek. If your body struggles with daily pain, confusion, and disease, little else matters, certainly not money. All attention is given to just getting free of pain. Without a healthy body (including our mind), life is limited. Human capital is the power and energy to fuel a full life.

The Capitalist archetype allows us to express our unique gifts and energy in the world. When we embody the way of the Capitalist, our belly is full of confidence, vitality, creativity, strength, action, right timing, passion, and more. We make things happen, and we get things done. We manifest.

Going further, when our unique, creative individual human capital combines with others', culture thrives. Gladwell emphasizes the necessity of diversity; the richness of our collective develops from differing views, abilities, and contributions. Diversity at its essence is our creativity. Our creativity, having different views, opinions, ideas, abilities, and perspectives is essential for human systems to survive. The Great American Dream is only great when we generate a welcome mat for everyone. Our melting pot of human capital explodes into a new way of being, where everyone is invited to the table to offer their creative expression. Yes. We fail often and badly in this collaboration of human capital. But let me emphasize, human existence is generated from each of us recognizing our unique precious gifts, finding our place on this earth, and connecting with others to express our gifts. In other words, we know our gifts and we share them. If these gifts are not expressed, as the fabulous Martha Graham wrote, they will be lost forever. She said:

> There is a vitality, a life-force, an energy, a quickening that is translated through you into action and because there is only one of you in all of time, this expression is unique. And if you block it, it will never exist through any other medium and be lost. The world will not have it.[5]

Put that in your back pocket. It's a keeper. This is the way of the healthy Capitalist. Bam!

By contrast, the unhealthy Capitalist closes down generosity, kindness, and strategic action in service of self-preservation and self-interests. An overzealous Capitalist is unable to see the benefit of connecting and the importance of clear vision. Scarcity and greed accumulate rapidly. This is the Capitalist that we might envision, but it isn't this archetype's true creative expression.

Tiny Practice

(Remember the demerits if you skip this!)
Notice where your mind is.
Bring your attention to your belly.
Place your left palm just below your belly button and your right palm over your left.
Give it a hug (release shaming thoughts of belly bulge).
This. This is your power center.
Give your engine generous breath and fill'er up!
Expand your belly like a balloon with each subsequent breath.
Do this up to ten times softly counting.
Feel the front belly, the back belly, the upper belly, the lower belly, the side bellies.
These six directions reach to infinity.
Love your belly.
Love your Capitalist.
Rejoice in your unique gifts and energy to share.

Imagine standing at the top of a mountain. Your feet are rooted firmly. Your belly grounds your being; arms are stretched wide with a smiling heart. What do you shout out to the world? What is the fire blazing in your belly that only *you* and your unique precious self can offer?

Get crazy. Shout it now.

I shout that I want to cocreate with you, and others, willing to set their genius on fire!

The Trilogy of Archetypes Dancing

What happens when the capacities of the three archetypes work together?

The way of the Academic produces fabulous plans and follows rules according to a narrow precise path, doing what is right, expected and proven. The Academic files taxes promptly, keeps meticulous records, and restructures an investment portfolio based

Figure 5.1 Illustration of Dancing Archetypes.

on a rigid formula. Estate plans are current, insurance protection is adequate, budgets are strict, and all the "shoulds" in the world are tended to. The way of the Academic holds money and finances in a tight box, separate from other aspects of life. By itself, the way of the Academic is hollow and stale.

But when the Academic dances with the way of the Philanthropist. . .

The strict genius of the Academic links up with the deep purpose of the Philanthropist. The ability to plan and strategize connects to visions of generosity, kindness, and community. This is vastly more well-meaning than the Academic alone, and more orderly than the Philanthropist alone.

But the head and the heart often do not move in sync. The Philanthropist gives without thinking of the consequences. The Academic contracts in frustration to do things by the book, determined and controlling the numbers. Plans fall apart in conflict. *Money is a source of pain, and why not give it away to feel better,* says the Philanthropist. *Money is a source of pain and now we really need to tighten our belt and control what happens,* says the Academic.

We are missing power, steadiness, vitality, and movement.

We are missing the way of the Capitalist.

And what happens when the Academic and the Capitalist take a turn on the dance floor?

The knowledge of the Academic and the power of the Capitalist make a formidable couple. This is the predominant energy we perceive in successful financial corporations and Wall Street. Vision, clarity, and organization move stealthily with determination, vigor, and results. Combine the precision of the Academic with the power of the Capitalist and you will see buildings built, money accumulate, finances flow, spending and saving and stretching—oh my! This successful, outcome-driven life looks favorable. So what's the problem?

Here's the problem.

Without the generosity and care of the heart, the Philanthropist, manifestations are hollow. They are harmful. Without regard to who is affected, visions manifest with force for the benefit of a few.

ALL money actions that do not include the heart are void of humanity. The purpose of our existence is missing, and we might as well be the illusions from *The Matrix. I'll take the blue pill please.*[6] All meaning in life is sourced from the way of the Philanthropist. You might have already felt the drop in energy as you read. You might now feel a tug pulling your heart down with the realization that this, a lack of attention to our heart—and a lack of the integration of all three centers—is the present predominant state of our money way.

Without the heart, humanity is doomed. Yes, that does feel bleak. Sobering. Stark.

It's also the truth.

But when all three archetypes are integrated, when the openness of our heart connects the head and the belly, we access to our capacity to feel sufficiency and operate with generosity. I call this the Virtuous Flow of Somatic Finance, the truth, the potential we have been waiting for.

Tiny Practice

Take a moment for these ideas to sink and settle.
Place the palm of your left hand on your belly.
Place the palm of your right hand on your heart.
It's okay.
We are here, right now.
Be in your body activating your expression of all three archetypes.

Take a final moment here. Give attention to the entire felt sense of your body—find your skin, the container of your body. Breathe through your pores and wash your body with love. Feel the sensations around your belly, heart, and spine. Make the connection to each center by giving attention to each. Place your hand on your belly, then your heart, and then elongate your spine.

In your belly find presence.
In your heart find connection.
In your spine find wholeness.

Set an intention to move with money from an integrated whole: Head, Heart, and Belly. Add to that intention to let the heart lead, let the head provide a vision, and let the belly energize action.

Your practice takes us one step closer to universal integration, which is a weird way of saying love.

Notes

1. Source: Joyce, James. (1914). *Dubliners.* London: Grant Richards Ltd. Fair use.
2. Source: https://www.drdanielpbrown.com. Fair use.
3. Source: Gandhi, 1940. *Harijan.* Public domain.
4. Source. "Carlos Doesn't Remember," *Revisionist History* podcast (2016). Hosted by Malcolm Gladwell. Fair use.
5. Source: de Mille, Agnes (1991). *Martha: The Life and Work of Martha Graham.* New York: Random House. Fair Use.
6. Source: *The Matrix* (1999). Directed by Lana Wachowski and Lilly Wachowski. Produced by Warner Bros./Village Roadshow Pictures/ Groucho II Film Partnership/Silver Pictures. Fair use.

Chapter 6
The Virtuous Flow

Instead of one step forward, what is the deeper step in?
—David Whyte

The Virtuous Flow of Somatic Finance is the capacity to feel sufficiency and operate with generosity in regard to our money, as well as other areas of a wealthy life. We are familiar with similar models for healthy relationships and healthy careers, but we exclude money. This model welcomes all of our life, sustaining all wealth, built through our bodies. When the openness of our heart connects the abilities of our head and our belly, we are able to be in Virtuous Flow.

We experience Virtuous Flow through somatic practice. It isn't only an idea; it's a state of being that arises from embodiment. Recall our illustration—"Learning to Knowing to Embodiment," on page 36. Our first moves are to read, study, and understand concepts with the head, and then with practice, we begin to embody the concepts in our belly and our heart.

I use the word "virtuous" on purpose. When we feel sufficiency and operate with generosity, our actions model our authentic nature. The Virtuous Flow is a way of being that sustains life; instead of killing it, we flourish as humans. I use that word, "killing," on purpose, too, for we know a world that runs on the opposite of sufficiency and generosity, a world of scarcity and greed. When scarcity and greed feed our veins, we suffer physical, moral, planetary death. The Virtuous Flow is a better way of life.

I want you to know, though, that Virtuous Flow isn't an end-point. It isn't an achievement or a mountain top where you arrive and say, "I made it." No myth of arrival. No one gets a certification in Virtuous Flow with pretty letters behind your name. But I will gladly blow you a kiss!

We move in and out of a feeling of sufficiency. We move in and out of generosity. We are human beings, with our complexity and contradictions. Instead, the Virtuous Flow gives us a practice to help us be fully embodied in this precious form as we use money.

I know these ideas can be slippery. (*Sufficiency* is what now?) That's because they aren't really ideas; sufficiency and generosity are experiences of the body. Please take my hand and, with curiosity and amusement, saturate your head with information, so you can begin to understand the elements of the Virtuous Flow.

The Virtuous Flow is shaped like a Möbius strip. Feelings of sufficiency loop around and lead to the actions of generosity, which loop around and feed into feelings of sufficiency. We don't stand still; we act and absorb, sense and reflect, give and receive and give. Consider breathing, a constant loop of in, down, around, up, out, and back in, again and again. Like breathing, virtuously flowing is a dynamic capacity that sustains life.

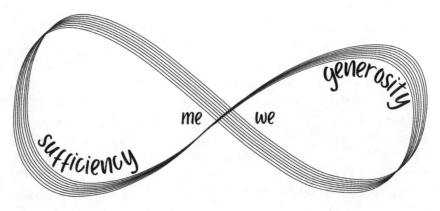

Figure 6.1 Illustration of Virtuous Flow.

Also, like breathing, the Virtuous Flow can move quickly or slowly. It can be interrupted, or it can be a struggle. We practice, gaining proficiency and awareness.

Let's get more familiar with the Virtuous Flow by exploring its two gateways: sufficiency and generosity.

Sufficiency

You never know how much is enough until you know how much is too much.

—William Blake[1]

Sufficiency is the ability to abide no matter what comes up. It's knowing, in your body, that you are okay. No matter what, you are okay.

It's also okay if you can't believe that such sufficiency exists, particularly around money. That disbelief rises in part because sufficiency is only known in the body, not a concept. It's okay to feel a lot of skepticism right now!

But stay curious, too. Think about some of the words we use in everyday life to mean sufficiency—having enough, or having plenty. That's often how we see things as "sufficient."

Yet these words can't get us to the true sense of "I am okay, no matter what." Having enough carries a smidge of lack, and the possibility of needing more just to make sure you have enough. Having plenty can tip us over into having too much, as eating plenty usually leads to an overfull belly.

In sufficiency, we are grounded in the present moment of *I am okay*. Nothing else exists but this moment of okay-ness. Pristine. True. Yes. Long out breath of reality. Our first direct experience of this sufficiency may only be for a nano-moment but a moment, nonetheless. Soon, through embodied practice, the moments begin to cling together for longer moments of *I am okay*. String together these clusters of longer sufficiency moments, and pretty soon more than fifty percent of your time is flowing in sufficiency.

From here, this ground of *I am okay*, it is easier to be fully awake to our life, our incarnation, our situation, who we are, our responsibilities and opportunities. We more easily recognize the ocean we swim in and others are swimming too. We are all in this together. We belong to a WE. And from here, there is a natural and easy opening to generosity.

Here, in embodied sufficiency, money makes the most sense. Our understanding of impermanence, coupled with our okay-ness, allows a bigger perspective on our human existence and the role money plays in the larger view. Money is a conduit for life to happen. Life happens among people. We are part of something much greater than ourselves. Money allows us to connect with the greater whole.

In sufficiency we come to realize that our body is essential in all aspects of life, including money. The body is a source of unique wisdom. As we relax, which happens in our body, we directly sense sufficiency, with all of our senses. We begin to integrate our personality traits with money; in this unification we move toward embodied sufficiency, which supports the release and healing of money habits, beliefs, behaviors, and traumas. The body allows for coherence and harmony, and money becomes coherent when our somatic wisdom meets each situation.

Generosity

It is only with the heart that one can see rightly. What is essential is invisible to the eye.

—Le Petit Prince

Authentic generosity naturally emerges from the space of sufficiency. It is the capacity to give and to receive with openness.

Authentic generosity gets distorted by "idiotic generosity." Some practice generosity from a place of lack, rather than sufficiency; lack originates in ego, a limiting belief or pattern. We are told early in our life to be selfless, not selfish. Practice the Golden Rule: "*Do unto others as you would have them do unto you.*" These embedded "should" ways of generosity harm. As mentioned earlier, it is idiotic generosity to give to others when you generate self-harm. When you give to your own detriment, whatever is given is challenging to receive. Self-sufficiency is a practice of self-awareness. When we give in harmful ways, particularly self-harm, it is an absence of awareness and an absence of embodied sufficiency.

Authentic generosity naturally emerges from the space of sufficiency. Many of us are generous, and we believe that our generosity is authentic. However, unless we embody sufficiency, our generosity contacts fragments of scarcity. We know this because we float from scarcity to generosity without a sustained presence of healthy me.

Sufficiency, interestingly, can be catalyzed by idiotic generosity. When in a state of giving and creating self-harm, an opportunity arises to learn self-care and experience authentic sufficiency. Remember our sweet mantra, "I matter too"? If we give to our own detriment, the pain caused from our excessive giving is the invitation to take care of ourselves. The best and most used example of this concept is reflected in the emergency instructions when flying on a plane. Always put your own oxygen mask on before you put the mask on a child or friend.

If you give with a condition, any condition, this is idiotic generosity. Authentic generosity is without conditions. "Aloha," the Hawaiian greeting shared earlier, means to give without the expectation of anything in return. This way of giving generates unlimited energy; it is boundless, vast, and inexhaustible. We gauge the authenticity of our giving by the energy sustained in our body.

Now that's a meaningful measurement! Vitality. Aliveness. Health. Vibrancy.

Sufficiency and generosity flow into and out of each other. But just as rocks in a river disrupt the current, two other states of being splash and disrupt money's Virtuous Flow: scarcity and greed.

Scarcity

Scarcity is a visceral feeling of "not enough" and "not safe." Scarcity is felt even if you are surrounded by resources. Scarcity arises from fear of not having enough (or not being enough). The lack of "enough-ness" produces discomfort, which typically translates into "I am not safe." In scarcity states, sufficiency is impossible, and generosity is as dangerous as death.

In this writing you are learning about scarcity as an idea, with our head skills. As we continue to learn and practice through our belly, the seat of safety, these ideas become experiences in your body. Using our body as a guide helps us explore fear with curiosity and perhaps amusement, developing a resourceful way of engaging fear. **Fear is the underbelly of scarcity—all money issues. (Yes, I did say all.)**

Fear is fundamental to our money because fearing for our safety ·is intrinsic to being human. Fear about money, about not being safe, is embedded in our DNA, literally in our bones and all bodily systems. Fear about money, about not being safe, is steeped in our family systems, from our family ancestry through our inception to our birth, childhood, adolescence, and adulthood. Our culture and the modern world, including a vast and complicated financial system, compound these personal and family fears.

Stories, beliefs, patterns, and behaviors develop out of all those experiences, and not having enough money or safety becomes a fundamental lens through which we see our world.

When we turn to the body, we see that fear is typically felt in the belly, the seat of safety. Safety is the first of three essential human nutrients for healthy development, followed by connection and dignity. (We'll dive into the three nutrients in the next chapter.) Our belly, which houses vital parts of our nervous system, adapts to feelings of safety and danger. In our early development if we do not feel safe, our body will assist by shaping—protecting—to keep feelings of danger or threat at bay. These belly-centered nervous system adaptations evolve into patterns, stories, and behaviors that continue to mute those feelings as we grow. Money is often a disruption pattern, found in the belly, that feels like pain, nausea, or any number of sensations. You have a signature disruption that only you can feel.

The vast majority of our belief system about money is in place at a very young age. As we grow older, we reinforce these beliefs through interactions and experiences with others and in various situations. The belief becomes our behavior around money. Have you ever heard money described as dirty? Do you believe that to be true?

Imagine Peter. Peter as a kindergartener walked to the bus stop with his mother. He spotted a round silver coin and enthusiastically picked it up exclaiming, "Look mom, I found a coin!" Just as quickly, his mother admonished him saying, "Peter, that money is dirty! Throw it away!" This experience creates a money imprint that deepens and scars for the rest of Peter's life. Beliefs about dirty money form so that Peter looks through a lens of money for "dirt." His beliefs are reinforced throughout childhood into adulthood. When he graduates from college and seeks employment, he undervalues his contribution because it doesn't feel good to earn a living. His belly aches, and in fact, his belly always bothers him when money is involved. His identity of being a good noble poor person, in contrast to a dirty person who has a lot of money, magnifies under that early childhood money lens. Decades of patterning through that lens reify and solidify the truth that money is dirty.

Consider the outcomes of our identity, our safety, being tied to this story and patterned scarcity beliefs.

But we can shift scarcity beliefs. The shift starts to happen when one or more of the following occurs: (1) the beliefs and behaviors are pointed out, (2) previously unfelt feelings and emotions are felt, and (3) a visceral sense of a shift happens with awareness and presence.

Once we recognize the belief, feel the feelings, and sense a shift, we practice maintaining the shift. Just because something is recognized doesn't mean we are finished. Our recognition is an opening to do the practices, gain more insight, and clear up the debris of all limiting beliefs, behaviors, and emotions related to scarcity.

Body practice offers a kind and compassionate invitation to shift from scarcity beliefs to sufficiency beliefs. In the Practice Guidebooks, you will learn and experience somatic belly practices as an antidote to scarcity. When practice enables you to live better than 50% of the time without scarcity tendencies, you activate the capacity to enjoy sufficiency. You are freer to step into the Virtuous Flow.

Greed

Money is the most powerful secular force in the 21st century.
—Dick Wagner[2]

When you remain in a closed constricted state of scarcity and lack, fear can crystalize into greed. Greed is a bound-up knot, an insatiable sense of deprivation, lust, desire, and aggression. In greed there is no recognition of others—there is only me. Whew!

After exploring our scarcity, we soften into befriending greed, often the "one who shall not be named" in us. Typically we avoid looking at our own greed because there is always someone or some situation far more egregious than our own. This statement is true; we can always find someone worse than us, and we can always find someone better than us. Comparisons do not matter. The consequences of our own ignorance, aggression, and desire make it necessary and important—dare I say imperative—for us to broaden and deepen our understanding and recognition of our individual and collective unconscious.

Greed is reified fear. Greed is the crystallization of fear. Greed could be described as the fossilization of fear. There is much to say about greed, and I devote a whole chapter to it. We cannot ignore greed anymore. Because, ultimately, greed is a slow way to die.

Greed holds the deep wounds of the soul. Greed is not natural. What is your greed? Are you greedy for information, chocolate, sex, attention, time, power, experiences? Greed is not just about money. To soften, greed requires courage, humility, vulnerability, light-heartedness, and fierce love. And the body is the best space to meet this powerful money force—particularly with greed.

Just like we practice when held in scarcity, we practice the somatic finance practices (get the Guidebooks!) if we are stuck in greed. But the practices are different depending on who is practicing. Greed may require the gentlest whispers of touch. Or it may require a fire-stoked sledgehammer. Sometimes the practices and attention don't look pretty. But then, reified fear isn't pretty either.

Here is a small written practice to give you a taste of what it means to face greed with care. We begin to face greed with head skills, often in the form of examine, experience, explore questions, to settle the confusion and anxieties of the Academic.

1. **Examine** the nature of greed.
   What happens to me, the individual, and others, the collective, when greed persists?
2. **Experience** practices to access my own greed.
   How can I allow the presence of generosity to meet my terror? Am I aware that greed flourishes with terror? What is my experience of these survival instincts on steroids?
3. **Explore** the power of love and acceptance.
   Am I aware the antidote to greed is love? Am I willing to accept and love what is? Am I willing to taste okay-ness, feel the depths of despair, sorrow, and disconnection? What happens when I allow the full expression of my worst feelings, and I arrive on the other side okay? What is liberated in me from the fear of those feelings?

You will learn more practices to face greed. For now, go with the following question:

What is my essential deep wound that wants attention?

We cannot make the journey unless we are open to all aspects of ourselves. Greed happens, and we cannot ignore it. Some stuck in greed require an ice pick or forest fire to shift; neither of these experiences is friendly or desirable. Not all will make the journey—some of us will be left behind, some of us will die, some of us will hold on to the illusion that we deserve more and others deserve what they get. Life is not a dress rehearsal, but we constantly forget. What do we do instead of standing idle? Light a candle, a gentle flame of care and concern, and watch the frozen grip melt.

In greed we open and wonder and give space. We allow what naturally arises and what is willing to show up to reveal itself. The slightest move to fix, change, judge, shame, criticize, blame, or resist will halt the melt. Our deepest wounds require tender touch. When we lovingly open ourselves, without judgment, our wounds, held in greed, show up.

Greed is a human condition. It does not arise from nature or our natural state of mind. Greed is human-made and our natural unfiltered body intelligence is our ally to teach us and heal us.

The Vision of the Virtuous Flow

Let me feel that love come over me. Let me feel how strong it could be. Bring me a higher love.

—Steve Winwood[3]

Given the intensity of greed, the scope of scarcity, is the Virtuous Flow ever possible for us?

Good question. The truth is, very few of us, if any, live on the Virtuous Flow. I don't. So let's give ourselves a break and lower the bar. Relax. The Virtuous Flow is an aspiration. A noble one, but still an aspiration, a vision. I am writing, and you are reading this book—not so we can congratulate ourselves for perfection nor hate ourselves for failing but to see what could be and to practice, in the body, the dance steps of human flourishing.

My **why** can be summed up in the Virtuous Flow. So let me spend a few minutes here. My dream is human flourishing, a higher love individually and collectively abiding on the Virtuous Flow—where each of us generates our gifts for the world, and each of us receives the gifts of others. We are not abiding there—not by a long shot, but I know we can.

The good, the true, and the beautiful of humanity come alive in our many, many, many differences, or geniuses. Consider a kaleidoscope or tile mosaic. Different forms, textures, and colors come together to create unique beauty. A symphony is created through myriad musical instruments—violins, horns, trombones, percussion, and more—conducted by the heart's inspiration. We are sounded into another world of truth. How can human flourishing not be good? Or, better queried, can we see and imagine the good in the flourishing of all humans?

When we are not able to flourish, we perish a slow existence; many of us are slowly perishing. When bright minds and generous hearts are not able to soar, we all miss out, and we need to change our systems, our connections, our views, our ways of going.

When we demand more from those who are unable to give more and we block the ability of those capable of giving more, we lose. We practice oppress-insanity—oppression and insanity.

Let's look at one system. Common beliefs in our society proclaim that higher education and academic rigor will garner a sound future with a solid career and lucrative opportunities, a trajectory filled with achievement and honor. We value education. I value education. But education is not opening our minds and hearts to why we are here and how to express our gifts.

Friends, a couple, who land in the gen X generation struggle financially. Well, they struggle in spirit, like many of us, which manifests in slow perishing where money limitations become the threshold of the struggle. This couple holds higher degrees. He earned a PhD investing significant financial resources, time, and energy. In the time of Covid, he performed odd maintenance jobs for people in his community. His potential is languishing, and he is not an anomaly. Many of our bright minds and hearts are not accessing pathways to flourish. His partner works skillfully in his excellence and genius zone to earn a sufficient income—but only so much because if he earns too much, their health benefits will erode and they can't afford to pay more. They are not saving for a future. They are getting by.

Please understand too, even if financial resources are rewarding, if we remain stuck in a comfortable financial position where we are not expressing our genius, we still feel scarce. We are too scared to make the leap into a life that brings us to our full measure. This choice, very common, results in the slow death I spoke of earlier.

What is this? We exist in a cluster of crap where decisions are made from a narrow scope of understanding that affect millions. Our planet offers nature's response in fires, floods, fierce winds— and a mountain-sized flip of the bird to all of us. Actually, nature is not saying this. Nature only mirrors our own oppress-insanity.

I assure you I do not have any solutions.

But I maintain a dream of human flourishing.

I maintain that we need a world where each of us can offer our gifts and receive the gifts of others.

I maintain that we need a world where our hearts lead the way.

I maintain that when we access our own sufficiency by balancing our Academic, Capitalist, and Philanthropist, we open the gateways for generosity.

I maintain that the Virtuous Flow is possible for all of us.

The Virtuous Flow of Somatic Finance is our potential when we welcome the wisdom of our soma to the party. Abiding as the Virtuous Flow is a rhythm of movement attuned to the moments at hand communicating a higher loving life. Virtuously flowing along the Möbius strip honoring our body intelligence as money flows—wherever money serves each situation, each place and all beings.

It's time to touch in to your motivation for reading this book, your **why**.

Has your motivation shifted or altered in any way?

What is new that nourishes your motivation to continue to read?

What has happened to your beliefs about money?

How is your body responding to tiny practices?

Where are the subtle nudges to get started?

I can't wait to play with you—in practice!

Notes

1. Source: Blake, William (1790–1793). From "The Marriage of Heaven and Hell." Public domain.

2. Source: Wagner, Richard. (2016). *Financial Planning 3.0: Evolving Our Relationships with Money*. Denver: Outskirts Press. Fair use.

3. Source: *Higher Love* (1986). Written and performed by Steve Winwood. Produced by Island Records. Fair use.

Chapter 6a

Love Letter Invitation

Dear YOU, my precious reader,

It is pure joy connecting with a letter. Imagine you are opening an envelope with gorgeous stationery of heavy weight paper. Take this letter to your favorite reading spot for personal letters. That's how I roll. Intimate. Personal. Real.

We are all different when learning something new. Somatic Finance is new. Some of us want more information, like the way of the Academic. Some of us want to get moving, like the way of the Capitalist. Some of us want to feel more connected, like the way of the Philanthropist. At this juncture in the book, you have read sufficient information—sufficient landscape—about Somatic Finance. You can continue to read more landscape details and information about Somatic Finance or you can begin to practice. If you recall, in the beginning of the book I shared that two sections constitute the book, along with a special companion site with practice resources and guides for your experience. Each offering has a unique feel and purpose. Practice is available at any time. Access the online Practice Guidebooks for guidance and instructions.

Take a moment to choose the way of engaging this book that feels most enlivening and aligned with your way. As you know, there is no right way.

For some, you are just getting started and settled and relishing information. You will want to continue to engage in Somatic Finance by reading in the order the book is presented.

For some, you might be antsy and feeling a vibe for deeper somatic engagement. You will want to return to reading this section after or while engaging in practices, jumping in the ocean and swimming around.

For some, you might be very full but not ready to engage in practice, and you want to feel more connected to our humanity. Take a big leap to the fruition section for more stories and wonderings and generous conversation.

The ocean is vast, and there are myriad ways to engage the lively body of water. Some of us dive deep into the dark mystery with scuba gear and sophisticated equipment. Some of us stay on the shore's edge playing and swimming, taking our time to get wet. Some of us travel the ocean surface in vessels that go fast and slow, water skiing, or floating on a raft.

What is your way? How do you know?

Come inside your body and ask.

How do I want to engage this book right now?

What response does your body provide?

Thank you, my precious friend. I appreciate you welcoming your body wisdom and cocreating with this reading, these practice invitations and conscious choices.

Oceans of joy,

Gayle

Let's dive deeper and a bit wider to explore subtler elements of the landscape of Somatic Finance. What nourishment do we need in order to experience the Virtuous Flow? Why is the heart essential for transcending the limits of individualism? How do greed and shame block us from living a wealthy life? These chapters let you relish in greater information and finer detail about Somatic Finance, preparing you for practice.

Part IB

Subtleties
of the Landscape

Chapter 7

The Trilogy of Nutrients—
Safety, Connection,
and Dignity

From birth to death, the human brain changes more than any other organ. And just as plants take shape according to the availability of sunlight, soil and water, our brains take shape according to the availability of three essential nutrients: safety, connection and respect.

—Amanda Blake[1]

We need three things in order to develop as full human beings and to build the capacity to tap into the Virtuous Flow. As author and scholar Amanda Blake writes, we need safety, connection, and dignity. I use dignity and respect as the individual and collective of the same idea, respectively. Dignity resides in me. Respect is received from outside. Both represent the same nutrient.

When we do not receive these essential nutrients from our family, community, or environment as we grow up, two things happen.

First, **our bodies** will adapt to help ensure our safety, make connections with others, and feel dignity. (Our bodies do this? Yes!)

Second, because our adaptations don't meet all of our human nutrients, we then look outside ourselves for safety, connection, and dignity; we often look to **money**. We turn to money to make us feel safe. We use money to help us connect to other people and to groups. We lean on money to provide us dignity. But money can't nourish us. We don't experience a truly wealthy life by using money, or anything outside of ourselves, as nourishment. Nutrients are generated and replenished by authentic safety, connection, and dignity allowing us to inhabit and experience a joyful thriving existence with money.

But before we go further, let's look at how the body becomes our developmental support system to source these three nutrients.

Think of the plant Amanda Blake references. Its essential nutrients are healthy soil, sufficient water, and ample sunlight. When a plant is missing sunlight, it grows in any direction required to find the sun. Its stem changes. When a plant is thirsty, it will take care to minimize use of moisture at the expense of creating more leaves. Its veins change. When a plant takes root in too-compacted soil, roots get thin to find open spaces. Its roots change. The body of the plant adapts in order to get essential nutrients.

Similarly, our body bends, armors, shrinks, bulks in varying ways to meet each situation for protection (safety), attention (connection), and worth (dignity). Do I feel safe? If not, our body contracts toward safety. Do I feel connected? If not, our body armors the spaces that are open and vulnerable. Am I fundamentally respected? If not, our body imprints unique ways that help us retain dignity. In short, where nutrients are not present or received or fully digested, from itty bitty babyhood to childhood to adolescence to adulthood, the body, our body, will seek to fulfill that need.

Tiny Practice

As you let these ideas of essential nutrients sink in, take a whole-body breath by breathing into all the pores of your skin and float these wonder questions through your mind, deepening in your body. Ask yourself, Hmm, I wonder:

What essential nutrient is asking for my attention?
What essential nutrients might be missing or depleted from my growth?
How my body is currently shaped to source nutrients?

Do you suffer from frequent belly aches, do you have a twitch in your eye, do you find your head tilting, do you lean away from people in situations, does one side of you turn toward something while the other turns away? Notice and trust your experience. No judging. There are endless responses, and we all have body responses to compensate for our lack of nutrients.

You may feel called to journal and explore the insights that emerge from the questions. Or wait until you enter practice and view the Practice Guidebooks where questions like these return.

The adaptations our bodies make to ensure safety, connection, and dignity show up in many ways: a twisted hip, the lingering head tilt, hunched shoulders, stomach pain, achy heart, or in my case, a funky left shoulder. Over and over, day-by-day, and year-by-year our bodies have provided what life could not.

This body response and solidifying happens through the nervous system. Often we use the term muscle memory as a way of saying, "My body remembers this action from past experience." In actuality, muscles remember nothing. It is the nerves located within our muscular system that remember. Our nervous system is the glorious linkage of experiences within our whole body.

Our nervous system is intricately woven throughout our brain, our spine, and our body. The central nervous system is located in the brain and spine integrated with the peripheral nervous system, which is divided into the sensory and motor systems. The motor system is divided into the somatic nervous system and the autonomic nervous system. The autonomic nervous system is divided into the sympathetic and the parasympathetic systems. Whew! Good stuff!

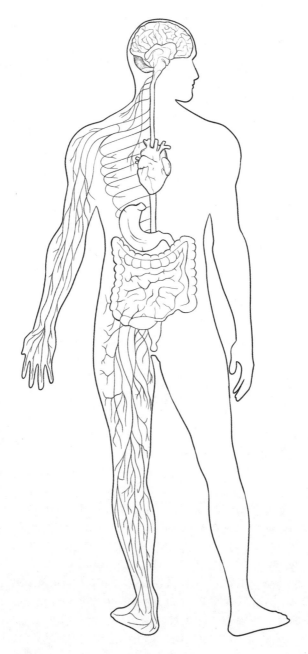

Figure 7.1   Illustration of Nervous System.

The importance of our nervous system intricately intertwined within our body cannot be emphasized enough. Continual discoveries in brain science, expanded by authors, teachers, coaches, and professionals reflect this importance and fresh opportunities available to learn and grow. We will return to the importance and connection of our nervous system regularly. As we learned from Amanda Blake in the chapter on the head, *"Your entire distributed nervous system evolved to take care of safety, connection and respect via sensation and motion. In other words, your brain—and by extension your entire body—is your social and emotional sense organ."*[2]

My body, my nervous system, my brain, adapted by having my left shoulder rest higher than my right. It has been this way for many years. Until well into adulthood, I did not know for certain when my body began to adapt. Reflecting on, feeling, and unwinding past experiences has allowed me a glimpse into my history and how my body supported me in times where safety, connection, and dignity were not present.

For the past several years I have been receiving structural and myofascial release to break up the scar tissue built up in my upper back, shoulder, and neck. This therapy attends to soft tissues, such as the skin, muscle, nervous (neurological), and connective tissues. I am attending to my body with intentional body support to sustain a high quality of life in my body. My intention is not to fix something that is "wrong" but to optimize my life by sustaining a healthy vessel. My shoulder movement has improved, my spine health has been nourished, and my connective tissue is smoother and offers optimal nutrients for my health.

As the treatments continue, I have also experienced "unfelts"—a term I first heard from Gay Hendricks in a live training when he directed us to feel body sensations in present time that were not felt when originated.[3] Along with experiencing unfelt emotions (sadness, fear, anger), I have unwound stories and beliefs. My shoulder carried unfelt experiences from my childhood when I was scared. My shoulder rose to my ear to protect me and provide a sense of safety. Over time, it stayed that way. I have caught myself holding my shoulder up in very safe circumstances. Now, more and more, my shoulder relaxes; there is no need for my shoulder to protect me. I access safety in my entire body now.

Pause for a moment. Digest these concepts.

You might recognize a similar place in your body that is off symmetry, or holds tension, or takes you regularly to medical care.

If you are surprised and distraught by these ideas, it is not a time to begin blaming others (parents, siblings, society). That is a different book. Give yourself the nutrients you need. Go take a warm luxurious soak in the tub. Fix yourself a soothing cup of tea. Take a long hike in the woods or stroll on the beach. Wrap yourself in blankets and lie down. Sink your feet into the earth. Hug your animal. Call a friend and tell them you care. Breathe into your belly while saying, "I am okay." Your hands hold a book chock-full of warmth, love, and answers in the form of information, practices, and inspiration.

If you are gobsmacked with a burning interest to learn more science, your brain is on fire, I suggest you check out the growing resources in neurological studies, somatic practices, or in my journey, Amanda Blake's work and her course Body = Brain.[4] She is wicked smart and amazing.

If you are wondering how your experience with money is tethered to missing nutrients, let's dive a bit deeper.

Looking Outside the Self

If we did not experience a seamless flow of nutritious attention that satisfied our safety, connection, and dignity, even though our body did the best it could to provide what we lacked, we still have a gap in our fulfillment. What do we do now?

In our modern world, we look outside ourselves for safety, connection, and dignity. We look for food, or relationships, or fitness, or hobbies. And we look for money.

We look for money because we live in a state of relative truth, believing that we are separate and distinct from all other beings.

The ultimate truth is that we humans, and all beings are interconnected in a web of loving filaments throughout time and space. This statement reflects Buddhist teachings of ultimate reality. Enlightened masters from all religions abide in all realms in all times and exist for the benefit of all beings. Ultimate truth is non-dual, it is just one. There is no inside or outside.

We can understand these concepts cognitively (chant "Ommmmm" with me), and perhaps we've tasted a direct experience, but in general, our day-to-day living, we dwell in relative truth. Relative truth, the relative world, is where we eat, sleep, walk, make love, work, play, spend money, and engage in our human experience.

Relative truth typically exists in duality—in separation. There is a you, a me, an us, and a them.

In this separation, we do not believe that we can source safety, connection, and dignity within ourselves, within our bodies, consciously (even though we do this unconsciously already!). We believe that there is no interconnected web of love. We believe the body is separate from the brain, and the dominant culture has believed this for generations. Therefore, we can only find those nutrients *exogenously*, from outside ourselves, because we believe we have no inner, *endogenous* source.

But we do. The body is our source.

Money is exogenous. Money is a popular external source for momentary safety. Money offers a false sense of connection. Money tries to ease the pain of no respect. Money is a poor antidote to the suffering we experience because of fear, lack of connection, and low self-esteem.

Money is not a source for essential nutrients. Our learning here, and practices, guide you to your body to source your nutrients. When you source your safety, connection, and dignity endogenously, from the inside out, three things happen:

1. You shift your relationship with money—it no longer becomes a false panacea for fear;

2. You begin a lifelong practice of sourcing nutrients and wisdom from the body, from the inside out. This inside-out practice is essential to experience the Virtuous Flow;
3. Your new capacities begin to nourish others.

Notes

1. Source: *Body=Brain,* Online Course (2015, 2018). Created and taught by Amanda Blake, MD. https://embright.org/body-brain. Fair Use.
2. Source: Blake, Amanda. (2018). *Your Body is Your Brain: Leverage Your Somatic Intelligence to Find Purpose, Build Resilience, Deepen Relationships and Lead More Powerfully.* Trokay Press. Fair use.
3. Source: "Conscious Loving and Body Intelligence," live training programs by Gay Hendricks (2000–2002). https://hendricks.com/seminars. Fair use.
4. Source: *Body=Brain*, Online Course (2015, 2018). Created and taught by Amanda Blake, MD. https://embright.org/body-brain. Fair Use.

Chapter 8

Our Heart—We Space

Our Western culture grew up steeped in individualism. "If it is meant to be it is up to me." Remember that saying? It's not that this view, and the generative powerful energy arising, is incorrect. It's that for a well-developed fully operative heart—one that truly opens and senses the world—this view and way of being is limited. Our heart wants to be the servant of "we." In heart money evolution, the way of me is called to open to the joy of we.

We is *and*. You and I. Us and them, in myriad forms. Call it collaborating, cocreating, playing, cooperating, teaming up, working/playing together, joining, communal, sharing, uniting, collective, combining—I love the thesaurus reference tool! These words all mean the same when we are developing **we space**. These words recognize expanding perspectives: individual, others, and collective.

When money doesn't weave with "we," a tainted and narrow path emerges in solo space. This path is riddled with shame, scarcity, doubt, fear and leads to the most harmful manifestation of all time: **g r e e d**. These feelings are embedded in an individual ego. When illuminated, they feel threatened and often paralyzed: becoming more solid in individual actions.

Financial systems are steeped in individualism, and greed permeates the field of finance. *We space* is a convenience. The organization uses individual motivation (scarcity, fear, desire) to feed an individual organizational aim that supports only a few power centers of the organization. I interviewed a bright young woman to join our small firm. She was miserable in her current position at a prestigious financial organization—a wire house, perhaps. This wire house, like many of the financial firms existing today (large and small) is rooted in individualism.

What can *you* do? How will *you* perform? Can *you* succeed?

Her job was cold-calling 250 people a day to generate new clients. Without getting into the merits or problems of this position, I ask you to look at how we continually reinforce individual behavior. The people (prospects) she contacted were not being met with an open heart of "I want to cocreate and serve you." These contacts were being drawn into a field of numbers, making quotas, and growing a "book of business."

It's not just for-profit organizations that suffer from individualism. For several years I served as a leader of a nonprofit professional financial services organization. On this board, in a desire to shift from individual work ethic to sensing the whole, I used the metaphor of individuals working as silos to groups working together in pods. The question posed to the individuals was, "What happens beyond your position? Where do the aspirations of your committee intersect with the aspirations of another committee? How does the aim of the organization get met by our efficient working together and become more effective by creating new ideas for the organization to flourish?" Progress happened. Then, over time, with new emerging leaders, patterns of old individual ways crept back in.

It is a **practice** to work (or dare I say, play) in *we*. If we don't practice, we return to well-developed individual habits.

My company struggles with *we*, and I am awake in the space—working with the concepts and offering developmental practices. Understanding, developing, and embodying *we space* is a practice; simple, not easy, and vitally important.

Do you wonder what this has to do with Somatic Finance?

Remember our cool elaborate illustration—the Virtuous Flow of Somatic Finance—showing the movement from sufficiency to generosity? The path to abiding on the Möbius strip is only possible with the heart's attention. The heart softens, opens, and recognizes others. The manifestation of generosity is only possible in the totality of *we space*. Our body wisdom is the only reliable ally that assists cleanly in developing *we*—in the heart—for ourselves, for others, and for all of humanity.

Greed crystalizes the heart in me.

Let's take a look at greed. Let's take a look at me.

Chapter 9
Greed

There is a sufficiency in the world for man's need but not for man's greed.

—Mahatma Gandhi

We are all greedy. We have all been greedy. I believe that any person lucky enough to have been born in the United States and modern world is here to resolve greed issues.

Greed isn't my favorite subject—perhaps I am reluctant to face my own greed—but it is necessary to our hygiene. The bits and bobs of greed hanging around in our shadow are not helpful and potentially harmful. None of us need to be **stuck** in greed. So let's get to it.

First, let's enter this conversation-exploration with a sense of sound dignity wrapped in humility, grace, and loving-kindness. This is how we meet and thaw greed.

What Is Greed?

Greed is defined by Google's dictionary as an "intense and selfish desire for something, especially wealth, power, or food." Let that sink in a few layers of skin.

Now take my hand and let's continue to chat with a couple of more dictionaries defining greed. Merriam-Webster Dictionary tells us greed is *a selfish and excessive desire for more of something (such as money) than is needed.*[1] Yep. That feels true. Wikipedia says greed *is an uncontrolled longing for increase in the acquisition or use: of material gain (be it food, money, land, or animate/inanimate possessions); or social value, such as status, or power. Greed has been identified as undesirable throughout known human history because it creates behavior-conflict between personal and social goals.*[2] Hmmm, this second definition offers a threshold for us to explore: behavior-conflict between personal and social goals. Remember *we space*? We space is both, and it honors the personal and the social. Greed rejects social goals, others, and relies solely on numero uno—me.

An internal focus on **me only** impedes human behavioral development stunting growth on all lines of development, but particularly, interpersonally, somatically, and emotionally.

Greedy behavior comes from the repeated contraction of emotion. It arises when an emotional experience is not allowed to fully expand, causing the mental and physical energy of the experience to contract in the mind and body, over and over again.

These emotional experiences might be sorrow and despair, anger and anguish, grief and disbelief, fear and terror. When we don't or can't fully expand into these emotions, we contract around that unattended energy. Contractions without full expansions solidify in our body and form into this greed, what I call *something*—sets of beliefs and behaviors, including scarcity, limiting beliefs, destructive behaviors, protective patterns, and dehumanizing actions. I call it *something* because it is alien to our true nature. This *something* fosters a need to protect, control, maintain, and figure out. Our rational mind (the Academic) takes over, grips like a dog to a bone, and it does not let go. Period.

Greed forms around fearful experiences in part because our body intelligence acts to protect us from danger. We feel scared—the boogey man resides under the bed, our parents are arguing, my belly is growling for food, your checking account is overdrawn—and our body skillfully responds with protection. With a physical and mental armor to help us feel safe to survive.

What happens when fear takes over, again and again, our body armors us, and we do not experience the felt sensations and energy of fear. Instead of climbing out of this protective hole, we begin to see and experience life as a solo protection game. There is false safety, no connection, much less joy, failing creativity, loss of dignity, and loss of love. The spiral in for protection forms into a callus that eventually becomes as hard as a diamond, impenetrable. There is only *me*. In other words, we make up shit to protect ourselves, and we cannot shake this truth.

Greed grows deeper and calcifies because we are cut off from the nutrients that make us healthy humans—safety, connection, and dignity. In this hard callused state, we are greedy because we are hungry (cold, angry, sad, scared), and we cannot find food (comfort for our situation or state of mind). There is not enough.

Greed in Action

So many in our society are stuck in the impenetrable place of greed that our society celebrates greed in a twisted way to survive. We need look no further than Wall Street. During the late 1980s, author Michael Lewis wrote *Liar's Poker*, a semi-autobiographical experience of his life as a bond trader on Wall Street.[3] Reading that book made my blood boil and my stomach curdle. Two clear reasons arise for my anger. One, of course, is the gut-wrenching filthy way clients were treated by greed-driven men (yes, they were men; I am calling it what it is) during this financial crisis. The other reason is the defamation of all of the trustworthy financial professionals who were left (and we continue to this day) cleaning up these messes.

But what fully undoes me is how many, many other readers reacted to the book: the author reports in one of his later books that readers were inspired to go to Wall Street and make money—behave just like the bond traders. They claimed greed, and the violent, depraved behavior of greed, as their own. They missed the original intended message.

We see the elevation of greed in other parts of our culture too, of course. And when a greed-fueled accumulation of power is combined with a lack of a moral code or outright psychopathy, the result can be horrifying. Think of the powerful men in entertainment whose monstrous behavior has been revealed in the last five years alone: Bill Cosby, Harvey Weinstein, Roy Moore, Roger Ailes. And they're the tip of the iceberg. Our society covered up the horrific, disgraceful, inhumane behaviors of these folks—the *greed* of these men to wield power, to control others, to cause fear, to dominate over and over again—because we deified their money, their power, their status. We celebrated their greed and overlooked their violence. We loved them, respected them—in part *because* they lived greed.

Now Let's Change

Our culture has celebrated greed. Until now. Now, the cracks of reality are arising. More humans are waking up and longing for more room. Enough of us are allowing ourselves to expand and see what is revealed.

Meeting greed with anger or fear won't work. Our move, our only reliable and meaningful move, is to go inside. Inside our body. We get to examine our own crevices of greed and clean them up. Yes, our greed welcomes us and with grace and loving-kindness, we are able to attend to it.

We start with the old banners like this one from Malcolm Forbes: "He who dies with the most toys wins."

What arises in your field of awareness when you read that line? Your field of awareness includes your thoughts, your body sensations, sights, smells, tastes, and sounds. In other words, does this statement ignite any response, particularly in your body, and if so, what is it?

Here are common phrases that tap feelings and beliefs around money and greed:

Bet on the wrong horse
Born with a silver spoon
Bread and butter
Break the bank
Caught short
Cheapskate
Chicken feed
Cold hard cash
Cook the books
Cost an arm and a leg
Deadbeat
A dime a dozen
Dutch treat
Feel like a million bucks
Flat broke
A fool and his money are soon
    parted
Foot the bill
Fork over
From rags to riches
Get along on a shoestring
Give them a run for their
    money
Gravy train
Midas touch
Doesn't have two cents to rub
    together
Highway robbery
Hit pay dirt
Hit the jackpot
In debt
In kind

In the black
In the money
Jack up the price
Last of the big spenders
Let the buyer beware
Live high on the hog
Living beyond one's means
Lose money hand over fist
Lose one's shirt
Made of money
Make a bundle
Make a killing
Make an honest buck
Make ends meet
Money doesn't grow on trees
Money makes the world go
    round
Money burns a hole in the
    pocket
Money is no object
Money talks
On a budget
On a shoestring
On sale
On the house
On the money
On the take
Pad the bill
Pass the buck
Pass the hat
Pay a king's ransom
Pay as you go

Pay in advance
Pay off
Pay one's own way
Pay through the nose
Pennies from heaven
Penny for one's thoughts
Penny pincher
Penny saved is a penny earned
Penny wise and pound foolish
Play the market
Pony up
Poor as a church mouse
Put one's money where the
     mouth is
Rain check
Rake in the money
Rolling in the money
Salt away money
Scrimp and save
Set back
Shell out
Sitting on a goldmine
Smart money is on. . .

Sock away
Sound as a dollar
Splurge on. . .
Squirrel away
Stone broke
Strapped for cash
Strike gold
Strike it rich
Take a beating
Take the money and run
Take up a collection
Throw good money
     after bad
Throw money around
Tidy sum of money
Tighten one's belt
Tight fist
Time is money
Turn on a dime
Two bits
Up the ante
Not worth a red cent
Worth its weight in gold[4]

Tiny Practice

These phrases represent a small portion of the way we
see money.

What are your favorites?
What phrases are familiar?
What phrases pickled you growing up?
As these phrases wash over you, pause.
Allow your attention to once again go inside.

Sense your heart, your belly, and your spine.
Do you feel a sense of energy and aliveness? Or, more likely. . .
Do you feel sticky?
Do you feel prickly?
Do you feel nauseous?

These idioms help us see how money and greed beliefs flow "innocently" into our conversation, our beliefs, and our ways of working. These reflect how greed begins to build and decay and stay.

Stand up and shake it off, whatever "it" is.
Wiggle and giggle. (Seriously. Stand and shake your booty!)
Breathe deeply into your belly.
Place your hands on your heart and speak out loud, "money serves my heart's motivation" and my heart is pure gold.

The Journey Is Up to Us.

The beauty of our courage to face greed is that we become the necessary leaders of transformation. We guide by example. We begin with ourselves by facing our greed directly. In doing so, without shame, blame, or self-flagellation, we free the most tender parts—the emotional experiences that most long to expand—and welcome them as long-lost friends. The spacious room we access in our body builds momentum and muscle to move through scarcity with ease. The old stories and by-lines melt. We understand that when scarcity is cleaned up and we choose to be on the journey, we gain access to sufficiency.

The profundity of our courage is that as we collectively grow, our development affects others, systems, policy, education, every situation that we meet. Our "clean energy," free of doubt, shame, scarcity, regret, and confusion, influences every person and single situation we encounter. There is no "trying" to influence; this gift happens naturally.

Greed is not inevitable. Not by a long shot. We are all in this together, and we each magnetize one another. But before we dance in the parade, I want to introduce you to our friend, shame.

Notes

1. Source: Merriam-Webster Dictionary. https://www.merriam-webster.com/dictionary/greed. Fair use.
2. Source: Wikipedia. https://en.wikipedia.org/wiki/Greed. Fair use.
3. Source: Lewis, Michael (1989). *Liar's Poker.* New York: W.W. Norton & Company. Fair use.
4. Source: http://www.idiomconnection.com/money.html. Fair use.

Chapter 10

Shame. . . Subtle, Seductive, and Searing

Quietly, moving on our tip toes and stealthy beneath the cement of greed, we find shame. Shame permeates our relationship with money. Here, we walk with tender care through the meaning of shame. We explore how money systems depend on our shame, and we look for the opening to lead us toward sufficiency and generosity.

Shame came to rest beside me on a bench. Somewhere in the crevices of my being I knew it would find me. Shame integration—if that is a thing—is necessary and essential for me, and for you, and for Somatic Finance. In the midst of writing this book, my father died. My mother died nine months after him. With their passing the structures that held our family system together collapsed—wildly, wickedly, wearingly. The fire of change and truth blazed. I have a few searing wounds, slowly healed. I see now that shame waited patiently to teach me what I resisted so far in my six decades of life. Writing about shame is part of my healing.

In the book *Conscious Luck*, Gay Hendricks writes about shame.[1] I have studied and trained with Gay and his spouse, Kathlyn, for over two decades. Teachings from the Hendricks Institute, as Katie

clarified for me, are reliably "rooted in thousands of hours of experiential research and emergent processes that then became processes and then got completely supported by scientific research."
Their "play to proof" approach met my body (Head, Heart, Belly)
and felt so natural—easy, fun, connected—that, at times, didn't feel
groundbreaking. Which is how I thought about shame for so many
years—with a familiar, unremarkable understanding. Imagine my
surprise when reading in Gay's book about shame struck me so
deeply, profoundly, alarmingly, this time.

Gay writes that we often mistakenly fuse together shame with
guilt. Guilt is feeling bad about something you did, he says. Shame,
on the other hand, is feeling bad about who you are. Big difference.
Read these lines slowly, with a gentle breath in between.

Guilt is feeling bad about something you did.

Shame is feeling bad about who you are.

Guilt can be addressed by taking responsibility with clear
action: apologizing, repairing, fixing, rectifying. Guilt is a little pis-
ser to shame, so let's face the Big Kahuna.

Shame is a beautiful concoction of fear, anger, and sadness mixed
together in your own special blend depending on the parts of you
that are deemed in need of control by another. Gay writes that we
are not born with shame, that it is bestowed upon us by others. That
may be true. I also believe that shame lives in our DNA passed along
generational lines. While I was in utero, when my mother felt a wave
of shame pickling her veins, how could my cells be exempt? For our
purposes, we simply recognize that shame is fear, anger, and sadness
ceaselessly bound together and reinforcing each other, and the result
of this intertwining is feeling bad about who we are, in mind and body.

I read Gay's line about shame shortly after reading a disturbing
text from a sibling about a difficult family situation. I felt triggered.
Simultaneously my face felt flush, my jaw tightened in anger, my
stomach churned, and my heart hurt. I recognized these body sensations of shame.

I stayed with the sensations in my jaw, heart, and belly.

I released any thoughts about why the news on the text triggered me.

Breathing, allowing, and honoring my body wisdom, these sensations moved along.

Practicing this body intelligence, I trusted that what I needed to know about the situation would reveal itself to me in perfect order as I gave kind generous attention to my present experiences without trying to change anything.

In future practice you will learn to be fully with your body sensations too. You will find that sometimes revelations arrive like a gentle creek, soft winding waters offering bits of insight. Sometimes revelations arrive like a torrid tsunami filled with gushes of power and a brutal cleansing.

Sometimes revelations arrive like rushing rapids testing capacities to paddle, twist, and turn navigating the scale of rocks, branches, and river debris.

And you will have your revelations that look nothing like the above but unique to you.

Keep going. Stay open. Trust your body.

What Was Revealed to Me

As I sat there, Gay's words in my mind and my sibling's text in my hand, experiencing the physical release of following my body wisdom, I remained open for whatever came next.

I recalled a brief encounter when I was three years old, right outside the front door of the log cabin I grew up in the west coast beach of Florida. My father and a man named Henry worked most of the day in the woods chopping down overgrown palm trees. We ate hearts of palms for months afterwards. Henry, a large strong Black man, towered over me like a mountain. He was drenched in sweat from head to toe, just like my father. It was dusk, and they were finished for the day. It was dinner time, so I asked Henry to join us for dinner. The nanosecond after I invited Henry to dinner,

I knew I did something wrong. I felt bad. But I had no idea why. Henry politely declined my invitation.

A few years later I overheard my father repeating the scene to a group of friends. Levity filled the room as he said, "Gayle invited Henry, our hired hand, to dinner. He knew better than to accept her invitation." I still did not understand the scope of the situation, but I was closer to understanding that inviting Henry to dinner was wrong. My shame strengthened, instead of releasing. Here's why. I saw with my own eyes that two grown men were tired and probably hungry. It was dinner time. I knew the right thing to do was to invite Henry to dinner, because I was told that we are kind and generous to others. Why was inviting Henry to dinner wrong when I could see he was tired and hungry?

Anger arose when I felt powerless to respond.

Fear arose when my safety was tied to staying silent.

Sadness arose when I saw harm to another being.

Confusion wrapped itself around my fear, anger, and sadness to supercharge my shame.

Fast-forward years, with similar repeats of the story, compiled with myriad experiences of shame. I knew my parents' actions did not match the words they spoke and the values they preached. I could see the incongruencies in my family system. And my powerlessness each and every time an event occurred created a self-perpetuating shame machine. My body received each and every nano-moment of shame to hold for me until now.

My parents were shamed.

Their parents were shamed.

My parents shamed me.

My siblings were shamed.

My siblings shamed me.

We had all been pickled, steeped, and broiled in shame.

Children are the most vulnerable to shame. Then when children learn shame behavior, and feel less than, they become shame perpetrators to feel the momentary power over another. Children do this to siblings, as I experienced with my older siblings. If we do not recognize this pattern, it repeats itself from parents to children for generations.

Imagine how money is a perpetuating shame machine. What are your shame experiences and stories?

Tiny Practice

Take a moment to hold shame and notice where, if at all, these statements ring true.

Pause and feel your body. Notice if any sensations are speaking to you.

Whatever is happening, just let it be.

If you are aware of shame and have been facing shame, well done. Bravo! Brava! I bow to you and your journey.

If shame is a surprise, and these statements feel foreign, no worries. We are in this together. You are not alone, and you may or may not have shame discoveries.

If you are somewhere in between the above scenarios, join me on the conga line. We are invited to a gorgeous dance.

I wish this story ended here. But shame is deeply entwined with money.

Money Shaming Systems

Money has capitalized on shame. Not money per se, but the money systems built by people pickled in shame. These systems are built to have power over people. Shame strengthens the systems, keeping us locked inside.

Let me start with a simple personal experience of our shaming money systems. I pay a hefty health insurance premium monthly to support my health and well-being in the event of an emergency and to sustain a healthy body. I receive chiropractic care to support my health today and tomorrow. Some treatments are preventative in nature—I want to be able to walk and easily move later in life—and some treatments are more acute in nature responding to natural wear and tear in an aging body. Each year I receive a questionnaire from my insurance company asking me about the origins of my need for services. The insurance company is seeking information about how I was injured. Was I injured on the job? No, I have not been injured on the job. But if my injury was job-related, then the insurance company would cease any benefits because it would be my employer's responsibility to pay for the injury. I do not question the validity and necessity of safe working conditions. Employers need to provide safe working conditions and respond to injuries when they occur. Stay with me here as we go a few layers deeper.

The message I am receiving from the insurance inquiry is this: I have done something wrong to take care of my body by going to a chiropractor. The suspicious and blaming nature of the system's paperwork asking me about my choices is very, very subtle.

You should not be going to the chiropractor to improve your posture and movement.
Your health and vitality do not matter.
Insurance benefits are only for sick people who have not taken care of themselves properly.

So if you need these treatments and want health insurance benefits, you are lazy, obese, and have made really bad health choices, and we will make it very hard for you to receive benefits as a punishment for your bad choices.

Shame on you.

Let's try another example. There are many to choose.

Are you familiar with credit scores? Those numbers that allow a system to calculate whether you are a safe and favorable credit risk? Can you imagine, or maybe this has happened to you, receiving a low credit score while applying for a credit card, a bank loan, or other financial assistance? Your choices and bad luck and negative financial consequences in the past calculate a low number and determine that you are a high credit risk. Not only are you told that you are not in favor, but to add insult to injury, the cost to do business, if even accepted, will be higher because you are bad.

Shame on you.

And one more.

You ask for parity in your salary because you recently discovered that your same job with the same responsibilities is paying $10,000 more to another person in your company. In your dismay and disappointment, you research desperately for the difference in your work so that you can squelch the questions mounting in your mind. But research only points to even more disparity. Not only is your work superior to your co-worker, you work longer hours, you receive more favorable annual reviews, and better results, but you discover additional company benefits not given to you. In the conversation with your boss as you reveal all of your facts, he argues with your conclusions, defends his decisions, squirms in discomfort as you meet each of his defenses with truth. You are the bad guy wanting to be paid an equal salary as your co-worker. Gender and age should not matter when it comes to performance. But it does. You get the raise, not the extra benefits, and the price you pay is contempt from your co-worker and a boss who sees you as a problem. Promotions are given to others. You should have been grateful for what you had.

Shame on you.

I could go on with many examples of money and shame. No doubt examples arise in your mind from your life money experiences. Let them come to explore later in practice. Let's dive even deeper in the torment of money shame.

What happens with fear, anger, and sadness when they are tangled up for so long? They get together like a weird collection of tainted energy feeding on negativity. Remember, fear, anger, and sadness are not evil. They are human energies reflecting an authentic human expression. But without the breath of truth, distortions slime these energies for days, months, years, decades, even lifetimes.

Picture this:

Fear grasps the ferocity of anger and the anguish of sadness with vibrating tentacles. As anger burns hot coals, fear intensifies like molten lava. As sadness wallows the depths of despair, fear seeps in pricking deeper wounds. If one feeling seeks freedom, the other two step in to take up space. In short, these feelings calcify each other with self-directed hatred so no space can break the tight seal.

On the Map of Consciousness in the book *Power vs. Force* by David Hawkins, shame lives right above death. Shame's vibration is as low as it gets before becoming a corpse. Shame around money prevents us from living, much less living a full vibrant enjoyable life. Shame can stop us in our tracks, for years. So here, we pause again to give reverence to the potency of shame.

Shame commands respect, and so does your sovereignty.

Shame will not release without unbridled, determined, loving open attention from your truest and holiest of holy parts of you. It is that important. But don't be afraid and don't give up. I am right here and the practice, the discoveries, and the realizations are so worth it.

Thank you. You are courageous. I'm right here with you.

I feel joy in my heart being here, writing for you, revealing my shame, and offering a light to lead us forward. The light is here—in us, you, me, everyone. Trust your body to lead the way.

In the next section, you'll learn about the five core emotions and the location of these feelings in the body, called somatic markers. We'll look at the concept of measurement through the lens of body response. We'll explore the extraordinary vagus nerve. The Academic, who likes explanations, information, and proof, will be very satisfied. But I sense the Capitalist and Philanthropist will enjoy the swim too.

Note

1. Hendricks, Gay (2020). *Conscious Luck: Eight Secrets to Intentionally Change Your Fortune.* New York: St. Martin's Essentials. Fair use.

Part IC

Science
of the Landscape

Chapter 11

Basic Body—Body, Emotions, Sensations

D id you see the animated movie *Inside Out*? The five main characters are the feeling of joy, anger, fear, disgust, and sadness inside a young girl's mind. Each feeling has a distinct character, a clear job, and a lot of jokes.

Plus or minus the jokes, the idea matches up with reality. We feel about five core emotions, with variations in kind and intensity. For example, *anger* holds frustration, boredom, annoyance, irritation, fury, rage, resentment, and wrath. Each of these emotions doesn't have a little animated character running around our brain, but each does relate to a location or locations in our body where we experience the emotion as a sensation.

What? Yes. All emotions have corresponding sensations located in the body. Our body is more than a stand for the head. The way of the academic is gasping!

In my study with Kathlyn Hendricks, PhD, I learned the five core emotions as anger, sadness, fear, joy, and sexual feelings. You may be familiar with four basic emotions as mad, sad, glad, and scared. Simultaneously, each of our core emotions has a precursor physical sense. Our body is a real-time map for our natural human emotional expressions. Our body doesn't contain or constrict these emotions, but painful or traumatic events can, and do, borrow our body to protect us when it is not safe for us to experience them. Our body is a welcome mat and open door for all of our emotions and the sensations that accompany them to be expressed.

Typically, the core emotions are located in the following body spaces, with sensations felt as pressure (tight, open, twisting), temperature (cool, freezing, sizzling), and movement (flowing, jangling, swirling).

Anger: back, jaw, shoulders;
Sadness: upper chest, eyes, throat;
Fear: belly, hands;
Joy: all over, core, and spine;
Sexual feelings: pelvic floor, genitals, and erogenous zones.

The body map of feelings is an excellent visual tool to assist us in becoming familiar with core feelings and where they are located in our body and what sensations arise when these emotions show up. Of course, each of us is unique, and our experiences are unique. This map identifies the typical spaces and places we can look closer to discover our signature sensations of emotions moving through our body. Check it out for yourself, and notice how your feelings arise and how you describe those sensations.

As you may remember in Chapter 2, "The Head," when we discussed the work of Dr. Jill Bolte Taylor, emotions and physical sensations have a natural ebb and flow. Research tells us that it takes approximately 90 seconds for a wave of emotion and physical sensation to begin, peak, and release from beginning to end. Just 90 seconds!

However, our rational mind often brings stories, beliefs, and ideas from the past and future fears that cause blocks in the flow of these energies. The body handles the disruption by physically contracting and distorting the physical sensation until another point in time that emotion can be fully felt. If we do not fully experience the emotion and associated sensations, it stays stuck in our body.

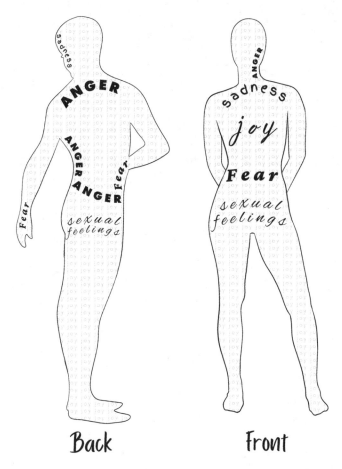

Back   Front

Figure 11.1   Illustration Body Map with Emotions.

Your opportunity, as you gain a deeper understanding of our human body, our core emotions, the location in your body these emotions arise, and what they feel like, is to get curious about two situations. First, when you notice sensations in your body, pause and consider your state of mind as these sensations arise. Ask, am I feeling a flavor of joy, sadness, anger, fear, or sexy? Second, when you are angry, sad, happy, scared, or feeling sexual, notice your body sensations and where specifically these sensations are located.

Do not:
Try to figure anything out;
Analyze the experience;
Come to a definitive conclusion;
Explain your experience;
Label the experience from the past; or
Project the experience to the future.

Simply, be open, get curious, and explore like a child in a new playground filled with dogs, squirrels, and chipmunks.

Neurosis versus Essence

Most of us did not grow up in a feeling-friendly environment. Our birth family had ideas about what feeling states were acceptable to express and which ones were taboo. To adapt and fit in, we learned to hide or suppress the "bad" feelings as they arose. This experience is a common example of blocking emotions. We judge some feelings as bad and classify them as neurotic states of mind. (Don't get me started on the long winding road of treatments to address "bad feelings.")

Feelings are not good or bad. Humans experience feelings and emotions. Feelings and emotions make us human. As we grow and accept the wholeness of our human experience, including feeling the entire wave of emotion for 90 seconds without blocking, we recognize the importance and benefit of all the core emotions. Each emotion possesses an essential quality or, as described in Buddhism, inherent wisdom energy. Inhabiting the essence quality of our emotions is the integration of our full experience. Figure 11.2 depicts what I describe.

Let's bring our body, our feelings, our nutrients, our archetypes together in an example. Fear is the underbelly of our money issues. Fear gets jacketed, covered up by other emotions, usually anger and sadness. Our Academic typically gets angry, and our Philanthropist typically gets sad. Yet, if we stay with concepts like this, we feed

Core Feeling	Essence Quality	Wisdom Energy
Anger	Determination	Power - Inexhaustible energy
Fear	Clarity	Awake - clear truth
Sadness	Compassion	Love - boundless heart
Joy	Gratitude	Peace - infinite equanimity
Sexual	Creativity	Emergence - ceaseless action

Figure 11.2   Chart illustration of feeling integration.

our brain more knowledge. When we give direct attention to our body centers, we begin to feel the sensations attached to the anger, sadness, and fear. Something happens. We begin to feel. We begin to heal. We begin to understand. Insights arise. Feeling safer, connected, and dignified we unite our somatic experiences with truth. Truth is clarity, which fosters power and action in determination. Determination shows us why this matters, and compassion naturally arises. Compassion generates boundless love, touching into our joy and creativity. But none of these results are possible without tending to the bedrock, fear. So we pay attention to fear always. Remember fear responds as fight, flee, freeze, and faint, or usually a signature combo of our very own.

Even if the above translation seems far-fetched, get willing to discover for yourself what is possible. You are always making the choice to close down or open. At the very least, watch *Inside Out* and introduce yourself to your own animated feelings playing in your head, your new best friends.

Chapter 12
More Geeking Out with Somatic Markers

Too often, in the field of economics, decision-making is deemed void of emotions. The best decisions are based only on logic. In other words, if it makes rational sense based on a cost-benefit analysis that one decision is better than the other, we will make the favorable financial choice based on reason alone. Emotion does not factor into making decisions.

But the reality is that emotions guide decision-making. Period. We've known this for years; it is not a hypothesis. Even if the financial decision is not complex or conflicting, emotions remain present in the decision-making process, albeit quieter.

Our brain—connected to every inch of our body through many neural networks—is vastly underutilized if we rely on rationality alone. Let's fire up more of our gray matter!

It helps us to learn about *somatic markers*.

Antonio Damasio, the David Dornsife Chair in Neuroscience and Professor of Psychology, Philosophy, and Neurology at the University of Southern California, developed the hypothesis of somatic markers. He writes: "Somatic Markers are feelings in the body that are associated with emotions, such as the association of rapid heartbeat with anxiety or of nausea with disgust. Somatic markers strongly influence subsequent decision-making. Within the brain, somatic markers are thought to be processed in the ventromedial prefrontal cortex (VMPFC) and the amygdala."[1]

In other words, somatic markers are places in the body where emotions are typically felt. Over our life, these emotions and their corresponding physical sensations can get attached to particular stories or meanings that we make about our worlds, often about money.

As Damasio writes, "Emotions are changes in both body and brain states in response to stimuli. Physiological changes (muscle tone, heart rate, endocrine activity, posture, facial expression, etc.) occur in the body and are relayed to the brain where they are transformed into an emotion that tells the individual something about the stimulus that they have encountered. Over time, emotions and their corresponding bodily changes, which are called 'somatic markers,' become associated with particular situations and their past outcomes."[2]

In this model, experiences with money activate a physiological change communicated to the brain and transformed into an emotion. With repeated experiences these body emotions become "somatic money markers" signifying, in the body, some kind of meaning we've made about our money situation.

Let's put the theory and life experience together. Let's dive deeper with a blanket of wonder inviting us into our own ancestral party. Here's one example of the many swimming in our ocean of money.

In more than one client experience, parents (or grandparents) have struggled with money management, one decision turned sour and the ability to make ends meet is impossible. The chosen solution is to declare bankruptcy. The stress and stigma and confusion surrounding this decision is devastating and lasting, for generations to come.

Consider this scene. A child in grammar school, just learning to read, write, and do arithmetic, comes home to tension and stress. Sometimes her parents argue, and money is always the subject. The tension spills over into dinnertime, conversations, the walk to the bus stop, even trips to the grocery store. "Can we buy some cherry

Jello and make dessert for tonight?" she begs. "No, young lady! That's frivolous spending, and we don't have extra for that!"

The field of tension, stress, and angst suffuses into the body and bones of this child. She does not understand what is going on with her parents and her family and how recent financial loss and the decision to choose bankruptcy is making everyone so unhappy. The cognitive pieces she picks up, unconsciously, are that money makes people angry and unhappy. *Money is bad*, and *I don't want to have anything to do with money. I do not feel safe around people when they discuss money. If I stay away from money, I will be happy and okay. I will earn lots of money and become rich so I don't have to feel this way.*

Her body holds unfelt emotions of fear, anger, sadness, confusion, and more in the form of sensations everywhere. These money beliefs, emotions, feeling states, and sensations are somatic markers, and with each unfelt occurrence thereafter as she matures, they become more solid and stuck.

If we held solely to a rational view of money, we might believe that with this lived experience the daughter would be extremely astute financially. Recognizing a poor financial path with ease and not wanting to feel the stress she felt as a child would catalyze sound financial decisions. Maybe. This is one potential result of being pickled in that childhood brine.

And here are others:

Frugality may lead her to withdrawal, the need to control, even to the extent of harmful body trauma like bulimia, anorexia, or cutting. Living in an out of control space, where money is a factor, may cause the opposite reaction to always "be in control."

The financial constraints may lead to overconsumption and the desire for more to feed the empty spaces that were never met emotionally, physically, mentally, or spiritually. Restrictions in experiences—blamed on money—may cause similar patterns to emerge that look different. Overconsumption of material goods, food, alcohol, sex, any addiction is possible.

Overzealous work, as in becoming an overachieving workaholic to avoid the possibility of financial ruin, may fill her days. The ability to enjoy life, relationships, and accomplishments are met with the crushing need to perform more.

Dependency on others for financial decisions may riddle her days. Even possessing a high IQ, healthy relationships, and healthy lifestyle can cripple her own decision-making. Smart people being taken by financial schemes happen because of this vulnerability.

Use your imagination to create any number of outcomes. Perhaps, this story is too familiar to you. If your nerves are activated, please pause and give kind attention to your belly, touch your heart, and lengthen your spine. Enter your body for kind attention and relief. Your body loves you.

You can see that while the rational mind arrives at one reasonable financial choice based on metrics, the nonlinear mind, connected to all of our experiences, and the experiences of our ancestors, offers myriad answers in the complex soup of life. Somatic markers are part of our birth family lineage. They do not disappear. They evolve as we evolve. And they evolve positively when we bring them consciously into partnership with our body.

This is fabulous news! We have our body, our lifelong partner, to work with us in practice to engage any questions about our somatic money markers and more. Open your financial decision-making skillfully. Embrace the partnership potential of your body and your mind. Allow your bright mind to serve your heart, which always offers the *right* decision.

Notes

1. Source: Damasio, A. R., Everitt, B. J., and Bishop, D. (1996). "The Somatic Marker Hypothesis and the Possible Functions of the Prefrontal Cortex [and Discussion]." *Philosophical Transactions: Biological Sciences*, 351(1346), 1413–1420. Fair use.
2. Source: Damasio, A. R., Everitt, B. J., and Bishop, D. (1996). "The Somatic Marker Hypothesis and the Possible Functions of the Prefrontal Cortex [and Discussion]." *Philosophical Transactions: Biological Sciences*, 351(1346), 1413–1420. http://www.jstor.org/stable/3069187. Fair use.

Chapter 13
Our Nervous System

S cience fascinates me when I am not required to dissect an animal or examine moving microbes under a microscope. Some of the most recent advances in science relate to our body, brain, and the vast territory of previously unknown connections between the brain and body.

Say hello to our nervous system, particularly the vagus nerve.

With our deep-rooted money fears, and again, we all have fear issues with money, learning about this powerhouse nerve while understanding the interconnection of our body and brain will support our progress as we skillfully practice integrating money in our life.

The vagus nerve is the longest cranial nerve. It contains motor and sensory fibers and, because it passes through the neck and chest region to the abdomen, it has the widest distribution of any nerve in the body. It contains somatic and visceral fibers that communicate impulses through the central nervous system. Take a look at the illustration in Figure 13.1. Are you turned on?

We are not necessarily trained scientists here, so let's get down to basics. We know what a nerve is, right?

A nerve is one or more bundles of fibers that form part of a system conveying impulses of sensation, motion, and so forth, between the brain or spinal cord and other parts of the body.

Nerves are communication systems located throughout our body systems—all body systems—and the vagus nerve is the mother

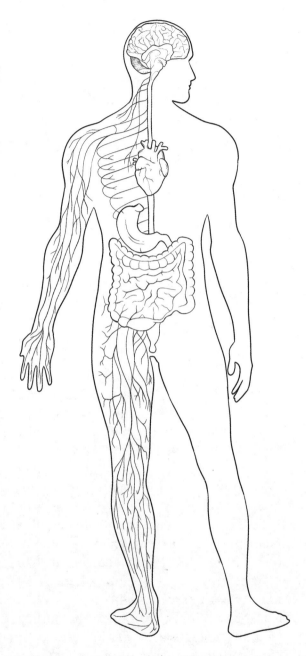

Figure 13.1   (Repeat Figure 7.1.) Illustration of the Nervous System.

lode of nerves; it is the longest communication system between our brain and our body.

Not only that, but vagus nerve research proves what many body practitioners have experienced for decades: the body informs and instructs the brain more than the brain informs and instructs the body. In her Body = Brain course, Amanda Blake describes the power of our belly and how it functions independently from the brain, different from any other nervous system. Our belly communicates to the brain 80–90% of the time, versus the brain communicating to the belly.[1] Who's got the power? Shake it!

For the skeptics, because skeptics have feelings too, this information supports your practice when doubt arises. Our body offers information consistently to stay healthy—in body, mind, and spirit. Let's listen directly to our body. We do not always need a blood test, a stethoscope, or a physical exam to learn what we need to know from our body. We only need to pay attention, build new muscles, and allow our integrated wholeness to lead.

How about a Tiny Practice?

Place your hand on your belly.

Breathe deep under your hand into your belly.

What do you notice when the mind is fed facts?
Are you able to synthesize and integrate?
Or do you get stuck wanting more information?
Or do you get stuck fogging out with too much information?
Just notice.
What does your belly say about this?
How does your body serve your answer and your next action?

If you want to integrate the information, reading the rest of the chapter *may* continue to enliven you. But check in with your body to see what you are feeling inside for a true answer.

If you are grasping for more information, give a nod to your way as the Academic and read on.

If you are tired of this science, skip ahead to the next chapter.

Zoom Out with More Juicy Nervous System Science

From Stephen Porges, the originator of polyvagal theory, professor of psychiatry at the University of North Carolina at Chapel Hill, and director of the Kinsey Institute Traumatic Stress Research Consortium at Indiana University Bloomington, we learn even more about our stunning vagus nerve and how it interacts with our four fear responses to a perceived threat: fight, freeze, flee, and faint.[2] Deb Dana simplifies this science in her Sounds True course "Befriending the Nervous System."[3]

The sympathetic and parasympathetic are the two main branches of the autonomic nervous system. These two branches respond to signals and sensations (our survival instincts at play) through three pathways. One pathway aligns with the sympathetic branch running near the middle of the spinal cord and preparing us for mobility. Responding to cues of danger, it triggers adrenaline to fuel our mobilized fight-or-flight fear response. The other two pathways are the vagus nerve aligned with the parasympathetic branch. The vagus nerve begins at the brainstem of the skull and travels down and up in two directions: down through the heart, lungs, diaphragm, and stomach and then up through the neck, throat, eyes, and ears. The vagus is divided into the ventral vagal pathway and the dorsal vagal pathway. The ventral vagal pathway responds to cues of safety and generates feelings of comfort and connection. The dorsal vagal pathway responds to cues of danger and generates disconnection and disassociation—our immobilized faint-and-freeze fear responses.

Understanding the biology of fear has direct implications for our money. When we are activated around money, our nervous system is either energized in the sympathetic branch in the back of our spine getting us ready to move or energized in the dorsal pathway of the parasympathetic branch ejecting us from body awareness. Mobilized fear (fight and flee) in finance will have action and movement. It may look like on the outside random risky investing or excessive frenetic spending. Our sympathetic branch is activated. Immobilized fear (faint and freeze) in finance will be still and silent. It may look like paralysis in confusion, avoidance, doubt, procrastination—ignoring a glaring call to make a decision. The dorsal pathway of the parasympathetic branch is activated.

Mobilized fear causes us to react to a money situation and make repeating bad decisions, one after another. While mobilized fear reactions are unhealthy, typically worse are immobilized fear responses that eject us from our body into freeze and faint as wired together traumatic survival patterns are activated. The way to reconnect to the dorsal vagal pathway is through somatic awareness and somatic practices—where the seat of the trauma resides.

Breath in our belly is one reliable way back to the body.

Our belly space and breath soothe our senses and calm our nerves so that we can return to a state of safety. Feeling safe, our heart lights up through our central channel as we recognize we are not alone—we return to a state of connection. Feeling safe and connected, our belly and our heart unite, strengthening and igniting our spine. Dignity comes alive. Landing and abiding in my body, I find my own safety, connection, and dignity, sourced within.

This chapter leads us conclusively to this essential point:

Learning the depth and breadth of body wisdom, backed by science, is the imperative to include our body with our money journey.

Notes

1. Source: *Body=Brain* Online Course (2015, 2018). Created and taught by Amanda Blake, MD. https://embright.org/body-brain. Fair Use.

2. Source: Porges, Stephen (2011). *The Polyvagal Theory: Neurophysiological Foundations of Emotions, Attachment, Communication, and Self-regulation.* New York: W.W. Norton. Fair use.

3. Source: "Befriending the Nervous System" (2020). Created by Deb Dana. Produced by Sounds True. Fair use. https://www.soundstrue.com/products/befriending-your-nervous-system.

Chapter 14

Measurements: Money and Body

My dear reader, I am offering *a lot* of information in the landscape section. Even the way of the Academic may be getting full. So if you are full, please move to practice with the Practice Guidebooks and start your big dive. If you want a bit more, keep reading here. My intention in this chapter is to highlight, in broad and clear ways, how much we rely on measurements to ground, stabilize, feel okay, and plan our financial future. While we may be seeking joy and well-being, our underlying "thing" with measurements is safety. We want *proof* that we are okay. Measurements will never offer anything except a measurement and a fleeting feeling of the deeper thing we seek. Hug your body, and let's get going.

Any measure is performed at a specific time in a particular place in evolution. We can only measure with present-day tools, present-day technology, and present-day proven science. Any new discovery can never be examined exceptionally with today's tools—because today's tools are based in a past time by the very nature of their existence. Measurements, all measurements, are always old and always changing. We only measure for a narrow point in time, yet we cling to measurements for future answers, to feel better, more certain, more in control. So let's not forget—what about the immeasurable?

Every situation and thing we encounter and we measure is partial. Yet we are whole people. So when we utilize present-day tools (sometimes held fiercely from the past) anything we measure can never measure up. Pun intended.

Measurements support knowledge creation; knowledge, as you know, is located in the head center by the way of the Academic. Measurements in finance, for the most part, are meant to alleviate the fear of a future unknown. Questions are consistent with our human experience: will I have enough to retire, will there be enough money to live comfortably for my life, will my kids be able to handle it, what will happen if/when I get old and decline? All of these can be summed up in the question: Will I (we/my family) be okay? And am I enough right now?

My daughter was born a few weeks premature. Before her birth, I was given an amniocentesis, where a needle is stuck in the womb and draws out amniotic fluid to measure the size of the baby. I was told my daughter would weigh about 3 pounds. In a state of worry, truly this was not pleasant, I asked, "What is the accuracy of the measurement?" The answer: 20%. I blurted, even in my distressed state—my Academic fiercely protective—"Why bother with such a low accuracy measure?" The response was it was the best available. My daughter weighed 6 lbs. 1 oz at birth. To this day I strongly question the merit of any medical procedure that not only offers a very limited result but additionally causes more stress and harm on our living vessel, our body.

Science, finance, health all use measurements as a reliable standard to create protocols, processes, procedures to advance and improve our human life and well-being—by giving us something to hold on to. For most of these systems, consistency and repeated use enable the measurements to have some meaning, credibility, and validity. This mode of thinking seems outdated. As a human culture we need to use measurements more intelligently—with our whole body and not just our brain.

Given that measurements are limited to a time and place where something can be measured, let's return to the seemingly immeasurable, which has a direct impact on our well-being and happiness.

Many countries, Bhutan being the most well-known, now measure GNH—Gross National Happiness—rather than GDP (Gross Domestic Product), as a better measure of economic prosperity. Gross National Happiness is a philosophy that guides the government of Bhutan. It includes an index, which is used to measure the collective happiness and well-being of a population. Enacted in July of 2008, Gross National Happiness is the goal of the government of Bhutan documented in their constitution. The term "Gross National Happiness" was coined in 1972 by the then king of Bhutan, Jigme Singye Wangchuck, when he said during an interview by a British journalist for the *Financial Times*, "Gross National Happiness is more important than Gross National Product."[1]

Can you imagine, just for a minute, a culture that cares about happiness to the extent that government policy is based upon human joy? Yes, my friends, take a moment to pause. A focus on well-being is real and worthy of our contemplation. Well-being, happiness, okay-ness, all of the states of being human that truly matter have very little, if anything, to do with measurements. But since we are not well versed in understanding the limits of measurements, Bhutan has taken what really matters and begun to measure it, to help connect the dots, to bridge perspectives, to expand awareness, to emphasize what is important.

Translating these "what really matter" measurements to finance continues to be met with barriers. Let's just name it. We are not open to new ways of measuring unless they confirm an existing belief. We are addicted to our comfortable measurements that allow fear to wiggle in the veins of self-interest.

In 2014, a best-selling book on clearing clutter, *The Life-Changing Magic of Tidying Up*, made its way across the globe. I devoured it from cover to cover. The author, Marie Kondo, describes her HonKari method simply as decluttering by discarding and organizing.[2] While she is respectful of traditional approaches to organizing and clearing clutter, she points out the limitations. She introduces the HonKari method as a game-changing approach, and I see this as the opening to a new kind of measurement, one that includes our body wisdom. First, segmenting similar objects together, her practice goes like this:

Pick up the object (clothing, book, pot, pan, cup—any item you steward) and ask: "Does this spark joy?" Simple. The only true answer naturally arises from your body wisdom. Joy is not a concept. Joy is experienced in the body. The question skillfully bypasses the rational mind, which typically offers any one or more scarcity thoughts:

a. Is it still in good condition? I am wasteful if I get rid of it.
b. I should keep it, just in case.
c. I did not get my money's worth; I should use it more.
d. Someday this will come in handy.
e. Or—the opposite—why throw away something that has been so useful, I may never find another like it.

What is your favorite way of rationalizing? (You do know you have a favorite, right?)

Rationalizing is a protective posture that limits the full brilliant joyful vitality of human life. Asking, "Does this spark joy?" opens up a whole new path for measuring that ineffable place, which, you guessed it, is immeasurable—perhaps.

The body assists in measuring that which is deemed to be immeasurable. When you ask yourself, "Does this spark joy?" immediately your body answers. For me, there is a quickening of sensations in my body, and these sensations signal—without interpretation from my left brain—yes, I feel joy when I tune in to this object, or no, I do not feel joy when I tune into this object. Immediately, with a commitment to this process, our ability to appreciate an object for its gift to us is available. We can release our attachment to it (our limiting beliefs about the object that foster shame, guilt, fear, regret, and confusion), thank it for its use to us, and send it forward to be of service to another being.

Tiny Practice

Let's locate joy in the areas of your body.
Breathe into the entire felt sense of your body.
Smile. Drop your shoulders. Soften your body tension.
Recall a happy and joyful experience. Lower your gaze to assist with visualization.
Supercharge your memory as you give attention to your body.
What sensations do you experience during a state of joy?
What is the temperature, pressure, and movement of joy in your body?
Our body helps us measure joy.
Joy results from being in a continuous state of well-being, wholeness, happiness, okay-ness.

If we can begin to measure joy, imagine the opportunities to measure sufficiency and generosity. The Virtuous Flow allows joy to be a renewable and resourceful fuel from our mere existence, breath, and movement.

In our company, we aim to engage in work that activates and sustains our genius. Interviewing a candidate for an open position, I shared our firm's "working in our genius" philosophy. Simply stated, genius is the intersection of activities that generate potent impact, unceasing energy in our passion, and mastery level output in our skills. We aspire to work in our genius because when we work in our genius, we are happy, feel good, and sustain health. Our body experience is palpable and energized. Our output is generative and alive. Our offerings are of value. When I asked this candidate about his experience of working in his genius and how he knew he was, his answers were *body-centered*. "I feel really good. I want to do more of it. I feel connected."

The questions to ponder are:

Does this spark joy?
Does this deepen love?
Does this expand generosity?
Now we're talking.
Now we're shifting paradigms.
Now we are catapulting finance to essential wealth of what truly matters.
How are the measurements working now?

*When we enter into practice, it is helpful to examine **how** we practice as much as it is to know the practice. In the next few chapters we tour the landscape of pacing, masculine/feminine, measurements, and methodology.*

Notes

1. Source: Wikipedia, https://en.wikipedia.org/wiki/Gross_National_Happiness. Fair use.
2. Source: Kondo, Maria (2014). *The Life-Changing Magic of Tidying Up: The Japanese Art of Decluttering and Organizing*. Berkeley, CA: Ten Speed Press. Fair use.

Skillful Response in the Landscape

Chapter 15

Productive Rest and Productive Action

It has been estimated that out of every million parts of information received and processed by our body, we humans only admit thirteen parts into our conscious awareness. That means we only allow ourselves to be conscious of .000013 percent of the data, of experience, known to our body.

—Reginald A. Ray, PhD[1]

O ur body is our lifelong ally. With uninterrupted attention, our body shows us explicitly where tension, ache, constriction lives, and our body generously offers us gestures for healing, clearing, and making room for useful energy.

But our body will not truly open up to us unless we give it our full abiding attention, and that depends on a skillful flow between *productive rest* and *productive action*.

Let's swim with these important words.

The rigorous coaching methodology from Integral Coaching of Canada (ICC) taught me the difference, and importance, in productive and unproductive mind states that affect our way of moving and our way of being.[2] Most often we consider productivity to be a result of action, something that is completed. We are productive when we take action toward the completion of a specific objective.

This is true. And it is partial. Equally important in our productivity is rest. Productive rest.

In the ICC curriculum, the lens for human productivity asks us to study and recognize four different states of mind or modes of going in our clients: high productive, low productive, high unproductive, low unproductive. Let me unpack this lens for you. The high and low reflects energy—lots of energy expended or very little energy expended. Productive indicates whether the energy expended is beneficial or not, toward positive development.

As we become more familiar with our soma, our body wisdom, and our energy, we are attuned to the necessity for productive rest and productive action. Let's look closer at each of these four ways and then link to the engagement of meaningful practices.

Most of us are familiar with and may be able to engage in productive **action**. We sustain a flow state, a term coined by Mihaly Csikszentmihalyi, also known colloquially as *being in the zone*.[3] Athletes are particularly attuned to these concepts and practice in their particular field of athleticism. It is operating from a mental state performing an activity fully immersed in a feeling of energized focus, full engagement, and enjoyment. Flow is characterized by complete absorption in the activity where we lose track of time and space. This is also where we "play in our genius." Recall genius activity is unique to each of us and represents the intersection on a Venn diagram of skill, passion, and impact. Flow, or genius activity, is a high productive state of being and going. It is productive action, vibrancy, and vitality that our body requires to optimize our well-being, happiness, and development. This flow state of being nourishes our Virtuous Flow of Somatic Finance. In other words, with this nourishing energy it is easy to sustain flow—moving to and from sufficiency and generosity—moment by moment. It is almost impossible to retract to scarcity; and even if you do, the momentum to return to flow is powerful and easy.

Writing produces a flow state for me. My writing is a natural skill that produces quality output. Not only do I feel energized, *more* energy is created while I write. After writing for hours, I have more energy. The output of my writing affects those who receive it. Is this book having an impact on you? I hope so. Positive impact is my intention as this book comes to form.

Recognizing when we are in a high productive mode of going is generally easy to do, even if we are not well practiced. If you are not aware of your high productive energy—what it feels like in your body *and* the activities you are engaging when your energy expands—please try the Tiny Practice below introducing the genius exploration. You cannot play in your genius and experience high productive energy if you don't know what lights you up. Period.

Tiny Practice

Choose to play in your genius!

Genius is the intersection of three embodied activities: skills, passion, and impact.

Skills reflect talent, any activity in which you engage that produces mastery level output. Explore your skills by answering: *What activities do I engage in that produce mastery level output?*

Impact reflects benefit, any activity in which you engage that produces impeccable contribution (to self, others, organizations, the world). Explore your impact by answering: *What activities do I engage in that make impeccable contributions?*

Passion reflects power, any activity in which you engage that generates unceasing energy. When you engage in this activity, vitality increases rather than feeling depleted. Explore your passion by answering: *What activities do I engage in that generate unceasing energy?*

To my precious reader, did you notice the above practice relies primarily on your cognition. Did you listen to your body for answers? What changes or clarifies if you do ask these somatic (feeling) questions: *What does mastery level output feel like? What does impeccable contribution feel like? What does unceasing energy feel like?*

The opposite of high productive is **high unproductive**. This mode of going is the frenetic, overwhelming, mind-moving, and blurring scene where we are running around like the chicken with her head cut off. We might be making some progress, but for the most part, our high-energy output is not producing effective results, more likely stress. Our production of stress is the most common contributor to unproductivity. In the high state of unproductivity, tension, aches, and constriction circle inside tying us in more knots of confusion, frustration, and anger. When we are in this state, it is best to stop trying. But let's face it, when money is part of our situation, urgency often has its way. Trying to stop only intensifies unproductivity. In these stuck flow states a beneficial move is toward a low productive state of silence, stillness, and space. In my experience, the quickest and easiest way to stop trying and slow-down is to return to our _____. (Yes, body. Breathe.)

A low productive state is rest. **Productive rest** allows us to feel and honor the fatigue in our body, restore and balance our energy, and expand our awareness. Common teachings on Western culture and spiritual exploration say that Westerners are culturally opposite from Eastern practitioners. Eastern practitioners typically suffer from laziness. In the West, we suffer from busyness. We do not know how to rest. We do not know how to *practice* rest. To top it off, innovative technology only adds fuel to a blazing fire of going, going, gone.

Productive rest accesses a slower pace. We give attention and awareness to our pacing in movement activities. It is not unusual for me to give practices to clients "moving at a 50% pace" or a 25% pace. Habitual patterns relish the constancy and monotony of repeated activity, and the faster, the better. But most useful skills are built through conscious sacred action, not unconscious habit. When we become aware of how we are going in the activity, we have a chance to change. When we become aware of the bombardment of more, we notice the claustrophobia. We recognize how tight and unbearable it is to live in our skin. Sometimes we want out.

It might surprise you to know that science informs us that our body is made up of molecules all attracted to each other, water, and atoms. We are not really solid but a unique beautiful constellation of energy floating together to make a whole vessel of yummy you and yummy other beings. I will not go into further detail here, other than to offer, we have many concepts about who we are that limit our potential. Science can only measure what it is able to measure, remember? We don't know what we don't know. Interesting? Let's get back to rest, which we do know about. When we slow our pace, we gain a better sense of ourselves, and the invitation to deeply productively rest becomes more appealing.

An old friend, Dan Howard, developed a unique methodology called, Intentional Resting.[4] What makes his practices unique is not so much the gentle breathing and meditations but his instruction to intentionally rest for a place in your body that is tense. Yes. Intentionally rest *for* your hip, heart, nerves, or knees. What a practice! Include rest in your daily schedule. Kindergarten teachers are brilliant; naptime for a good reason! It is more common for us adults to be exhausted and require our fatigue to be the indicator to go rest. Our body informs us with lethargy, pain, stupor, listlessness, or dullness to go lie down and sleep. This response is not restorative rest; it is exhaustive rest. We want to be both resting and aware of the resting that produces a still, spacious, and silent mind state and somatic relief. In this way we inhabit an experience that balances important neurotransmitters producing feelings of peace, stability, calm, equanimity, and sufficiency. Or let me say that these are my experiences of productive rest. You may have other words to describe your experience. It is always my invitation for you to have your direct experience.

When we are able to practice productive rest, our band of potential nourishing experiences expands. I just made up that interesting phrase. What is a band of nourishing experiences?

It is the ability to inhabit strong muscles and to experience any situation as nourishing—regardless of what is being delivered. But if the immediate experience doesn't feel nourishing, it is possessing the ability to quickly return to a space of nourishment. Productive rest is supported most effectively through a meditation practice that allows us to still the mind. When we pause all (or most) thinking activity, our body relates to us differently. Our body senses a beautiful opening to connect, and something new begins to happen. We don't just slow our pace, we learn to halt. The band of nourishment expands through practice on the polarities of productive action and productive rest. With a healthy band of nourishment, we abide more easily on the Virtuous Flow.

Before we explore the fourth state of being, unproductive rest, I want to ask you: When you read these states of being and ways of moving—productive and unproductive—and think about how you work with money,

What happens in your body?

Did you notice an immediate tension arise just reading the word "money"?

Are your money challenges in the high unproductive state or the low unproductive state?

Your recognition matters when choosing practices to build useful muscles. Often we are drawn to what we already do well or have familiarity with. Let me say this in a different way. Practice requires openness and patience in developing a new muscle that may not seem necessary, friendly, useful, or possible.

As I emphasized above, most of us do not have a clear understanding of the importance of rest, much less embodied productive rest.

Tiny Practice

What does rest and ease feel like in your body?

Do you feel at ease in your body right now?

If not, what is one way to move closer to ease? Write it down.

Was your one way a thinking move, from the Head?

Was your one way a grounding move, from the Belly?

Was your one way an opening move, from the Heart?

How was your move familiar?

How was your move original?

Pick another center. What is a new move from this space?

These somatic reflections offer new insights to support choices for new practices that will fit you. In other words, the best practices for you to engage will arise from your discovery. I could offer suggestions. They might be fine. But when you come to your own realization about how you are, adding your inner wisdom, your motivation to practice for your benefit increases. It is the way we are wired.

Take a breath, nod your head, and smile. I am.

The last of the four mind states and mode of moving is **unproductive rest**, which could be labeled as depression. But it doesn't need to be a full-blown medical diagnosis of depression. We have all encountered some form of depression, and what it means in this context is lethargy to the point of loss of will for any period of time. Our willpower loses its mojo, and we are foggy, groggy and soggy. Yes, our mind is murky, our state of being is deeply, unsettled, and our body is limp. Low unproductive doesn't have to last long, but it affects us. It is worthy to note the way we move and our physical posture when we have low energy that produces minimal results.

If I neglect to practice productive rest in my way of going, the risk of falling into a low unproductive space is high, for me. Let me say this another way, when I neglect my meditation practice, I tend to do addictive, low-energy activities such as streaming stupid TV for way too long or munching on Cheetos or chocolate (something savory or sweet when I am not hungry). Another way of describing low unproductive is curling up into a ball and hiding out under the covers like Greta Garbo, "I want to be alone" persona. Lingering in this low unproductive place, my appetite fades and circles form under my eyes. My body gives me indicators when I am here.

What indicators does your body offer you?

Isn't she generous?

A beautiful ocean with waves lapping to the shore comes to mind. Imagine now sitting on the beach watching a vast blue green ocean. Each wave before you is a present to engage what most wants attention in your body—right now.

Polyvagal Theory and Productive Unproductive Action

Earlier we covered the basics about the four states of fear and poly-vagal theory. Recall the four ways fear manifests as fight, freeze, flee, and faint. And recall Steven Porge's illumination of our vagal nerve and what happens physiologically when fear arises, to survive we either move (fight or flee) or we stop (freeze or faint).

Productive action and productive rest relate to the two ways our body responds to life events. Productive action attends to the mobilization, and productive rest attends to immobilization. Money frequently causes us to unconsciously (we are unaware) ignite a fear response into an unproductive movement (fight, flee) or unproductive stillness (freeze, faint).

Overreacting to a money situation with mobilization looks like selling securities when the market drops and we are fearful that the investments will not recover. Underreacting to a money situation with immobilization looks like ignoring accumulating bills and incurring hefty interest charges and late fees. The financial systems, banking systems, money systems, and global financial events are not controllable in any way. They will continue to move, change, disrupt in response to political, social, evolutionary, and planetary pulls that we have no control over and have never had any control. These systems are changing more rapidly than ever. I don't need to inform you, the reader, of this truth.

Our body systems and our mind like stability, balance, and certainty, particularly around money. When our body is activated from a surprising financial event, and we have read about and currently experience many money events, we can react unproductively from survival habit if we do not become familiar with productive action and productive rest through practice.

Productive action engages—with confidence, integrity, and dignity—the fundamental money practices that we in our present culture are asked to address. They include for most of us activities such as filing income tax returns, budgeting (earning, saving, spending with awareness), managing debt, and executing estate documents (wills, durable powers, health care proxies), among many others. When attending to these activities, we want to be fully embodied by knitting together the importance of these activities to our life.

In other words, money activity is not separate from our body. Money is not a pile of paper over there that goes to the bank or the cashier. Money moves through us with intention and, hopefully, right action.

Productive rest engages the interior in a creative loving generative way where money is invited to the experience. You access the deeper whys and what matters most by understanding your own money psychology, beliefs, and behaviors. Cognitive conversations lay an entry point for going deeper. Somatic Finance takes your hand and guides you further into your physical systems that supercharge your valuable psychological insights and heal unhealthy money patterns.

When we bring money into this map, I point to the necessity for us to build new sacred rituals and routines that allow us to be productive in all situations with money, to be ninja warriors with the many responses and actions we encounter around finances. When our practice is stable, we are then called to support others in this new way of going with money.

Constrictions in our body are present because of an unresolved money thing.

Some might challenge me on what I am about to reveal. But experiment for yourself and come to insights that resonate for you. In my direct discoveries, in the beginning of exploring money issues, being engaged in low productive practices allowed me the slow generous space to become more familiar with my body, my tension, where energy flowed with various emotions and how to befriend my beautiful vessel. Engaging my body intelligence with curiosity and appreciative inquiry gave me new insights about my limiting beliefs and behaviors. After gaining access to these insights, the opportunity to ramp it up, so to speak, with high productive practices became a natural evolution and aspiration.

To be more explicit, consider my prescription that has brought me to writing this book.

Introduced to somatic meditation in the early 2000s in meditating with the body, I experienced slow, deliberate, soft, still, and gentle body practices for the first time. Somatic meditation was my threshold for whole body awareness. With somatic awareness, other practices, courses, and modalities such as Appreciative Inquiry, Imagination Made Real®, and Byron Katie's The Work provided access to deeper insights, growth, healing, trust, and creativity. I discovered that it did not matter which course or practice I chose. Far more important and essential was my somatic awareness as I engaged in each practice, which always informs the best pace. Holding this view and motivation to bring healing to our money collective, earlier teachings in my life clarified and expanded meaning. As my nutrients were well fed, openness allowed me to bravely engage life pursuits and obstacles skillfully (e.g., career shifts, transitions, parent's demise) and to include money with equanimity.

There is no one-size-fits-all way to engage. Paying attention to your body wisdom and the openings that arise when building this relationship offers you the best path forward, for you.

So, my friend, what calls you?

How does your body respond?

Productive action or productive rest or both?

Notes

1. Source: Ray, Reginald (2016). *The Awakening Body: Somatic Meditation for Discovering Our Deepest Life*. Boulder, CO: Shambhala Publications. Fair use.
2. Source: Integral Coaching of Canada (ICC). https://www.integralcoachingcanada.com Fair use.
3. Source: Csikszentmihalyi, Mihaly (2008). *Flow: The Psychology of Optimal Experience*. New York: Harper Perennial Modern Classics. Fair use.
4. Source: *Intentional Resting—How to REST NOW* (2010). Created by Dan Howard. https://www.youtube.com/watch?v=eNLvaBX5w7A. Fair use.

Chapter 16

Masculine and Feminine, Focused and Spacious

We might have read or heard information about masculine and feminine energies. And in the context of Somatic Finance these concepts can be helpful to how we engage our practice and to expand our perspectives. Relating to the masculine and feminine, we examine how they both work for us and they both work against us. Just like our three archetypes have both strengths and weaknesses in money situations, masculine and feminine ways do too.

Finances have long been worked in the masculine: a laser-like focus on a target to solve the problem, get the job complete, mark a big check on the page. After careful analysis with a rational mind—full of tactics and strategies to accomplish a specific financial objective—actions are taken with focus, clarity, and intensity. These are important activities to make progress. And yet, there is more to the story.

While the masculine is focused and gets the job done, the feminine casts a net wide and far, to see the rest of the story. The feminine is capable of holding all perspectives—that allow for more human data and optimal actions to follow. All too often in finance there is no casting. Known strategies are activated with a whisper of intention, and before any contemplation or reflection or conversation, an answer, a conclusion, a course of action is made, and focused direction begins. Because there are results (positive and negative), and because there are metrics, we think this is fine. We counter correct with more strategies and actions, like a chess game.

We can visualize the masculine and feminine by returning to the common actions of our ancestral humans. The masculine way of going is akin to a hunter stalking food with a spear. A laser-focused intention of killing to survive directs the hunter to heave the spear in the center of the heart of the buck. The focus is single-minded and may not account for the danger and damage of the actions. Meanwhile, the feminine has a view of the entire landscape. With a wide-angle lens, this person sees that this buck is the father to four fawns, who have a lame mother. Without this buck, the entire species may go extinct. The masculine perspective doesn't know this broader truth, but the feminine does. Both are needed for survival and thriving.

Purposefully I am using masculine and feminine rather than male and female. This is not a gender thing in the male-female context. This is an energetic way of moving, sensing, seeing, and going in the world—depicted in masculine and feminine. Masculine agency is focused action, and feminine care is spacious insight, both necessary for us to be whole.

We will go into more detail and nuances about masculine and feminine and the different situations in our personal and financial lives that call for a more masculine or feminine approach. Before these nuances are presented, it is necessary to gain a strong foundation of masculine and feminine principles.

It will seem as you read that I am favoring the feminine in my writing. That could be true. I lean toward a feminine way of being. Our money systems are so far skewed to the masculine that the balance for feminine focuses my attention. The body is the essential space of the feminine. To meet the arguments that the mind is our body and for purposes of understanding and practice, let's use "bodymind" for a knowledge-based and masculine way of orienting. For the feminine way of orienting, we will say "wholebody."

In most of the subjects you are reading, we are pointing to the feminine. Practices in the soma are more feminine but never exclusively. Masculine and feminine co-occur; there is no separation. But in order to abide in wholeness, we gain clarity with the parts. The feminine is offered to gain access to more space, more room, and more possibilities. Wiggle room provides relief. Expanded breath provides relief. More options provide relief.

As I write this piece, I am attending a financial conference. For sure there are many more men in attendance than women. It reeks of masculine energy, and I do my best to stay present and allow the dense focused energy of each presentation to move and settle. I recognize a pattern of masculine energy with my intention to be present with all that is arising.

If I am not careful, I interpret the intensity as direction and progress. In reality there is some of that, but there is a high percentage of sucking, consuming, draining energy that brings fatigue. Too much intensity doesn't necessarily build new muscles; it only tires us. Fatigue is what I believe permeates our money life. With pervasive masculine in the financial systems, we are all f***ing tired. (Remember productive rest, and the need for balance?)

The evolution of the financial services industry paints a picture of how it has been held in the masculine.

- 70s—insurance (sell life insurance, annuities, to fix a perceived threat and instill more fear needing this product to be safe).
- 80s—tax sheltered investments (sell illiquid real estate partnerships with 4-to-1 tax write-offs to minimize taxes for fear of paying too much in taxes).
- 90s—AUM (accumulate assets under management and charge a percentage to drive wealth growth as the target of security).
- 2000s—life planning (ask pointed questions in a structured linear process—yes, closer to the feminine—yet without integration and a dynamic flow).

- 2010s—technology, AI (access technology for efficiency and control while fluctuating trust and comfort with money and advisors).
- 2020s—evolutionary shifts are upon us we cannot escape, nor do we want to, because these shifts ask us to develop our feminine care and open our hearts wider. While I am not an oracle, who doesn't have stories and experiences of the first two years of this decade that harbor big changes, questions, and choices? Who isn't tired of working harder, faster, and with fierce agency? Perhaps it is the potency of these shifts that make the balancing of our body centers in Somatic Finance so important for our success—survival, connection, and flourishing.

The masculine leads in the forces of money evolution. It just does. Relief comes from relaxing into a broader space of feminine care, as in productive rest. Do you want to be held with love and kindness? Do you want a place to let your hair down or prop up your feet? Do you want a process you can explore that offers contemplation with curiosity and wonder? Do you want finances to be fun?

What do I mean by the above?

Our actions in life want to be tethered to what deeply matters. Everything that deeply matters is recognized in the heart. Information shared from our brain requires time, care, and practice to drop down and integrate into our body. Our wholebody offers wisdom that helps to shape what deeply matters with our bodymind. When we are able to connect our deepest **why** to the information swirling in our head, our ability to skillfully, full-heartedly, pleasantly, openly, smoothly take action becomes easy, if not an ecstatic dance. Reconnect to your **why** discussed many chapters ago. How is it for you to read new concepts with body awareness and touch in to your **why**? Engage this question right now.

Tiny Practice

Express your why out loud three times. (Return to page 14.) Notice what's happening in your Body.

Does it feel dense, tingly, open, stuck? Just notice.
How might your masculine agency be showing up?
How might your feminine care be showing up?
Feminine energy softens sharp edges.
Feminine energy fills in the gaps of fear and confusion.
Feminine energy allows for the unknown to be the journey,
until clarity arises.
As we move through the 2020s, the feminine will no longer
take a back seat.

The feminine keeps the heart connected to the power of our belly and the knowledge of our head. The feminine aligns tight with our deepest heart *why* and allows for our why to flourish.

Bringing a popular map from Ken Wilber's integral theory to our conversation, we note how the integral quadrants relate to Somatic Finance. Beginning on the left side of the quadrant inside our individual body and heart connections, we examine, reflect, open, cry, sense the tender spots, feel into the values that hold us, the communities that shaped us, to discover beliefs that have directed our harmful actions—whether we know them or not. In this generous space, relief emerges because we are seen—as we are—completely without judgment or pressure. For some of us, it might be the first time of beholding. This authentic experience is scary because it is so naked, and yet it is what we all long for as humans.

Our *why,* known on the interior, gives direction (*how* and *what*) to follow for our unique personal integrated financial plan on the exterior, the right side of the quadrant. Our life is held together rather than compartmentalized. Perhaps for the first time, our money makes sense to us, and we possess genuine energy to take action. Even men are drawn to this way. In truth, men long to be held here too. Society and culture have demanded that men be strong, take care of things, make great decisions, never make mistakes, and certainly never make financial mistakes, that they are too scared to do anything other than take action solely from knowledge

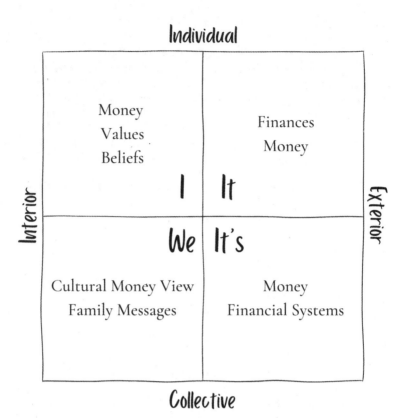

Figure 16.1   Illustration of Integral Quadrants.

held in the strategic brain. And when we ignore the intelligence that rests in our body, we are all doomed to fail.

We are doomed to fail not because the decisions made and actions taken are bad. We fail because when we only consider the best financial result, without walking in the interior, we miss the mark. We ignore the essential point of our hearts' desire, our hearts' longing, and the place that makes our lives worth living, the core of *why* we walk on this earth. We miss the Virtuous Flow from sufficiency to generosity over and over and over again.

What happens when we roam the interior? We learn who we really are in context to a bigger situation. Instead of repeating habitual inherited or societal behavior, or taking a shortcut just to get it done, we slow down, take a beat, and reveal important answers from powerful questions.

It's scary. It is scary because it is unfamiliar and perhaps uncomfortable to consistently bring our why forward with money. But the more we play, explore, open, and walk in this territory, the more comfortable we become, and this integration becomes our natural way.

Again, what does this look like from a practical place?

Before we make financial decisions and take action, we step back, as far as we are able, and we dive deep, as deep as we are able, to name our truth of existence. Why am I here, really? Yes. This is the big question that is asked of us from all walks of life. If this question is too scary or too big, take a few steps forward to connect to your heart with a narrower question. Why do I really want to fund my retirement plan (renovate my kitchen, visit relatives, start this business)?

Activities we engage to assist us with our deepest and deeper truths are widely available.

With interior truths, we skillfully meet exterior answers to *our* life. Repeating my words earlier, when we embody our **why**, the flow of our actions becomes easier and comfortable.

Chapter 17

Wider Masculine and Deeper Feminine

It is not sufficient to just understand the landscape of masculine and feminine and the integration of our deeper **why**. Our understanding gives us access to continue to merge money well with the endless winding road of life. Different times and situations emphasize masculine over feminine and feminine over masculine. Other times and situations we favor movement over stillness and stillness over movement. Some times and situations we favor form over formless and formless over form.

Earlier we clarified feminine and masculine. Let's add *dynamic* and *static* as two terms to exemplify movement (productive action) and stillness (productive rest). Dynamic is like water, constantly moving. Water can be highly intense and compelling like a rapidly rushing river, or it can be gentle and caressing like a soft moving stream. Regardless of the liveliness, dynamic is always active and always changing. Static is like a mountain, immovable. The energy of a mountain is fixed, steady, and stable; there is little to no change, even as the weather shifts and seasons come and go. Movement and stillness happen in space.

From study and training with Integral Coaching of Canada, Inc., we are taught that masculine and feminine are dynamic and static, and these energetic patterns flow with our life experiences relating to each other in polarities. This distinction provides us a view and a way to move with practice. Our money experiences, just as our life, flow on this map of static masculine, dynamic feminine, and static feminine, dynamic masculine. Different periods of our life call for different emphasis in order to progress with our finances, meet the truth of the moment, and effectively make decisions.

The wisdom of Laura Divine, one of the cofounders of Integral Coaching of Canada, Inc., among other trained coaches and researchers, offers more depth and nuances on this subject. The static masculine (systems, structures, order, balance) holds its polarity with the dynamic feminine (spontaneous, flowing, unknowing, lively), while the dynamic masculine (goal oriented, achievement, exploration, determined) holds its polarity with the static feminine (wholeness, beholding, affirmation, acceptance). Recall the previous introduction to masculine and feminine and

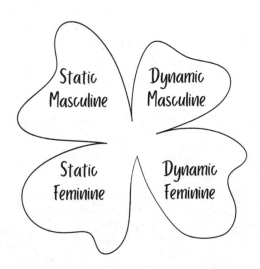

Figure 17.1   Illustration of Flow of Static-Dynamic and Masculine Feminine.

my calling attention to the current money systems held in the masculine.

Can you connect our present-day money structures to static masculine, where precise accounting, defined budgets, strict financial rules, and a rigid stake in the ground keeps our financial systems intact? Can you connect present-day money flow to dynamic masculine, where fierce direction driving toward goals, achieving, growing, accumulating, winning, and figuring out keeps us focused forward moving in determination? Gosh, I have totally lost my breath writing these two sentences.

Why?
Pause.
Breathe.
Open.
Where is the wonder?
Where is the laughter?
Where is the freedom of pause and digestion of creative emergence?
Where is our weaving with others' wisdom?
Where is our savoring of accomplishment?
Where is love?

The feminine, static and dynamic, energize our **why**, our hearts pulse that bleeds attention to the edges and rigidity of the masculine. Without feminine care, greed poisons the well of humanity. We lose all perspective with focused attention that rarely, if ever, illuminates consideration of others.

Let's give attention to a few common life and financial situations:

- Preparing to retire;
- Changing careers;
- Buying a home, a car, furniture;
- Saving for a goal (education, car, vacation);
- Giving to a cause;
- Tending to elderly parents;
- Raising children;

- Developing a business;
- Volunteering for wildlife;
- Finding employment;
- Healing disease.

It's helpful to locate where we are and in what direction we are going when certain financial situations are present. Bring your current financial situation to mind to examine in our exploration. Note, a *big* note: all of these situations optimally or eventually touch all of and flow with the static and dynamic masculine and feminine energies. All of these situations feel different in our body experience. Allow these examples to support your felt (in the body) experience of the situation and the benefit of that particular way of being. Pay particular attention to the preponderance of masculine energy in our money field.

Static Masculine

Saving for a goal. In order to save for a goal, we require a clear structure to accumulate money. Most commonly we use a bank account to receive and tally money for a specific goal.

Developing a business. In order to establish a business, a declared entity defines the business structure, and systems align around that declared legal structure.

Static Feminine

Tending to elderly parents. In this precious time, deep, dignified care holds our loving actions on behalf of our elders. Our time and energy is currency flowing.

Giving to a cause. In this sacred stance of generosity, we unite with something bigger than ourselves. Our dedicated heart magnetizes generosity.

Dynamic Masculine

Buying a home. In order to locate a new residence, we explore toward a specific end. We research a preferred town and search for homes within our price range.

Changing careers. To shift our career, we take authentic initiative to achieve power, shift our situation, and demonstrate ambition.

Dynamic Feminine

Preparing to retire. In this powerful life transition, we open to vast possibilities from life as we complete a specific season of work and yield with the next arising change and season.

Raising children. During this important phase of parenting, we navigate all waters with a deep knowing of love and recognition that we might know nothing in these fresh waters.

I repeat, this bears repeating, we do not stop the cycle from one pattern to the next. Each example moves on the map, and the focus of movement changes. Planning to retire as dynamic feminine moves to static feminine with a resounding clear *yes*. The affirmation of a clear *yes* to retire moves to dynamic masculine where specific goals and retirement plans activate. The activation of retirement then moves to static masculine for strong structure to hold the change. Abiding in retirement, dynamic feminine arrives as the spontaneous space for retirement to unfold over and over as the concept of retirement fades to "this is my current situation, I occupy life here."

We might recognize that one way of being may feel easier than another. Our productive rest and action and unproductive rest and action mirror these energies. Practices in productive rest and action assist us to skillfully move in these polarities.

We move quickly or slowly, for days or years, on this cycle. We always move, unless we are stuck. Bringing an emphasis on the feminine allows stickiness to loosen and effectively move to what is needed in our financial life.

Now, let's look at what is present for you, in your financial life, right now.

Please refer to Figure 17.1. The illustration of the flow of static and dynamic, masculine and feminine on page 158.

Tiny Practice

Pause.
Breathe.
Open.

What is your money sore spot or singing potential?
When you reflect on your money situation, what gender pattern is most alive?
When you reflect on your money situation, what gender pattern brings you closer to your objective?
Are these postures the same, close, or far apart?
What needs to shift, develop, and awaken in order for you to get from where you are now to where you want to be?

I'm tingling with excitement for you. If you are not excited, start breathing. Play with this good stuff. I am right here.

Are you struggling with a budget, a spending plan, a "where do I allocate my resources" plan?

What stands in your way?
Have you connected to your *why*? (feminine)
If not, start on the inside.
How does this experience feel in your body? (feminine)
If you know your *why*, access your head for knowledge (masculine).

What form will hold your why? (masculine)
Does this form match you and make sense to you? (feminine)
How does this inquiry feel in your body? (feminine)
If you know your *why* and your form, access your belly for dynamic strength (masculine).
Where is your discipline to activate progress or a practice? (masculine)
Are you willing? Have you committed? (masculine)
How do you re-commit? (masculine)
How are you feeling in your body? (feminine)

If you know your *why*, your exploration defined a form, and discipline is energized, access your belly, heart, and spine for sufficiency. Sufficiency, as you are aware, is the gateway for the Virtuous Flow.

What are you seeing and experiencing?
What are you measuring?
How does this experience feel in your body?

Embodied sufficiency supports clarity and progress, with a beautiful integration of masculine and feminine.

One more reflection before we move on, unhealthy masculine and unhealthy feminine produce the worst of the worst in finances. Unhealthy masculine is rigid, contracted, narrow focused, and makes many arrogant mistakes. Unhealthy feminine is chaotic, ungrounded, confused, and makes many ignorant mistakes.

We need both masculine and feminine energy.

We need both healthy masculine and healthy feminine energy now, in finances.

Our body is the best path to get us there.

Note

1. Source: Sophie, Josephine. (2018). Coaching Grounded in the Masculine and Feminine Principles. *International Coach Academy.* https://coachcampus .com/coach-portfolios/research-papers/josephine-sophie-coaching-grounded-in-the-masculine-and-feminine-principles.

Chapter 18

Money Madness
Made Mindful

Seeing, going, checking.

Perspective, action, results.

View, conduct, realization.

These methods, maps, and motivations say the same thing, which is:

Seeing, perspective, and view—name our beliefs.

Going, action, and conduct—demonstrate movement.

Checking, results, and realization—verify our beliefs and movement.

Integral Coaching of Canada's methodology for a client's way of being is held in seeing, going, and checking. Human development maps hold perspectives, action, and results. Spiritual teachings are motivated with transmissions of view, conduct, and realization.

Our way of seeing, perspectives, and view is how we engage life with concepts.

What ideas, beliefs, limitations do we carry about money as we move through the world and verify experience?

Our way of going, taking action, and conduct is the manifestation of our beliefs.

How do we move with money such that verification of our movement aligns with our beliefs?

Our way of checking, creating results, and realizing verifies beliefs and movement.

When we verify money experiences, we solidify beliefs that support our moves.

This trinity cycle is humanity's play. It does not matter which methodology, map, or motivation carries you. They all work the same. You choose what resonates. More important is recognizing that multiple teachings are similar, and when multiple sources say the same thing, we pay close, intimate attention. Attention to wisdom offered in multiple languages and veins and times lends credibility.

Beliefs can be limiting or generative.

Movement can be draining or resourceful.

Verification can be constricting or insightful.

Let's unpack these concepts to gain comfort together before bringing money deeper into our conversation.

Beliefs

Beliefs are the lens through which we see the world. Our beliefs (opinions, views, perspectives, etc.) viewed on a continuum—at one end can be held as definitive truth crystalized into a hard diamond, or on the other end can be held like a bird's feather floating through the wind never landing. Let's choose to believe where we locate ourselves on this continuum is not good or bad, right or wrong. Reflect now on how you hold beliefs. Are you more in definitive truth? Or, are you laissez-faire, comme ci, comme ça?

My unscientific guess is we all land somewhere in the middle of this continuum. Depending on the situation, our movement of beliefs on the continuum moves one way or the other. The cool part about movement is not tightening or loosening—it is the movement. It is the realization that our beliefs are not static. Beliefs change. Drum roll. Mic drop.

When we add money to beliefs, what happens to your tightening or loosening? Identifying money beliefs and examining how tight they are held is a valuable exploration. If your body nudges you to pause and explore further, check out the Somatic Finance Practice Guidebooks for resources. Yet you may have noticed with the Tiny Practices a few realizations about your money messages. Bring your discovered messages with you as you play in these pages and in practice.

Movement

Our beliefs often guide how we move, and the opposite is also true, how we move supports our beliefs—like two sides of the same coin.

With tight beliefs, our movements support tightness. Our body shape, texture, and posture reflect less space, more constriction, and a pacing—fast or slow—that maintains tightness. If we move holding our breath, tightly armored, in less space, our beliefs mirror our physicality, firm.

The converse is also true. If our beliefs float in the wind, our movements support slackness. Our body shape, texture, and posture reflect more space, looser, and a pacing—fast or slow—that maintains slackness. If we move like the wind with no center, freely chaotic in open space, it is likely that our beliefs mirror our physicality, floppy.

When we add money to movement, what happens to your tightening or loosening? Again, a valuable exploration—examining how our body in movement and tension presents itself—when money shows up. These seemingly unrelated aspects—beliefs and movement—work together to verify each other to keep the trinity in play.

Verify

Verification is nothing more or less than our bright mind validating a belief as the way it is or disrupting a belief with new insight to expand perspective. What? Did I lose you?

Because this book dives deep into somatic teachings about money, keen awareness necessitates understanding this trinity as an entry point. Let's look at beliefs and movement with an example.

Tiny Practice

Let's try this:

Bring to mind a recent money event.
What is the belief attached to the event?
What were you doing (movement) in this event?
How was the experience verified in the event?

	Belief	Movement	Verify
A	The amount of money spent does not equate to its value.	I was searching for blankets for the bed in our guest room.	Shopping I found expensive cheaply made blankets. I found well-made blankets on sale for the same price as the cheaply made ones.
B	Money conversations are challenging.	I was talking with my spouse about our cash flow and our preferences for spending this year.	Conversing with my spouse, I felt tense, tired and defended my desires.
C	Freedom gets tangled with money.	I was reading (yes reading is movement) articles about third world countries, animal rights and political events.	Emphasis on the need for more money rather than better solutions permeated the articles. Often less expensive solutions are eschewed in favor of costly solutions due to a belief that money is always necessary.

Figure 18.1   Chart of Belief, Movement, Verify.

(Note: According to a *60 Minutes* news report with journalist Scott Pelley, a Russian climate scientist developed an inexpensive way to combat the melting of the Arctic tundra. His discovery is groundbreaking for our world climate change and a beautiful remedy to our existing climate issues. The funding of this generational solution is on a shoestring.)[1]

Back to your discoveries.
Review your answers.
What do you notice regarding your trinity play?
Is the way you see, go, and check in harmony?
Identifying beliefs is important.
Recognizing movement is important.

Practicing, with somatic awareness, allows us to make leaps and bounds in our development, which displaces trinity play and we join the Virtuous Flow, a different atmosphere of life altogether.

In the Practice Guidebooks, we will explore these types of inquiries:

How is your body shaped, and what sensations do you notice inside your body?

Which lead to these types of responses in the examples above:

A. My spine is elongated, and tingling light, cool energy moves up my torso.
B. My head falls forward, and my belly feels woozy.
C. My shoulders hang loose, my jaw quivers, and my chest feels soft and warm.

In the practice, we engage in somatic practices with clear attention on gross, subtle, and very subtle body awareness. Which leads us closer to our body creating sustainable stable change. Curiosity takes us deeper into our body. Our body responds for us to see more, move more, gain new insights, and strengthen our confidence making decisions, all about money. How cool is that?

Our head keeps the trinity cycle cycling. But when we welcome our body, our capacities and enjoyment flourish. Let's cycle on a different ride, like our Möbius strip on the Virtuous Flow.

Note

1. Source: "Siberia's Pleistocene Park: Bringing back pieces of the Ice Age to combat climate change" (2019). Hosted by Scott Pelley. Produced by *60 Minutes*/CBS News. https://www.cbsnews.com/news/siberia-pleistocene-park-bringing-back-pieces-of-the-ice-age-to-combat-climate-change-60-minutes Fair use.

Chapter 19

Wants, Aspirations, Goals—What Are Mine?

Financial planning, and any kind of planning, requires us to be clear about our objectives. It is virtually impossible to plan without a focal point and direction. Before more commentary, please note that being open to spontaneous magical serendipitous experiences is welcome, always, even if I am not explicitly discussing how the universe conspires for us.

What am I talking about here?

Research suggests that most of us regularly do not know what we really want. Our decisions are riddled with hidden beliefs, "shoulds," societal pressures, fabricated debris from ancestors, and more; we don't have a clue these barriers linger in the crevices of our mind. Dr. Shlomo Benartzi, a professor and co-head of the behavioral decision-making group at UCLA Anderson School of Management, an expert in the field, had his own story to tell. He shared his mistaken preferences for dining out versus home-cooked meals. For years on his work travels he visited fancy restaurants, until one experience with a friend and a home-cooked meal shifted his awareness. He realized that he preferred home-cooked meals but had never stopped to consider or, in his work parlance, to test his assumptions, as to his true preference.

He writes in a *Wall Street Journal* article:[1] "We might **think** we really want a big house over a smaller condo, or that we want an aggressive investment portfolio rather than a conservative approach. But if we don't test these assumptions, we might never know that we're wrong." Then he delivers a very cool assumption practice: the A/B test, an essential tool used by highly successful technology companies such as Amazon, Google, and Expedia. Using this tool requires a version A and version B—of whatever test being conducted—to determine the true preference. Dr. Benartzi, along with other fine luminaries, conducted A/B tests to explore different versions of the same basic financial offer.

They created a savings app that assigned users to one of two groups. Group A was asked if they would like to save $5 a day. Group B was asked if they would like to save $150 a month. Our Academic knows the amounts are essentially equivalent. He believed the $5 a day option, which makes saving seem less painful and more doable, would exceed the $150 option. Indeed, this option was preferred but he was astounded at the significance. The users given the $5 question were four times more likely to sign up.

His article continues encouraging the use of self-experimentation with three keys to success. First, the alternative choices have to be random. Second, aim to scale the test by repeating it as many times as possible. Finally, track the results. Seems clear, but let's get practical. What are we testing, and what am I doing in the test?

We can test anything that matters to us and is helpful for our money management. He suggested there are five areas about money worth exploring to gain clarity on what you really want. They are:

1. Basic goods versus luxury goods;
2. Frequency of portfolio monitoring, more versus less;
3. Retiring now versus later;
4. Spending more now versus less in retirement; and
5. Spending on the usual versus new experiences.

Briefly, these categories examine the (1) preferences of really well made and expensive goods over general less expensive goods, (2) looking at our investments many times or moderately, (3) stopping work earlier rather than later in life, (4) spending more or less after we stop working, and (5) the allocation of our money toward usual purchases or new experiences. In the Practice Guidebooks we return to these areas, and a few more, to experiment, in a new way—including our body wisdom. You didn't think we would leave our precious unique body intelligence?

Which brings us to the new opening related to A/B testing and the potential for superior practice. First, the simplicity and academic intelligence of this tool is a welcome relief for nonscientific folks. It is a fine example of borrowing a business practice and adapting it for other purposes. In this case, for individual clarity on preferences that relate to money. Second, it gains credibility with us because it offers a scientific way to arrive at a better answer. However, it is also a very clear example of how we innocently, or unconsciously, exclude our body.

Did you know—and yes you do!—that our body offers a clear true response for our wants, aspirations, and goals?

More important than, or in addition to, the results from these A/B tests is accessing our deepest longings through our heart. When we are truly able to reveal and receive our utmost precious reasons for being here in this world, the clarity and energy that emerges for our life explodes. And our money follows.

Yes. It is this simple. Yes, it is this profound.

In our client conversations, we use the three questions or scenarios from George Kinder's Seven Stages of Money Maturity:[2] The scenarios explored, I paraphrase, are:

1. Imagine that you have plenty of money today and in the future. How would you live your life? What changes, and what stays the same?
2. Imagine you have between five and ten years to live. What will you do in the time you have remaining to live?

3. Imagine you have one day left to live. Ask yourself: What did I not get to be or do? What legacy is lost?

These interior explorations lead us to what matters most. After courageously exploring and naming our hearts' desires, freedom and longing emerges from that clarity, with a fierce determination to move toward that truth.

My heart isn't faking it when I put other wants in front of my own, for instance. As writing this book for you is my deepest truth and heart aspiration, any time I am not able to write in a day, and most definitely in a week, I get *really* cranky. My heart hurts. As time unfolds, the hurt blossoms to angst, pissy-ness. To meet my goal, I am building new muscles of focused clarity, setting, and maintaining boundaries. Most recently I am energizing a fairly radical—if you are not part of my writing journey you are not in my journey—view. Even writing this statement a power surge moves up my core from my belly, lighting up my spine. See? Our body is powerfully present each moment assisting us in clarifying our wants, aspirations, and goals.

Back to our interior exploration, when we identify what matters most to us and a heart longing is activated, the two truths link together. The more we attend to the link, the happier we are. We supercharge that link when we tether our attention to money. In other words, the clarity of what we want, aspire, and our named goals make it easier to link our money decisions to those goals. In truth, this is the most integrated holistic way to operate with money, but we have not had a clear path—until now.

The pith instructions or short path is this: skip all of the other beautiful concepts and go straight to your heart. Just do it.

Tiny (Advanced) Practice

Your resonance with this practice depends on the openness of your heart. If your heart's not open, that's not a problem. We're just getting started. Establish clear choices to know what you want (e.g. I choose to clearly know what I want).

Bring unwavering attention to your heart center—relaxing, opening, releasing.

If this is hard, put your left hand on your heart and your right hand over your left.

Ask beautiful questions about what you want. (e.g. What do I really want?).

Drop your shoulders. Unfurl your brows. Soften your jaw.

Give attention to breath under your palms.

Abide in your heart with the beautiful questions.

Receive answers about your true wants, aspirations, and goals.

Trust your direct experience.

Now, feelings may arise, sensations may pop up, tensions and aches may surface. Maybe no answers came. These human experiences are our glorious journey. As long as you are sincere and practice, trust that the answers will arrive, just maybe not in the way you expect.

The payoff of practicing and embodiment is that our body loves to cocreate with us. When a trusting relationship is established and sustained, our body signals us in unique ways to let us know what we want, in the moment! Yes. You read that correctly. I don't need to engage in long drawn-out practice for many of my wants. My body tells me. For example, when I am choosing a meal, or grocery shopping for food, I pay attention to my body signals. My mouth salivates, tingles arise in my arms and belly, heightened happy lights in my eyes—these are "yes! signals" that give me positive answers. Conversely, my body will contract, get heavy, and my breath tightens when an answer is negative. My guess is that you have similar signals and others unique to you but may not have paid attention.

More practices are revealed and offered in the Practice Guidebooks. But I couldn't wait to share these truths a moment longer. Building a strong foundation is practice in itself. As you integrate these landscape chapters into your mind stream, your foundation is strengthening for what is to come.

Notes

1. Source: Benartzi, Shlomo. (2018, June 10). "It's Time to A/B Test Your Life." *Wall Street Journal*. Fair use.
2. Source: Kinder, George. (2000). *Seven Stages of Money Maturity*. New York: Dell. Fair use.

Chapter 20

Trust

We can't explore money without delving into trust. Any meaningful engagement in life requires trust. The next step, next breath, next leap, all require the inner sense of something beyond and unknown. At my late teacher Dr. Dan Brown's weeklong level 1 meditation retreat, the first couple of days cover foundational teachings to support meditation practice.[1] Just like a good recipe requires specific ingredients to produce an optimal dish, meditation requires important ingredients to make progress on the path. The ingredients in this meditation course include concentration, equanimity, light-heartedness, discipline, calm abiding, and trust. While we all possess these ingredients, sometimes we need emphasis on one or more to get the right mix. But, as Dan noted during our retreat, of all the ingredients, Trust (with that capital "T") is the most important. From my own experience, I wholeheartedly concur.

Here's why.

Trust is the first move releasing certainty, a solid self, our ego holding on to hope and fear. Trust enables us to take, as David Whyte expresses, *that next step, close in, that we don't want to take.*[2] Faith gets me out of bed, in the shower, filled with food, connected to others—when all I may want is to ball up under the covers or hide out in a cave. (Yes. Sometimes I long to sit in a cold damp stone space by myself.) Money stuff fosters these aches in us.

Money requires trust. Our money experiences for eons foster anything but trust.

Working with a new client who has experienced money trauma pointed directly to this need. I don't use the word trauma lightly; we have all experienced trauma, and repeating the experience unskillfully does not support healing. Perhaps there is a beneficial therapeutic diagnosis of money trauma gaining traction in the therapy world. We can offer pages of antidotes, processes, conversation topics, activities, and more to meet money trauma. But by far the most effective gateway is trust, trusting that there is something beyond and, of course, trusting our body.

Our new client experienced several noteworthy negative experiences with previous financial advisors. Her investment account suffered three different market declines due to, well, the market declining but also due to a lack of connection with money, her money, and her life. Her fear and lack of trust create a constricted dust ball barrier to being able to support her optimally. Our work with her required enormous energy to meet the dust ball pervading each connection and the actions that needed to take place in order for her to make progress.

The catch-22 is trust develops over repeated direct experiences that prove trustworthiness. But no matter how many experiences defy and deflect prior negative experiences, unless we tap into the depths of our body, open our hearts to the dust balls lingering in our system, all trust building will be partial. And the slightest perceived repeated negative experience can reactivate the trauma. Our brain is highly attuned to repeated patterns. You can't win for losing. Two steps forward, one step back, and another notch on the measurement. All of "it" is held in the body.

The joy of embodiment and bringing body wisdom into our way with money is that we learn to trust our body. Yes. I am most interested in our clients trusting in their own innate wisdom, held in their body rather than anything or anyone outside, including me.

Because when we are able to trust our interior, trust becomes available to us in an extraordinary way, always right here.

No longer are we held captive by past experiences, the "deal of the day," market forces that do what they do, bad financial advisors, past mistakes and poor decisions, detrimental monetary policy, embedded fears of doing it wrong, fake commercials subtly selling something. We transform the outsourcing of money to the most reliable source of trust intelligence, our body.

Of course, our relationship to our body needs building, developing, and mastering in order to possess the confidence to trust body wisdom, our body wisdom. This is another catch-22. Our head will never fully trust without the heart and without the belly. The head is not wired that way. Think about it.

How do you trust?
What does trust mean to you?
What is required to trust?
How does the way of the Academic process trust?

I'm smiling as I tune into my own Academic. My mind immediately looks for trust in past experiences that focus on exterior people, places, and pursuits. My mind is performing perfectly.

We need that next small step, the one we don't want to take, and yet, somehow we do.

Dan often pointed out to students specific instructions to support their practice. No doubt. No doubt. No doubt. No doubt—these are frequent words offered as loving adjustments to practice. These two words apply potently here. No doubt, my friend.

In order for us to evolve a new way with money, we require *no doubt*. We require trust in our body—so that we can build trust in money. Not trust in me, or the bank, or our parents, or our estate lawyer, or our friend, or numbers printed on paper or a screen displaying figures. And don't forget Oprah, the president, spiritual guides, a Ouija board, or the newest best-selling self-help book or online course.

Trust, and trust in body wisdom, and the co-emergence of this truth, is the essential ingredient for every recipe.

Tiny Practice

Pause.
Breathe.
Open.
Take a deep breath.
Go for a walk.

Let these pages introducing Trust, with a capital "T," sink in and down before reading further. Really, I mean it; GO FOR A WALK.

More on Money Trust

Trust and money is a love-hate relationship, and these kinds of relationships have their work cut out for them. It doesn't take much to turn away from trust. We require, in the words of Chogyam Trungpa, a leap to the situation. A leap in any situation means that we release past fear or future hope; we simply leap in wholehearted faith. Faith that life is an endless invitation cradling our back with love and devotion.

Money is a complicated exchange system that holds thousands of years of human situations abiding in skepticism, corruption, competition, greed, regret, and doubt—all of the ingredients that work against trust. In our love-hate relationship with money, we are faced with a mountain to climb, an ocean to swim, a sky to fly, and yes, a gorge to leap.

There is a sound and beautiful reason—the mind's reason—not to trust money. Money, as I said before, doesn't care. Money is an integral part of experiences going wrong in present life. Money is an integral part of experiences gone wrong in our ancestry. Money is an integral part of experiences that do not foster trust. Money is *not* the reason for less than optimal results. But it is an easy scapegoat to blame.

Even when money works well for us, we don't trust it.

Yes. Let me say that again. Money—not enough, too much, sufficient—we do not trust money regardless of whether it is flowing waterfalls or whether the faucet has run dry. Yet we are riddled daily with money decisions. Every day we must make at least one money decision. I am making this up at this moment and as I do, I am reflecting on a typical day. Do you engage in any of these activities in a day:

Enjoy a cup of tea or coffee.
Fill up your tank of gas.
Satisfy a bill, by check or electronically.
Buy groceries.
Pick up laundry.
Pay the road toll en-route to work or leisure.

Let's try this experiment another way. Is there a day that you do not touch money—cash, credit card, or electronically? Try a bonus practice: Intentionally do not touch money for a day, or a week!

To build trust, first recognize how pervasive money is woven into our life, no judgment of good or bad. This is what is. We become familiar with the way money moves in our world, all of the time. Our investigation and discovery allows us to begin to trust in a new way.

When we see clearly the way money permeates life, we join in the relationship celebration with fresh eyes. We are able to collaborate rather than compete. We see an opening to nurture what works. We follow openings to make better choices. Openings allow us to be more discerning in decisions that matter most to us.

Our self-confidence deepens, and money is not a foreign object but a partner in the biggest collaboration—our own life. Our body is essential for this partnership. The skillful leap we make grounds us in body wisdom. It is here where somatic practices create the bridge for money trust.

Pause again.

Take another deep breath in your belly.

Give attention to the breath in your heart.

You can go for another walk if you want.

Sometimes ideas can be too much for our mind to digest. So we generously allow our belly to expand space and support our Academic's muscle to fully receive. Notice how relaxation—even just a little—is possible with breath when you read something that might trigger doubt.

These steps, close in, pave the way for the giant steps and larger leaps coming next.

Trust is a powerful ally.

Trust is worthy of our attention.

When it comes to money, we can't make the journey without Trust.

Notes

1. Source: Daniel P. Brown, PhD. https://www.drdanielpbrown.com. Fair use.
2. Source: Whyte, David. (2012). *River Flow: New & Selected Poems*. Washington: Many Rivers Press. Fair use.

Chapter 21
Feedback

The friendly way to grow as a being is to listen and receive feedback. Feedback is a form of accounting, a report of what is, and feedback arrives in many forms. In the financial world we have reports that "account for" the holding and the flowing of money. These reports, cash flow statement, income tax statement, balance sheet, to name a few, are neutral. How we interpret and what we do with the reports, or feedback is the key.

True&Co is a start-up company selling lingerie. They claim to have produced the perfect wireless bra—for any size breast. They listened to and received feedback from 6 million women to create this perfect bra. I've been longing for this bra I never knew. Even at a price range of $34–$68 the value is aligned for me. Viewing the picture of the bra, and the news that 6 million women chimed in with their wisdom, I am very confident this company has created a positive result. When we listen to feedback, and we digest feedback, the natural outcome is a generous expression of that listening.

Feedback is a gift. Plain. Pure. Simple.

Another clothing company, Bombas, produces the perfect sock. A couple of guys, tired of the feedback they received from their feet when they wore traditional tube socks, determined they could make a better sock. Fast-forward two-plus years, several designs, listening, receiving, and digesting feedback, Bombas now creates the most comfortable sock for every occasion. The men in my life, as well as I and my daughter, enjoy the comfort of their creativity and openness to feedback. A gorgeous bonus is that for every pair of socks purchased, another pair is donated to the homeless. More feedback in the form of research told them the number one item of clothing requested in homeless shelters was socks. As of August 2022, 50 million pairs of socks have been donated to others.[1] Very cool.

If you are weaving the benefit of feedback, with these two stories, and the motivation of this book, you will quickly notice that the body gave the original feedback for these innovations. Women's desire to wear a comfortable bra on their breasts and men's desire to wear a comfortable sock on their feet. Six million responses of feedback for the bra and who knows how many moments of feedback for the socks are impressive. More impressive is the trillions and trillions of cells located right here in our body that give us feedback all of the time.

Yes. It is true. Our body is the most exquisite, reliable, and comprehensive feedback pal in our life. Makes me quiver and tingle. Yes. Chills and tingles are happening to me right now—body feedback—to the statement I just wrote. Feedback telling me what I wrote is true. Now, I am softening with weepy eyes feeling the joy and gratitude of how my body loves me, how our body loves us—if only we would listen to and receive feedback.

Returning to the accounting reports mentioned above, walk with me here. Isn't it fascinating that we have these very meticulous, precise, elaborate sometimes, accounting reports that tell us whether we are saving money, generating deficits, building an optimal financial picture—and yet, if we live close to home in our body, we already have a strong sense of our saving, or spending, and whether things are okay or not so.

Have you ever had a pit feeling in your stomach when purchasing something?

Have thoughts ever run through your head—I really should not be buying this?

Has your breath caught short in a checkout line with a basket filled with more than enough?

Have you ever signed a document—lease, loan, or financial agreement—where you felt stiffness in your neck or back?

Tiny Practice

- Take a moment to reflect.
- Reflect with the care of your body by asking your body to join the tour of memory lane.
- Come into your body by giving attention to the envelope of your skin.
- Breathe a bit deeper.
- Consider your money actions in the last year or two; does a particular situation arise?
- If so, return to the situation painting a vivid picture of what happened.
- Intensify the experience while noticing the sensations moving in your body.
- Allow your body to offer insights by opening and receiving your body intelligence.
- What are you discovering?
- Just notice and let it go.

Let me also be clear. Including body wisdom is not a suggestion or recommendation to ignore and eliminate the practical financial reports we use to navigate life in our modern world. Quite the opposite, this is my suggestion and strong recommendation that you allow your body feedback to be the wellspring of wisdom first, such that when reports are manifest for you, your ability to receive body feedback while engaging financial information and utilize that feedback is skillfully deployed.

Trillions and trillions of lively cells are speaking to you right in this moment.

What are they saying? Take this beautiful question to your practice.

Note

1. Source: Bombas. https://bombas.com/pages/50-million-donated. Fair use.

Chapter 21a

Transition Points: An Opportunity to Pause or Go Directly to Practice

I f you want to practice, now's your chance to hop off the page and move your body! Check out the link and download the Practice Guidebooks.

If you want to pause, we're going to slow down.

Slowing down opens choices for what the pause looks like, what is most important for our pause, and how we want to feel in a pause.

Poetry is a favorite way for me to pause. Let's enjoy a breathtaking poem from my new favorite poet, John Roedel. We'll follow his poem with stories and examples of practice and how to be fully engaged in practice and close our pause with inspiration and deeper insight into embodiment.

John's poetry was introduced to me by a friend in early 2021; poem #1 electrified my being. Fast-forward to meeting him at his writing retreat and asking for his written permission to use his work. Without flinching, his generosity poured out as a living example and expression of the Virtuous Flow. "Absolutely," he said. "Where do I sign?"

Poem #1 from the book *Remedy* by John Roedel

Pause. Breathe. Open.

my brain and
heart divorced
a decade ago
over who was
to blame about
how big of a mess
I have become
eventually,
they could, be
in the same room
with each other
now my head and heart
share custody of me
I stay with my brain
during the week
and my heart
gets me on weekends
they never speak to one another
—instead, they give me
the same note to pass
to each other every week
and their notes they
send to one another always
says the same thing:
"This is all your fault"
on Sundays
my heart complains
about how my
head has let me down
in the past
and on Wednesday
my head lists all
of the times my
heart has screwed

things up for me
in the future
they blame each
other for the
state of my life
there's been a lot
of yelling—and crying
so,
lately, I've been
spending a lot of
time with my gut
who serves as my
unofficial therapist
most nights, I sneak out of the
window in my ribcage
and slide down my spine
and collapse on my
gut's plush leather chair
that's always open for me
~ and I just sit sit sit sit
until the sun comes up
last evening,
my gut asked me
if I was having a hard
time being caught
between my heart
and my head
I nodded
I said I didn't know
if I could live with
either of them anymore
"my heart is always sad about
something that happened yesterday
while my head is always worried
about something that may happen tomorrow,"
I lamented
my gut squeezed my hand
"I just can't live with

my mistakes of the past
or my anxiety about the future,"
I sighed
my gut smiled and said:
"in that case,
you should
go stay with your
lungs for a while,"
I was confused
—the look on my face gave it away
"if you are exhausted about
your heart's obsession with
the fixed past and your mind's focus
on the uncertain future
your lungs are the perfect place for you
there is no yesterday in your lungs
there is no tomorrow there either
there is only now
there is only inhale
there is only exhale
there is only this moment
there is only breath
and in that breath
you can rest while your
heart and head work
their relationship out."
this morning,
while my brain
was busy reading
tea leaves
and while my
heart was staring
at old photographs
I packed a little
bag and walked
to the door of
my lungs
before I could even knock

she opened the door
with a smile and as
a gust of air embraced me
she said
"what took you so long?"

Tiny Practice.
Pause. Open. Receive. Rejoice.

Final Points

Before we move to Fruition:

Completing the Landscape section, with myriad chapters laying the foundation of Somatic Finance and pointing to the companion site for you to engage in practice, may bring up interesting feelings.

You may feel enthusiastic and joyful about your understanding, Tiny Practices, experiences, insights, and progress with money.

You may remain scared in a very anxious place about your money, still churning and burning discoveries that are simply terrifying.

You may have unearthed a deep money wound carrying anger and frustration that cracks sideways at the worst possible moments.

You may be ho-hum chugging along.

Whatever mind state you are experiencing, well done. Take a moment to register your newfound knowledge about money and body intelligence. Take another moment to register the unique experiences you may have discovered in practice, even if you're feeling flawed and your time in practice has been sparse. Breathe in your belly. Wrap your arms around your torso.

Let's revisit the illustration of "Learning to Knowing to Embodiment" that accompanies us on our journey. Give yourself the joy and jiggle of celebration. You have made significant moves to understand Somatic Finance. This pause reconnects us to our **why** and inspires us to the next move, Practice, and the move after that, Embodiment. We don't want our celebratory "pause" to become a "stop." (A "stop" would be like reading about an orgasm versus having one! I don't know about you, but I'm interested in that whole body experience!)

Learning to Knowing to Embodiment

Before every move there is choice. Your choice. I want you to clearly grok that you are in charge. When you realize you are in charge, two very important "empowerments" happen. First, you feel stronger and yes, empowered. You boost your agency and dignity, which are money superpowers. Second, your slippery victim—who tends to point a finger outward—finds her seat of authority.

Our way of being is how we show up in every situation to the best of our present ability. Our responses, our movements, guide either regressing in repeating patterns or evolving with embodied decisions. Money is desperately asking us to evolve. In order to evolve, we first learn new concepts. We review and study these concepts for comprehension and the ability to cognitively apply them. Understanding and knowledge is wonderful and important. Understanding and knowledge about body intelligence and money improves reading this book. But these ideas are not embodied and integrated into your way of being. Embodiment only happens with consistent intentional practice.

It may be obvious to you by now, but let's delve more into practice. What exactly is practice or a practice, and more importantly, why do we practice? Practice leads us to deep embodied roots planted, growing and influencing our way of being for the highest good of all.

Our first three moves toward embodiment are read/hear, review, and understand. With understanding, we now make a fourth move to practice, and with our body a fifth move, to embodiment. These five moves are not singular linear stages; they repeat over and over again, spiraling, dancing, weaving. Here's our illustration again.

Understanding is (just in case you were listening to rap music or scrolling on your phone earlier, here's a reminder) a concept (the

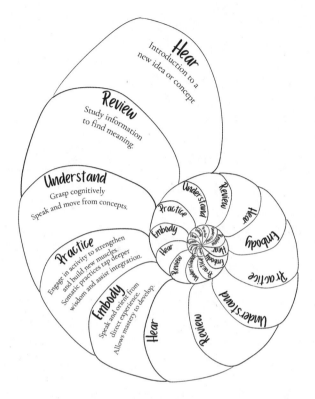

Figure 21a.1 (Repeat Figure 3.2.) Learning to knowing to embodiment.

head) and thinking (operative word: *think*) that we know something and therefore can "do it," "apply it," and, in the worst circumstances, "teach it" has led to much harm. Our deeper wounds are never met by facts and figures.

My promise, everything you read I am either practicing or I've embodied. My words are not theories or concepts or nice ideas that someone told me about or that I read on a billboard or a recent Facebook post. Any unpracticed ideas are like the way of the Academic, really important knowledge, studies, theory, and research and also partial. All reading is an academic guide and a powerful invitation to **practice** toward **embodiment**. Enjoy your body! Use it. Honor it. Cocreate with it. Grow with your body, who has been with you all of this life.

Let's take a tour of these five gorgeous moves.

Read/hear is simple enough. The first move to embodiment is to hear (or read) an idea about something that you have never considered before. Perhaps this is what you have been reading so far. The *essential point* is innocence. New concepts are the beginning of an opening to gain interest or let go.

Pause. Tiny wondering.

What does *innocence* feel like in your body?

If your interest is strong enough, you naturally progress to the second move, **review/study**. Here you gather more information in your own particular way. Are you a researcher and reader? Are you an inquisitor? Are you an "osmoser"? Regardless of how you digest information, the *essential point* is clarity. A review of interesting ideas and concepts begins to deepen your connection with other concepts. Study can be swift or lengthy, depending on your unique cognitive learning style. Bring attention to your body right now and sense your cognition. You may feel dull in your body. Or you may also feel a cool sense of curiosity in the process of learning and the cognitive line of development.

Pause. Tiny wondering.

What does *clarity* feel like in your body?

Just like the transition from hear to review, the next move evolves after synthesizing information. Confidence is the marker for the third move, **understand**. Understanding is a vast ocean of information, synthesis, connection, meaning, relating—it's big. We can stay in understanding for a long time, and many of us do, in fact, stay here. The *essential point* is confidence. Clarity rests in a stable foundation that promotes confidence to see new perspectives, find purpose, gain motivation and momentum for, yes, P R A C T I C E. And then here's the problem, the big problem: our disembodied culture relies heavily, sometimes solely, on our brilliant mind. Our mind becomes confident of information and fools itself into thinking (there's that operative word again) that understanding is the end game.

If you get nothing else from these statements, get this: Put your devices down. Merely understanding a concept is a painful partial existence. When you live from your head, you waste your life, your body. You live life through an idea, a movie. You suffer. Once you deepen understanding, nothing interesting happens—unless you begin to practice.

Pause. Tiny wondering.

What does **confidence** feel like in your body?

Entering **practice** takes courage. The essential point is humility. The confidence we gain in understanding needs to soften with humility. Our belly embraces humility, and in humility we begin to touch our heart. We become beginners—over and over again—in practice. Confidence buoys us sufficiently to practice, and when we practice, our body enters the game and whoa—look out. Life becomes magical and mysterious. Practice takes us to the edge of life. Here we get it: practice *is* life. The right practice matters to directly affect our inquiry. The right inquiry matters to point directly at seeing something new—gaining insight. In practice, insight cocreates with our body, entertaining an infinite loop of discovery and wisdom—which eventually leads to, yes, embodiment.

Pause. Tiny wondering.

What does **humility** feel like in your body?

Embodiment digests the previous four moves and the qualities of each move: innocence, clarity, confidence, humility, and courage.

Embodiment breaks your heart.
Embodiment tickles subtle spaces.
Embodiment is tense and thrilling.
Embodiment is tender and fluid.
Embodiment shivers and sizzles.

Embodiment senses energies, feels feelings, opens to the nanomoments of existence. Embodiment meets each and every situation with eyes and heart and belly wide open to feel and heal, so nothing latches on—because ultimately there is nothing to latch onto. Embodiment includes everything and everyone. But, don't take my words, these words, as truth. Experience yourself what embodiment looks like and feels like—for *you*. Welcoming your body with intention, invitation, recognition, and realization, your life will never be the same. Whether we are knitting, cooking, biking, hiking, swimming, reading, kissing, breathing, we carry our awareness of how our body is in the experience—that's the beauty and blessing of our human existence.

Embodiment allows us to effectively balance with our three archetypes, our body centers in every situation. We naturally emphasize one of the centers for a skillful move. Sometimes a situation calls for more knowledge; sometimes it calls for us to soften and connect; sometimes it calls for more action and determination. When embodied, our next moves are evident, a natural expression of clarity and attunement, titrating to the present moment.

I want you, my friendly reader, to know, I trust you. I am not the ultimate authority. You are, and *you have this*. I'm here for you, and we are in this together.

As you embrace and continue the Practices of Somatic Finance, allow yourself to be young again.

What does a beginner's mind, heart, and belly mean for you?

And the bigger question, ***What moves are you choosing?***

When you choose to practice, take leaps—small hopscotch leaps or off the cliff leaps, but leap. Leap into practice. Let your openness to learning and trust be your courage to practice in the space of the Head, Heart, and Belly, as your way of the Academic, Philanthropist, and Capitalist learn to dance new moves.

Coming to the end of our pause, let's take another breath and appreciate our kind pace.

We'll start again with our fruition stories, which show potentials and realizations when we practice, consequences when we don't practice, and possibilities for a new world with Somatic Finance flourishing.

Release any worries about needing to do anything.

Open to aimless wandering on the page.

Enjoy the offerings from a place of delight.

Digest what touches you.

Note tensions that alarm you.

Be inspired to supercharge what calls you.

Fruition arises after we choose, or choose not, to practice. It is that simple and profound.

Part II

Fruition

The Fruition Introduction

In this section, you get to stroll with your results of practice and understanding. These chapters are a few of my discoveries from swimming with Somatic Finance, from the depths of the ocean floor, where the whales call home, and to the splashing surface of wavy waters. As you enter, here are a few suggestions for you—you knew I would offer suggestions, right?

Return to the beginning of your reading and your **Why, How,** and **What.** What are the words you scribed as answers to your **Why, How,** and **What** for reading Somatic Finance? (See page 19.)

Pause. Breathe. Open.

What do you notice, right now? (Of course, in your body.)

I want you to have the opportunity and benefit of a first response. Meaning, how lovely to be invited to a fresh page without any other ideas to influence your journey. This is and has been all about you, your understanding, and your practice.

Pause. Breathe. Open.

*What has happened with your **why** and your experience?*

Write a few phrases or sentences in your notebook.

What capacities are stronger in you?

How are the way of the Academic, Philanthropist, and Capitalist living in you?

What does your head say about money?

How does your belly hold money?

Where does your heart connect with money?

How are the essential nutrients nourishing you?

What is money progress to you?

What remains in your basket of money to dos and don'ts?

What wonder question pops for you as you enter these pages?

What are you really curious about?

What do you know—by heart—as certainty without a shred of doubt?

What excites you?

What inspires you?

What scares you?

What ignites you?

These, and more, are the tendrils of wonder that keep the conversation alive, and perhaps never ending.

Spirit says you need to find your home in yourself.
Spirit says you haven't dropped into your body yet.
If I'm not in my body, where am I?
Five feet to the left and unhappy.

—*Mistress America*[1]

As we enter Fruition, I offer this quote as one more chance
to find and experience the wisdom of your body. I am confident
that you have read and practiced to get here—unless of course you
began with this section first, hoping for a quick fix and immediate
results. Which, in this case, you're busted! You can't get the goodies
without making the journey, one step at a time.

Our body creates pathways—both neurologically and
somatically—that eventually become, after practice, seamless and
integrated. When we get stuck, neurological transmitters linked to
the systems in our body open, activate, and move through our body
and brain. We prevent new emotional clutter from lodging in our
body and we clean up old emotional clutter ready to release. In this
way, the shadows see the light as we appreciate stuff emerging from
our darkness.

Our joy expands as we fully inhabit the territory of our human
body. Because emotional energies are welcome and appreciated,
life is enriched when we occupy the entire space in our body that
amplifies our experience. This means that when tension—in the
form of thoughts, feelings, or sensations—arises, we have a direction to go that reliably produces a bigger space to alleviate that tension. Truth and integrity are viscerally, immeasurably ecstatic as
our body is involved.

Our body is the ultimate tool, technology, process, and vehicle
for our money stuff and reliable relationship. You need nothing

except the interior of your skin to access the intelligence you seek. But don't take my word for it. You're a practitioner and can see this for yourself.

Consider what new moves you want to make with your realizations as you receive the remaining words I have to offer. Consider what new moves nourish your **Why** in ways that you understand and in ways that you cannot even imagine. Then, share your inspiration with others!

Note

1. Source: *Mistress America*. (2015). Directed by Noah Baumbach. Produced by RT Features. Fair use.

Part IIA

Fruition in Action

Chapter 22

Money Moving through the Heart

Yesterday I received a blessing, an uncensored gift from a client.

Kathy had been working with us for six years. She is a single mother of two teenage daughters from a successful, intelligent family lineage, riddled with money stuff. We all have money stuff, but we may be unaware of how money permeates the deep lines of our DNA. Our client is committed to developing. She is a long-time meditation practitioner. She moves her body in exercise and activity. She nourishes her body with healthy food. She is consciously raising her children with their father in a space of love and generosity. She volunteers her precious life energy in myriad ways. She is a cancer survivor. She's a badass. She is not average, though she is humble in her sense of herself.

Our client stays in the space of what arises. Her sense of self, held lightly, yet skillfully, navigates these points of connection with grace, ease, and healing. Stunning. Her words below illuminate the journey of birth family healing where judgments, assumptions, and withheld truths created estate documents filled with mistrust, control, secrets—the worst money bruises. Working with us she has strengthened her money maturity muscles. Gaining knowledge, understanding, and energy about finance—money flows, money investing, money giving, and money utility—have given way to money liberation. With stronger muscles her confidence has grown right beside her wisdom.

In her situation with two older siblings, her widowed mother recently remarried, with estate and fiscal matters revisited, the veil of her long-held sense of being misunderstood, untrustworthy, and utterly confused is shedding. She is engaged in deep and reverent conversations with her mother and her two siblings. Read on allowing your belly, heart, and spine to soak in Kathy's offering.

> You know, I'm not experiencing much emotion, about all of this. I'm feeling a lightening, opening, clearing. Sometimes there is a flinch, an urge to go into the old melodrama sorrow, and then the slight ache of not clamping down on that. Then the gentle joy of staying open. The gentle wonder of seeing it all unfold, the wide-open space in which my mom can speak and listen, reflect and return for more. The appreciation (but not surprise!) of my gradually embodied capacities to speak and listen and stay open, to see/feel my mom's reactivity and allow space, rather than clamping down in provoking her.

Can you feel the pulse of somatic experience ripe, alive, and fresh?

Do you notice the space, all of her open space that allows for real movement and response?

And do you recognize the generosity of her space that allows her mother to speak?

Are you tuned in to her gratitude for embodied capacities and the gentle delights unfolding?

Her body is attuned and awake to each arising and dissolving moment.

Here is more detail in one conversation with her mother.

> Recently, she was talking about fiery teens, and kids in general, how they supposedly provoke their parents "for entertainment." I said that I see it as the child's and the parent's patterns of seeking

the connection they truly need. These patterns can be unhealthy or destructive, and they can be transformed.

They are responses to the real and good impulse to connect.

Now it is clear that is what she and I are doing—transmuting the old muck, opening channels of real connection. And it all has been opened at last by communicating about money!

All about things officially called Trust. Woosh!

As Kathy abides and holds generous space, she taps the essential truth of connection. Humans are nourished by connection. In authentic connection she and her mother heal family wounds and the opening of their connection is money. How delightful. Did you ever imagine?

Kathy articulates her physicality in her direct experience.

I was so glad to be walking, while she and I spoke.

That physical motion, fresh air, sunshine, the arboretum—all supported me, helped me keep flowing.

Notice Kathy's awareness of the importance to be moving. Our body optimizes experiences when we stay in motion with the rhythm of the moment, a pacing that invites our awakeness at the same time. Aware in motion, insights pop, ease arises; we reap the rewards of our commitments, our practice, and our precious human birth.

Kathy is given the opportunity to read the restrictions on her parent's old estate documents, which identify her sister and brother as trustees of a trust created for her at her mother's demise. This trustee appointment means that she must go to her siblings to ask their permission for use of the trust assets. Imagine being a grown independent adult and relegated to a childlike position. Discomfort at the very least and the antithesis of money maturity. She continues describing her conversation with her mother.

I acknowledged that it was rather refreshing to see, in black and white, their distrust of me, as I'd always felt its unspoken undercurrents. I had long introjected their judgment, shaming myself, doubting myself, and that in the past several years I've come to really know and trust my strength, intelligence, intuition, resourcefulness, growth.

That the journey had been painful and difficult, but full of goodness.

I told her that when she and Dad clearly did not trust me and were upset about things I'd done, I did not feel connected to them, did not feel they were on my side, did not feel respected, did not feel safe.

Even though now, at 50 and as a mom of teens, I see that they were doing their very best to hold onto their connection with me and to support me. Otherwise, they wouldn't have been so worried about me.

The pain, mistrust, judgment, shame, and doubt from years gone by are melting away in a flow of loving connection held in space. Money grips itself into energetic knots that feel painful in the form of judgments, shame, confusion between people and with ourselves.

But here we see that money is really the catalyst and offering for a better connection.

Are you with Kathy and her mother?
Does your belly soften and your heart ache?
Where are your judgments, shame, confusion, and doubt?
What has shifted with your Somatic Finance practices?

You are allowed to cannibalize Kathy's experience for your own.

Just saying it's cool to see emerging fiscal maturity in action.
I kinda wish you coulda heard that conversation.
Just because it so clearly exhibited each of our idiosyncrasies and our family money story.

Go ahead and bask in emerging fiscal maturity.
Give a radical shout to idiosyncrasies and family money stories.
Kathy concludes with these powerful lessons.

So. The upshot. I don't need to pick up every strand and straighten it, or even shine my flashlight on it. I don't need to pick up the tangled mess that only exists if I maintain it.

Yet letting it all into the light allows the connection, respect, and safety we want to flourish.

Being able to speak transparently about deeply personal experiences—with my mom!

Goodness. Without now taking them personally is a gift and an achievement.

The spaciousness and freedom of movement are stunning.

My mom's increasingly free and increasingly non-defensive responses are stunning.

The more I don't clamp down on her reactivity, the more it falls away. I'm so grateful.

Kathy is flowing on the Virtuous Flow. Gratitude oozes from her words. The three essential nutrients are flourishing and fully absorbed. Rejuvenated rejoicing crowds out reactivity.

While it may not be like this for us, it won't be like this exactly, we can feel sympathetic joy from her experience. We may engage diligently with varied results, and our fruition will look different. But can you get a sense of what's possible? Does Kathy's story give you a boost, a sense of the potency of our journey?

Thank you, Kathy. I'm winking at you with a generous smile and open heart. Girl, you totally rock! We all thank you for showing us that this thing called the Virtuous Flow is not really a thing. It's a moving experience generating surprise, depth, and meaning when we abide on this ride.

Chapter 23

Humor and Humility on the Virtuous Flow

When we tip toward scarcity or contract in fear, what energies meet us and expand us back toward the Virtuous Flow of Sufficiency and Generosity?

Humor and humility. Let's explore them here so that when we contract in fear (as we certainly will, tomorrow, or Tuesday, or an hour from now), we can find and feel humor and humility nearby. We'll look at them in the context of arrogance, one surefire way to fall into scarcity.

Arrogance is tough for me and a common way of being in the financial profession. Arrogance stands next to confidence and gets turned on and up when unconscious fear surfaces.

My family story about arrogance goes back to my great-grandfather, a very accomplished entrepreneur who founded several companies and developed Florida land. But the stories about him were not flattering or happy. Most stories portrayed him as extremely arrogant. As a high achiever, he expected the same of everyone around him, which produced unhappiness, jealousy, fear, uncertainty, and more. Writing, I feel heaviness in my chest.

I believe arrogance is confidence gone sideways. It is not confidence but fear surfacing as arrogance donning a familiar mask to make one feel safer in an "I know" armor. I have a visceral response to arrogance. Really. My family beliefs pickled me good. Arrogance mismatches the truth. Being out of integrity and the subtle judging (self and others) embedded in arrogance creates a huge cognitive dissonance in me, along with jaw, shoulder, and back pain. I see and feel the fear. Instead of acknowledging fear, bullshit spews forth as something of value for the pitiful person being slimed.

Well, that is a bit dramatic, but it makes a good visual. Simply put, arrogance is an armored heart scared of being vulnerable.

We know how to soften arrogance. We feel our feelings. We move our emotions. We attend to the sensations flowing in our body giving us new information and insights. Rough edges are sanded smooth, like broken glass in our oceans becoming round and velvety.

Let me share a secret. My confidence debris is cleaning up as I write. One of the ways we grow is seeing triggers as teachers. Arrogance teaches me to fully embody my authentic confidence, my growth edge to take my seat. Stake in the ground. Full on presence unabashedly here. So yeah. I confess and I love this!

What do I love, besides seeing my shit? I love simplifying complexity. I attempt to create a linear path. But do you notice that everything swirls? For example, we move in and between haughty, humility, and humor like an ice puck in a hockey game. That puck is going to touch every surface of ice before the game is finished, but it is not happening in a straight line. Do not mistake linear writing with Möbius strip life—that's nice.

Arrogance and money get into trouble. False confidence makes weak decisions, disconnects from reality, separates from friends and family, and pretty much drives fear deep into our financial belly wounds. Money does not care if you are arrogant. Yet money commands respect—being arrogant is synonymous with being stupid. Doctors are notorious arrogant money people. Sorry, not sorry to generalize. Medical doctors—in general—earn high salaries and generate significant net worth for their ability to make astute good decisions. Their work and decisions are important life-and-death matters. Their focus is on their patients and practice. (Thank goodness!) When they are sold financial products that do not serve them well, sometimes it is very difficult for them to admit a mistake. Confidence in their medical skills spills into arrogance around money. I recall decades ago informing a doctor he had purchased so much life insurance that he was worth five times more dead than alive; his spouse might slay him. (Kidding.) But seriously. Ten whole life insurance policies with face values totaling $25 million was too much. While he understood this fact, his pride stiffened his poor and expensive decisions, though they made no sense in his financial planning.

Pause and recall an experience of money and arrogance.

What was happening?

Who was present?

Where were you located?

How were you feeling in your body?

If you can't recall a moment of money and arrogance, look for money and fear—arrogance might be hiding behind the door.

What can you learn, relearn, appreciate, gather—right now?

Integrating our practices strengthens embodiment.

Within the softening of our arrogance, humility peeks in the window.

Humility

Humility, genuine humility, feels delicious. It feels delicious to be humble, and it feels delicious to be in the company of someone who is humble. Notice I am talking about embodied humility, which just is. Easy. Humility is embodied sufficiency seeing friends, lovers, foes, black, brown, white, earth, sky, ocean—as invitations for connection, along with the realization we are always connected and with the realization that we are all the same, in this life together.

Humility teaches us we are lifelong learners and all of life is our teacher. We welcome what life presents—in all forms.

Being humbled is a different experience than being humble. The letter "d" at the end is a big deal.

Being humbled is another process of smoothing arrogant edges. In addition to feeling and opening on our own, we count on a little help from our friends to blow us open. Being humbled rubs elbows with shame. Touching pride causes shame to flare and generate heat to burn through arrogance, a false sense of self, and douse our ashes with humility.

As financial experts, opportunity abounds for us to be humbled in our career. While we know much information, some of the most important aspects of our clients' lives are unknowable until we humble ourselves in service to them. We cannot genuinely help our clients or the public by maintaining a know-it-all, power over, parent/child posture the financial industry has been built upon.

Humility and money are childhood friends. They kid each other and know each other's secrets. Being humbled allows us to rectify harmful money choices with new moves and rehabilitating decisions. I am fortunate to live with a man who is generous and nonjudgmental when I make mistakes. It is through his generosity my humility grows and self-laughter sparkles. He is not so lucky: another growth edge for me is to appreciate the mastery of others with sympathetic joy and aspire to develop those skills in myself with discipline and compassion.

Pause and recall an experience of money and humility.

What was happening?

Who was present?

Where were you located?

How were you feeling in your body?

Are you able to locate an experience? If not, be kind and gentle with your attention. Consider taking this query into one of your favorite somatic practices lying on the ground with the earth's support.

What can you learn, relearn, appreciate, gather—right now?

And then dear humor can appear when humility softens our edges and takes a bow!

Humor

Humor, from the hurts-so-good bellyache guffawing to the gentle breeze lips-turned-up and locking eyes, is a sure sign of integration. We don't look for humor; it simply shows up and smothers us with love.

Humor arrives when we have been at our worst, in the kindest view (I am learning how to love my crispy parts and the one who feels that burn).

Humor arrives when we see more than intended—something surprises us or deeper motivations reveal more.

Humor feels so damn good.

Who doesn't like a good laugh or a sweet yes of affirmation?

It is humor that says, "Well-done, grasshopper," sneaks a hug, and slips out the back door.

No more needs to be said or done.

When humor is consistent, the ability to love our money journey comes full circle and we grace the Virtuous Flow with our vital energy. Money situations easily express themselves with thoughtful skillful decisions, resonance relating, and peaceful closures.

Pause and recall an experience of money and humor.

What was happening?

Who was present?

Where were you located?

How were you feeling in your body?

Can't remember an experience? Then get willing!

What can you learn, relearn, appreciate, gather—right now?

Integrating our practices strengthens embodiment.

When heart smiles are not forthcoming, we look at our fear, which often manifests as haughty, or we look at our shame that is met with humility.

Returning to the essential point—we flow and continue to learn and grow, with money. Arrogance, humility, and humor are teaching points to look for in your direct experience.

Happy humble flowing!

Chapter 24
Money Mastery

Money mastery is our collective calling.

Mastery holds embodied wisdom that can never go away. Mastery changes us. Edges soften. Hearts swoon. Feet dance. Eyes glisten. Legs stride. Hips swing. Spines reach to the sky and spread wings. These vibrant ways of being are expressed through open, clear, loving channels of the Head, Heart, and Belly having been tested, trained, stretched, torn, cut, washed, bruised, and yes, in some situations ground to a devastating pulp.

Money mastery is no place for sissies either. Mastery takes its toll. Mastery can be quite painful. Your truth is known through direct daily experience, through the somatic realities of being present in your body. You are not distracted by fascinating ideas woven with hardened concepts.

Mastery can be and eventually is easy, not painful, flows of rhythms like a rushing river—mastery moves. You might also know this easier way—typically the fruition of doing it hard and learning a better way. The Virtuous Flow feels like this.

We are moving slow; remember go slow to move fast. Taking a sweet stroll on a rooted path. I want you to feel the gravitas of your life, your money life.

And this just happened. Writing takes its own flow—like the river mentioned above—and when I wrote about it, tender weepy emotions surfaced. A significant memory in my money mastery development returned to this present moment. I eased the old memory by going to the refrigerator and found hummus. Seriously, I just ate a fistful of Tostitos dipped in hummus. No, I am not hungry. This drift is what we do. The shift to awareness is how we return.

As a child, my siblings and I were steeped in a field of yelling. My parents were young and overwhelmed raising a young family. Frequently my father would scream, "You know nothing" to his four children. We are open porous vessels as toddlers and growing adolescents, and words sink deep; these words saturated deep into my body. Knowing nothing served me well for decades. And then it did not. It was time to grow up, mature, and develop my spine of dignity and self-respect. My body quivered and ached with recognition.

My mastery came online at the beginning of my integral coaching certification. Our group had just completed an intense experiential activity in the presence of each other. Afterward, the instructor, Joanne, asked, "So what did you learn?" I quipped that I knew nothing. Just as swiftly as I answered, my heart felt sliced painfully wide open.

Joanne looked at me with her strong steel brown eyes as she said, "Just because I know a bit more than you, doesn't mean you know nothing. You know a lot, in fact. You have a moral obligation to recognize it and use it." I wept uncontrollably and said to myself, "The jig's up, Gayle. It's important to share what you know." That moment—penetrating and painful—I saw so much. I saw the thread that held me safe under the radar. That moment was in 2009.

My friends, the tenderness remains. I stopped writing to feel the soft tears, my tender heart, the importance of what is being asked never goes away. . . it only deepens. These tears are a gorgeous mixture of joy, truth, love, service, and recognition. Joanne's fierce sword skillfully and lovingly sliced my heart open. My tears are the touchstone to what really matters to me, to you, to all of us. May you have the blessing of being here too.

Pause here and drop your awareness down into your body.

Come into your body—as you are well practiced, this move becomes second nature.

What do you see, feel, experience?

Are there lingering pops of debris calling for attention?

If something is here, put the book down and go lie on the floor.

Engage in Somatic Grounding found in the Practice Guidebook.

Enter your heart and enter your belly.

Ask, "What wisdom will expand my money mastery?"

Write your discoveries in your journal or notebook.

My embodied limiting belief of knowing nothing gave way to my depth of knowledge and the necessity to look beyond myself. Mastery leads us to others and the world at large. We taste our insignificance, and we don't look back—it's futile; it's also boring, constricting, lonely, uninhabitable, horrific, and repulsive. Yes, as I saw my insignificance, I was also horrified at how my lack of awareness caused harm to others. My lack of knowing, opening, seeing, and holding a limited view of prosperity, optimism, the glass half full, was my protection to not feel the depths of pain right in front of my face and beyond.

Integrating from my partial view toward the broader truth took several years. The journey of mastery has this flavor and feel. As I claimed my knowing, I could no longer pretend that I did not see by saying positive affirmations, platitudes, and cultivating my happy place. After falling apart, being in the mess, gaining access to beautiful wisdom, I came back in a less solid form ready to engage again.

More mature, with a few scars and a big dose of humility, my morality aligned closer with money. It is no wonder to me, given the pervasive lack of money morality in the world, that it can take years in my field to stay awake. I did not want to see it. But my body, and your body, are strong enough and wise enough and love us enough (sufficiently) to get us there.

Money mastery strengthens our moral obligation to the money systems in all ways. Our individual money systems get attention. We mature. We exercise important muscles of saving, earning, spending, giving, investing—consciously. Awareness expands, and we begin to see how anywhere money touches there may be wobbles of corruption to care for and clean up. Our heart's expression to care for others sees we are all in this together. Our belly's strength of character will not allow capital to cripple the future of all species and our planet, the place we call home.

Money mastery begins with the practical basics of finance, and eventually, money is recognized for the tool, the concept, the mechanism for which we navigate our modern world with grace, humanity, love, and acceptance for all beings.

We are all in this together. We will either all be together or not. How many of us are willing, able, and choosing to walk the money mastery path?

Chapter 25

Integrity Is a Direct Experience

I'm a little crispy, emotionally. And sometimes my crispiness turns into shards of glass. You are forewarned.

Many well-intended, bright, and prolific academics produce valuable work, research, white papers, books, journal articles, and speak eloquently about their work to audiences filling thousands of seats. Their work about money—behavioral finance, psychology, emotions, the interior space we have been exploring—is important. Yet these fine folks continue to fortify knowledge as the territory of exploration rather than the map. Recall, the map is the landscape of knowledge. We learn facts, figures, and ideas. The territory is where we directly engage our understanding of concepts in order to experience and inhabit in our whole body—for ourselves—what these concepts mean beyond our brain.

Just this past week I received a gift from the CEO of the CFP board, a new book published by the CFP Board Center for Financial Planning entitled, *Client Psychology*. This book presents seminal work with 50 studies supporting what we can all attest to: emotions, psychology, behavior, decision-making, biases, self-awareness, and money are linked together. We need to pay attention to money and how money relates to all of these human conditions.

The list of 24 contributing authors is impressive. All have multiple advanced degrees and have or are about to receive their PhD. Most are professors at American colleges. Most are academics, which may be redundant, but one can be an academic without teaching and focus solely on research. Most are in the profession of talking about their studies, what to do with clients, what the client experiences, what client problems arise, and how to manage, navigate, make sense of the client experience.

Of this list of 24 researchers and scholar-practitioners, only two have sat in the seat as a financial professional across from clients directly engaging in financial planning. Of these two, only one is practicing financial planning with individuals and families. Only one of 24 represents about 4%—where not only is the interior side of finances addressed but also the practical nature of money and the myriad ways money is managed.

Some might quickly say that investing, saving, retiring, the work of financial planning, is no place for our interior landscape. Which, if you have been absorbing this writing and engaging in practices, you know to be impossible to separate.

If 96% of these contributing professionals have never sat in front of a precious person, facing real monetary issues, their work is partial. Research lends only one perspective and covers the object of this work, because if we are not in the work, meaning, if we are not face-to-face with the rippling energy exploring our money matters, as experience happens in our body, we miss the authentic responses our somatic intelligence provides in the here and now. The work and results are tempered without engaging real people and the work directly. The work is an object sitting across the table. Conducting studies, writing papers, and making the lecture circuit gets us to the third move of our learning to an embodied way of being. We aim for all five moves, where money integrity lives.

No doubt I've pissed off a bunch of people reading these paragraphs. But hey, I said I was crispy, so let's all get a bit fried.

Never sitting in front of another human delving into the complexities of money while engaging the interpersonal, moral, emotional, and cognitive lines of development, *and* being held accountable to arrive at optimal money decisions and the implementation therein doesn't give you a direct money experience on behalf of the other. If our somatic line of development with unique wisdom is not engaged with another in those money moments, mental constructs remain fully in charge of the situation, and all research remains partial. Partial is not bad. It is just not whole.

While I really look forward to reading this research, I am preparing myself for disappointment—and a few spurs too.

Just two days ago I attended a half-day financial conference and was gobsmacked with an example of this experience. The presenter, well-educated and well-spoken, teaches applied behavioral finance—where he was explicit about taking information and doing something useful with it. He shared his mother's love of words and admonished us to be impeccable with our word choice. So it was deeply troubling and surprising when he used words and phrases to shame, instruct, and condescend his audience.

Let's pick one. Say, "book of business."

Do you know what a book of business is? Let me define it for you, it's one of my all-time least favorite phrases in financial services. Book of business means the number of accounts held in your book. In other words, you and all of your financial person's clients are summed up into a book. You and all of the other clients added together are called a book of business. It is a lousy shortcut describing important work, but mostly it is a disgusting way to define precious human lives.

Did you know that financial professionals receive many thousands of dollars for transferring their book of business from one firm to another? In other words, a broker can be enticed to leave a present firm by receiving a large signing bonus based on the value of the book of business they bring over to the new firm. How does it make you feel to know that your investment account is being used to benefit a move for your financial professional? It may not make a difference to you. It may.

It makes a difference to me. I know it bothers me because my jaw gets ornery and my belly shouts HUH? I imagine myself as a cow lined up in a barn with all of the other cows. Just put the whole container on the auction block please. It doesn't feel personal, and money is personal. Book of business is a way for dignity to remain in the shadows or one step removed from a direct experience and many steps away from integrity. Dignity, as we've touched on before, sets us apart from all of the other beings on the planet.

Safety, connection, and dignity, our three necessary human nutrients. Safety allows us to connect. Connection opens up dignity. Without safety we cannot connect. Without connection there is no dignity. Book of business is not a human connection. Therefore, no dignity.

Back to our presenter who is halfway through obtaining his Financial Therapy certification, another credential asking for somatic training. He continues to share the results of behavioral finance and ways to incorporate strategies.

For example: if the behavior is over spending, ask:

"Tell me how your mother taught you about money."
"Why do you do what you do?"
"Why are you overspending?"

Most of us get stuck at the question, Why. . .? "Why" can go narrow to a quick conclusion. "Why" can also take us wide into dire confusion. "Why" has a subtle blame attached to it. The most helpful "why" is tied to the heart and nourishes meaning.

Our presenter continued, saying people forget data, which means that if you show someone a cash flow report producing deficits, review the income and expenses, and determine where the expenses are over budget, people will forget. He coached the need to connect emotional impulse with the data. Very true. I wonder where the emotional impulse is located. Do you?

Another strategy he offered, to meet the behavioral knowledge that people remember the first thing and the last thing, is to start meetings with an important piece of information and end the meeting with important information. Then in the middle determine how they can feel.

. What?

It is dangerous to implement a new tool without a level of awareness that can adapt—in the moment—with a new experience. We practice in order to improve our skill and eventually embody the way of engagement. All experiences are new when we bring our body online, but sometimes habits make us fall asleep.

What happens when in the meeting there is an intense feeling, in the middle, and the opportunity to state the important last bit of information is not possible?

Any set of tools, questions, activities, processes, strategies, structure, formula, please fill in this blank _____ (the name that is used to define a static system for engaging a dynamic person or situation), is only as effective as the energy of the person engaging the tool.

Said another way, it is not the strategy or formula that makes connections, it is our heart and direct experience energized by the person aware of their body in present time. Scaffolding allows for energy exchange to deepen an authentic connection. But authenticity requires somatic intelligence. And integrity requires authenticity.

I've singled out this fine presenter and I've singled out the esteemed authors of a valuable book. It is not these people I am critiquing. I am critiquing what we all do. We prefer knowledge in the form of studies or formulas, rather than our direct experience. Direct experience by its very term means that our body is engaged. Awareness of the engagement and our body experience is our practice.

I want to end with a drum roll. But would a nail in the coffin be more apropos?

Can we all agree that knowledge is important, but it is not experience giving us what we authentically seek? It is experience that will assist us in making progress with our money aspirations.

It is our job, our duty, our potential to take the beautiful work of others and supercharge it with our soma. I do not expect researchers to jump for joy accessing their body wisdom through innovative somatic practices. It may not happen. It is not going to happen fast enough (for me). So, let's do the world a favor. Let's step onto the conga line and dance our way swinging our hips and kicking our legs to new glorious meaningful ways of integrating money with our whole body wealth.

Part IIB
Heads Up

Chapter 26
The Three Toxic Myths

When we think of fruition, we naturally move toward an optimal result. We gravitate to the best positive experience. Fruition illuminates the potential when we understand the landscape, we practice and build new muscles, and we reap the benefits of a choice and action to grow and create positive outcomes.

But fruition can also illuminate what happens when we *don't understand the landscape,* when we *don't invest time, energy, and resources in practice.* Results still manifest from ignorant action. Life continues to unfold, and what unfolds may or may not be optimal for you, others, and the world. The three toxic myths taught to us by Lynn Twist in her renowned book *The Soul of Money* offer a useful backdrop for our review.[1]

Simply named, the three toxic myths are:

More is better.
There is never enough.
That's just the way it is.

Myths are an unconscious set of assumptions that shape our view of the world, and toxic myths mean that they harm us individually and collectively. In the case of these three toxic myths, they demean human life, exalt more of anything and everything, perpetuate the pain caused by the belief that we are not enough, and have us convinced this is as good as it gets.

Let's take a tour with clear eyes and an open heart of these myths.

More Is Better: Aggression Poison

Our Western culture is steeped in more is better. Every turn of our attention we are faced with a jolt of, "If this _____ (thing, experience, person, situation) is pleasurable, just think how much more pleasure potential is possible with more of this." But since you have read and practiced, and since you are more embodied, you know that more food, more breath, more liquids, more exercise are not better and can lead to an overstuffed stomach, hyperventilating, loss of electrolytes, and torn ligaments, as examples. More has a flavor of scarcity, but the toxic subtlety of "more is better" is the emphasis on *me*. *More is better* amplifies a binary two-part view of *I win, you lose*. No other option is possible. Without the consideration of another, a cruel and distinct personality of this myth comes to fruition. A person who cannot attend to their embedded money fear and holds this view will begin to add the energy and emotion of anger. Anger adds power, force, and determination. Anger infiltrates fear, and the potency has superhuman strength. This contraction feeds greed and amplifies greed to an impenetrable marble. The poison of aggression explodes.

These folks prey on vulnerability, seen as a weakness to get their way. It is not so much about need or want as the aim of "I have more than you. I want more than you. I deserve more than you. I win; you lose." The filter of relating follows: it doesn't matter how much there is as long as I get more. Whether the situation has only a little or a lot, I will always get more. Remember, "He who dies with the most toys wins"?

This embodied toxic myth produces a person who has a crusty dried-up heart. This person bullies others with force, shame, and charm to get their way. These ways of seeing illuminate the eyes of "more is better."

As long as I win, I will not harm you.

As long as I win, we can remain friends.

As long as I win, there will be harmony.

If I don't win, I will wreak havoc, until I do.

If I don't win, we will argue, until you give up.

If I don't win, there will be hell to pay, until everyone caters to me.

The challenging part of this embodied toxic myth, as with all ignorance, is the person who holds this view has no capacity to see another point of view and has limited ability, if any, to see the effects of this behavior on others.

Because this view holds power, there will always (I ponder the word "always") be followers—people who cling to this personality, even if being in a relationship is demeaning. Followers will not see the limitation and harm because fear and need of a powerful force to save them tolerates the abuse. It is an enabled relationship. It is toxic.

Ripple the world with this manifested way of being, and corporate leaders place profit over people, profit over planet, profit over purpose. I don't need to give you examples.

For those of us who are aware (*you*—because you are reading this book, you are aware) we abide with a soft heart and recognize more is **not** better. A person who is well endowed with charisma, power, certainty, and resilience can intimidate us. Our heart practice becomes even more important. We, all of us, can never be harmed when we abide in our embodied truth that resides in our heart.

Our body wisdom informs us in each situation we encounter a person stuck in the view of "more is better." Our body tells us whether we stay and connect through our heart or we walk away.

There Is Never Enough: Desire Poison

Scarcity behavior is common, and as far as I have seen and experienced, every human walking holds at least a whisper of scarcity. You know more about scarcity from earlier reading and perhaps by engaging in your own practice. Scarcity is implanted in the zero-sum game. There is only so much, I see how much you have, and I need my share; I do not have enough. When we studied scarcity earlier in our reading, you might have discovered the ways that scarcity has crept into your life. Most of us are able to work with scarcity and release the bits and bobs and even deeper wounds that have held us captive. But if we are not able to examine our scarcity patterns, we can get locked in the Buddhist realm of the hungry ghost.[2] No one who sees through this lens will ever be satiated. Once a meal is consumed, they always want more, there is never enough.

This embodied toxic myth produces a person who has a bleeding sore belly riddled with fear and anxiety. This person whines, cries, and pleads, while comparing with others. *There is never enough* may seem similar to the way of "more is better," but the difference in view is looking out to compare with others. The "more is better myth" is *me* focused. "There is never enough" is *you* focused.

These ways of seeing illuminate the eyes of **there is never enough**.

If you have that, then I do not.

What you have is better than what I have.

If that is available, I want it.

My situation is worse than yours.

I need this more than you.

You have this, and I do not.

Perhaps you can see the difference in focus and feel as you contemplate these statements. With contemplation, *feel* how this personality grips a partial view—focusing only on "the other." When we cannot recognize what we have, acknowledge the benefits of what is here, and even more so, be grateful for the food we have consumed, for example, there will never be enough, because we are not giving attention to the blessing right here in front of us.

Folks who embody this toxic myth might use multiple storage units to hold extra furniture, clothing, household goods, just in case, or fill rooms with useless belongings, house treasures, and valuable collections—to ease the pain of fear and anxiety of not enough. I could write another book about behaviors and outcome, but you get the point.

For those of us who are aware (and yes, this includes you), we abide with a vast strong belly and recognize there is enough. A person who complains, cajoles, manipulates beyond reason can frustrate us. Our belly practice becomes even more important. We, all of us, source patience in the belly of sufficiency and abide in sufficiency found in our belly.

Our body wisdom informs us in each situation whether we meet a hungry ghost with our confidence or we stop engaging because the fear and anxiety has infected the edges of this person mired in the view that there is never enough.

That's Just the Way It Is: Ignorance Poison

Lynn Twist expresses this toxic myth as the most dangerous.[3] "That's just the way it is" paralyzes us. It holds the mindset in place without producing any energy to do anything different. We stop trying. Resignation is an energetic give up. When we give up, we typically don't look back. These are the lost souls, the wallflowers, and the personalities that fall away. Oddly enough, the best of circumstances holding this view, one lives a life of quiet desperation and resignation. Life is closed, quiet, and we get by, we make do, we are invisible. How many people are living in quiet desperation? I wonder. My guess, as you are reading and digesting this book, you wonder too.

The worst of these circumstances, the quiet desperation fosters an anger filled with pus, blood, and guts igniting bouts of rage that go sideways. Let your imagination float as you see where desperation, held in an energetic pool of fear, rage, violence, trauma, suffocation, can go.

This embodied toxic myth produces a person who has a crumpled spine leeching, "Oh, woe is me" and "I don't want help—I'd rather be left alone licking my wounds." This person whines, cries, pleads, but not to change the situation, only to intensify the whines, complaints, and pleads. While it may seem similar to the way of "there is never enough," the difference in view is in the desired outcome. The "there is never enough" view really wants and needs something. The "that's just the way it is" view requires nothing to change in order to perpetuate this view. If something did change, the personality would implode.

These ways of seeing illuminate the eyes of *"that's just the way it is."*

I can state my case, but nothing will change.

It doesn't matter what I say, what I want, how this is, it doesn't matter to anyone.

Since nothing will change, I will stop trying.

There is no point in asking or speaking out; no one listens to me.

The situation is _____ (unfair, broken, rigged), and I am powerless to do anything about it.

Whatever happens, happens, and I will not be considered.

While the view of "there is never enough" is a victim posture, the Grand Puba owner of the victim is "that's just the way it is." The lens of "that's just the way it is" sits squarely in victimhood and doesn't budge.

For those of us who are aware (you, the reader), we stand with a bamboo-like spine—strong and flexible—a sufficient belly, and a connected heart. A person who whines without taking responsibility and action wears us down. Our belly, heart, spine practice becomes even more important. We, all of us, source presence, wholeness, and clarity in our posture.

Our body wisdom informs us in each situation whether we can stir the soul of one who sees through the lens of "that's just the way it is" or we allow this soul to take its journey on its own.

Reflect, Wonder, Digest

Somber, pensive, determined, and clear—these are my present feelings and motivations. The toxic myths are offered as truth—not to instill more fear in a topic already stuck in it. The toxic myths are given as touch points—so we continue to develop ourselves and recognize our own crevices asking to be scrubbed clean. The toxic myths illuminate skillful means—where we activate right conduct to support others when they may be plagued by this toxicity.

My experience with these myths has become deeply personal. My first, second, and third reading I cognitively grasped and appreciated these myths as important. I wrote about them in my MoneyMoves® Online Game and highlighted these ways. Speaking one-on-one and in workshops occasionally mentioning them supports the growth and experience of other learners. I've explored and examined my own tendencies for these views and continue to do so.

But it wasn't until my direct personal engagement with close relatives that I knew by heart the danger that can arise from these views. It is heartbreaking. It is terrifying. It is shocking. It is the reality of our times. Be awake. Allow these words and these statements to support your wake-up calls.

If you are reading this book, you are one who is called to understand, practice, and ignite optimal fruition. May all of us benefit from this work, this journey, and this call to action.

Notes

1. Source: Twist, Lynn. (2017). *The Soul of Money: Transforming Your Relationship with Money and Life*. New York: W.W. Norton & Company (reprint edition). Fair use.

2. Source: Wikipedia. (2022). https://en.wikipedia.org/wiki/Preta. Fair use.

3. Source: Twist, Lynn. (2017). *The Soul of Money: Transforming Your Relationship with Money and Life*. New York: W.W. Norton & Company (reprint edition). Fair use.

Chapter 27
Unrealistic Expectations

My friend, if you read this whole book and you practiced and you understood and you practiced more and life doesn't go well for you, I'm truly sorry.

Because that happens. We do everything "right." We do everything we can, and still, you know, the proverbial s*** happens. I'm so sorry.

When we say that part of the work and practice of the soma is to feel all feelings moving through the body, you might expect the movement to be swift and completely scrub clean the emotional state attached to the old unfelt or the current flow. It is true that if we give full attention to our feelings and the expression of an emotion energetically, this flow of energy and feeling typically lasts for about 90 seconds. Yet not all of our feelings will be experienced this way.

Years ago, a fist-size pain and knot was lodged in my lower right back. I was grumpy. This knot reflected my grumpy nature. I chose to "play with grumpy" and my knot began to change and move. When I encountered co-workers, friends, and family, I was up-front expressing my grumpiness. I said, "Hey, I am grumpy. Whatever is happening here, my response has nothing to do with you, or our discussion topic. I am grumpy. I don't know why I am grumpy. But I am."

My grumpy experiment lasted six days. Six days of grumpy is a long time. Six days of being in and with and intimately meeting grumpy: the texture, the hiss, the scowl, the jaw tension, the tight shoulders and, of course, the knot climbing, pulsing, throbbing, changing, and releasing up my back.

My patience and practice held this experience where I recall wondering with horror, What if I remain grumpy? What if this experiment doesn't end? What if I like grumpy too much? Recognizing more, I began to love my cute and adorable grumpy. The experiment did end. On the last day of being grumpy, the tight-fisted knot on my lower back released itself through my right shoulder and down my arm. Poof, the pain was gone, and so was my lousy disposition. But I still get grumpy.

When we talk about money, it helps us to calibrate our expectations. Disappointments and frustrations with money often rise from unrealistic expectations, which are born from beliefs, ours and others'. Say you looked at the last 50 years of rates of return on stocks. If you expect that you will get that rate of return, but you're not taking into consideration current economic reality or an era of upheaval, you might be disappointed. This is an unrealistic expectation.

Instead of giving you a story about unrealistic money expectations, just look in the news. There's a fresh story every week, every day, every hour.

To practice, to live, with commitment and wholeheartedness, in regard to money, our body and every other part of our lives, requires us to accept that we live partly (a ginormous part in fact) in the unknown. We use expectations to try and control our experience and feel comfortable. Sometimes it works, often it doesn't.

Hold onto nothing, especially expectations. Trust and be patient, allowing the middle way to guide you. Stay awake to your insights offering recognition for your pure pleasure, amusement, and delight. No experiences are the same—but we gain momentum from each experience that leads us to the next, and the next, and the next.

You have money expectations begging for patience, lightheartedness, and recognition. Begin to reap more benefits from your practice.

Where are your unrealistic expectations?

Where are your unrealistic expectations about money?

What are you willing and choosing to see?

When we embody sufficiency, unrealistic expectations about money surface and show themselves with bright lights. Do not put on your shades and go inside. Face the light with embodied courage and take a tiny step forward and a deeper step in. You've got this. We've got this. Remember patience and recognition.

Or put your shades on. See what happens. It is your choice. The Academic will try to save us. Our rational mind is a beautiful savior—particularly when the vast majority of finance supports all mental tricks of the trade. The Capitalist will grab hold and belch a position of strength and a control posture or two. Sufficiency does not tango with force, tentacles, or dreams. It is the heart center reaching deep, opening wide, and standing tall that allows our head and belly to do their thing. It is the Philanthropist who brings together the knowledge of head sufficiency with the somatic experience of belly sufficiency and manifests the purposeful truth of embodied sufficiency all around us and in us. Our heart integrates sufficiency with the power of love, and the Virtuous Flow gushes with goodness.

Money will never meet your expectations. Money is not meant to meet any expectation. Unrealistic expectations reside in the corridors of your soul, found in the crevices of your body. What does Rumi say, "Out beyond ideas of wrongdoing and right doing there is a field. I'll meet you there."

Here, within the confines of our skin, are tangles of right and wrong, a breath away is the vast space of sufficiency. I'll meet you there.

Chapter 28

There Is No "Right" Number

A client recently asked what is the right amount of allowance to give her daughters; I recognized the myth of the "right" number. In a desire to teach her daughters healthy money skills, she wants to give them an allowance, a sum of money periodically they will manage—spend, save, or give away. Sounds simple enough. But it isn't.

We are saturated with the myth of a *right number*, a correct amount, a best figure for all of our money decisions. As I spoke and witnessed my client's paralysis, self-deprecation, and confusion, I assured her that her intention regarding the money lesson was most important, not the number. The motivation to teach her daughters healthy money skills was far more important than the allowance amount. I also saw how the myth of a right number gets started early, earlier than grade school.

For ease of conversation, we all join one of two camps:

1. The camp that loves science and math—these folks enjoyed adding, subtracting, calculating, and loved the competition for good grades. They loved arriving at the right answer because there

was only one right answer, right?—along with an addictive hit of adrenaline that fills membranes matching achievements.

2. The camp that despised math and science, the classes where numbers never made sense. These folks hated or in the best view tolerated the work and did well enough to get by but were never in the top of the class. Shame of not getting the right answers created a barrier to numbers. Most were happy to get by with a passing grade—arriving at enough right answers. Elders might have expressed liberal arts as a calling.

3. A bonus camp catches those who do not identify with the polarity above. But can we all agree on finding the right answer?

Between the ages of five and seven children start to learn math. And if your parents were overachievers, well, you were hit before "real" school began. How does this story feel? After identifying your camp, recognizing the addiction to being right with numbers, or the shame of not getting right numbers, what does your body offer for exploration? Go back, slower paced, and take a tour in your camp. Whatever you believe, or were taught, is a myth. There is no right number.

Repeating a sentence makes it potent. I repeat, there is no right money number.

Can you relax into this truth?

Does your body lead you toward relaxation?

When your heart and belly relax, your head can follow.

Or are you so pissed off your head is spinning?

The way of the Philanthropist is relieved.

The way of the Capitalist is cautious.

The way of the Academic is miffed.

Speaking mostly to the way of the Academic, being able to calculate problems and arrive at an answer that meets certain criteria of accuracy is important. It is not personal. It is partial.

When it comes to money and building healthy practices, we need to expand our view. Money does not have any right answers. *Many* possibilities exist for money to meet a personal aspiration, and this is one reason our money relationship is plagued with difficulty. Furthermore, it is no surprise that when we grasp the myth of a right answer, those who like to provide "right" answers no longer hold power over you. (Now maybe a few financial professionals are annoyed.)

Knowing there are many answers to paralyzing money questions, what happens?

Is this news a relief or a panic?

Isn't it interesting how someone is relieved when another may panic over the same situation?

When the possibility for multiple reactions arises to a particular situation, we are signaled to look inside. The best, optimal, suitable answer is found in whole body intelligence.

Those in relief bask in space and maybe tack on a smirky "I told you so."

Those who lean toward panic are walking in circles thinking, *unless you have been practicing*, in which case you are feeling the sensations in your belly and heart.

I told my client there is no right allowance. Arriving at a number that works for her daughters continues with conversations. Answers to the amount going up or down are dictated by age (capacity), character, and intentions. Of course the number changes with new situations!

What is the age of the child? An 8-year old and a 16-year old have different capacities to manage money.

What is the character of the child? Every person has a character, and a money character is not good or bad, it is what it is. Is your child a saver or a spender? Understanding character allows us to be skillful with our intentions.

Intentions are meaningful when they include appreciation and muscle building. Appreciation honors the character of our child. If your child is a spender, what are they buying? In my client's situation, her 13-year old daughter chose to donate to a women's shelter. (My children at the same age were buying electronic games; I shake my head with momentary shame and realize they are still good people and I am a good mom.) A 13-year old giving $50 to a women's shelter touches my heart. We get curious about spending habits and preferences to appreciate that which can be appreciated and to see where new healthy habits support stronger muscles.

For the savers, we make the same move. Appreciate the ability to save and get curious about what we are saving for, in order to build stronger money muscles. Every child is unique, and money practices are a beautiful way to give unique skillful attention to loved ones.

For the adults, remember we are children too; we loosen the grip on right numbers in our seasoned life. How many ways do we stay fixated on right numbers?

How much do I need to retire?

When will I have enough?

What is my number?

What is my number? Oh my, don't let me flare up! My number is the subject of a long conversation I had with a conference attendee plagued by the notion of a right number. Her financial advisor said that everyone had a number, and she needed to find hers. When I said there might be a different approach, she was intrigued, albeit skeptical. Go with me. Imagine that you arrived at your number. Pick a number in your head. It sits in the bank.

Now, what happens?

Do you stop? Do you continue? What changes? What remains the same?

Does life continue to move?

Then what?

And, oh, by the way, does the number mysteriously begin to move too?

What happens when you are striving for your number?

Do you work harder?

Does spending your life energy to meet a number bring you closer to joy, peace, well-being?

Do you give up—it's too far away from possibility?

Is the number a motivation or a depressing pill?

You see the myth of a right number can bring misery.

Let go of your right number.

Open wider to what works for you, unique, precious you.

What works for your children, unique, precious them?

Disclaimer: I frequently have a disclaimer to meet many perspectives. I do not want your children to fail calculus or for you to store currency under your mattress. For children, please study and do your best to learn math skills; they are important in our current culture. Will great grades in the subject (or any subject) bring you lasting joy? Probably not. But the discipline of learning and responding to money questions builds capacity to function well in adulthood and find fulfillment. For adults, please allow financial reports, calculations, and projections to serve meaningful conversation to connect what matters most to you, in planning, choices, and the fruition of your most wealthy life.

Do not seek and strive for the right number.

Allow numbers to reflect everything that is right.

Chapter 29

Love Your Victim

There are times when we are victims. Something happens to us that was not of our making, out of our control, and we choose to recover from the experience.

But other times, we adopt the position and the energy of "victim" as a way to *not* deal with, look at, or move forward from what happened. It's the energy of collapsing and blaming and sucking up everyone else's energy.

Staying in this "victim" posture is another way of staying stuck in scarcity and booting yourself off the Virtuous Flow. What's more, we begin to hate this "victim" energy in ourselves, even as we adopt it! And who gets the blame for how awful we feel?

Money. Money is the easiest bad guy, always at fault, always causing us problems—and always the potential hero if there were more of it! But then a bad guy because there's never enough of it. Is this circular logic? That's the victim at play.

It's hard to acknowledge and even love this victim self, and yet what they want is love. Unconditional love that says no matter what, they are seen, okay, and not alone. They are allowed to romp around in self-pity and then, make another choice. Simple, not easy, like many aspects of our human journey.

Let me show you what I mean.

A divorced person can easily fall into victimhood. Several divorcees are clients in our practice. Sometimes the planning and practices go well, and our clients move on to very satisfying thriving lives, with or without a partner. A few continue to struggle no matter what conversation, analysis, care, attention, and answers arise.

You might wonder whether professionals are always heroes to victims. Frequently we are. And if we are not self-aware and have little interest in interior development, we remain heroes. But once familiar with this potential, bringing conscious attention to client situations becomes more fulfilling from every vantage point.

Healing from a divorce is not my direct experience. I remain in a loving committed marriage. So I tread lightly and respectfully writing about divorcees. It is not the divorce that causes victimhood; divorce magnifies the areas of victim that never received attention in the first place.

In other words, our victim wants love whether we are married or not. But divorce gives our victim a grand dramatic story to be bold, front, center, and claim big territory. The choices are: (1) love your victim, or (2) stay stuck in victim patterns.

Working with an unhappily married client recently was a challenge for me. They were stuck deep and thick in victim patterns. As skillfully as I could, I pointed to the places and spaces of exploration using encouragement, clarity, curiosity, and truth telling. The meeting went 45 minutes longer than planned as I struggled to love the victim in front of me. The conversation repeated several of our conversations earlier in our year-long engagement. Just when I thought that the issue had been addressed and progressed beyond it, the same issue resurfaced along with an even more powerful victim posture.

My presence became more potent when money would "solve their issue." Red alert, my friends. If you believe money is the answer to your ills, stop. Just stop.

Pause.

Breathe.

Open.

Selling their non-liquid real estate to free up cash to buy more support, love, and care will not address the core issue screaming for attention. In fact, in their situation, it would make it worse—more complicated and stickier—while still married to a person they did not love. Divorce illuminates this example, but the truth of loving the victim is universal.

No amount of money spent on a victim will meet the victim's root issue. In most situations, perhaps all situations (I like to leave room for the exception), money only makes victims, *victimier*. For a period, improvement may be seen, but victims never let go, and money appeasement expires.

When my client expressed their willingness to now sell their property—having realized that their ownership was an expression of their independence and ability to survive on their own—I turned the conversation back to their current reality. It is remarkable to realize the meaning of this property. No one can take that realization away from you. And if these other aspects of your life were healthy, selling might be a viable move. But the reason for selling was to free up cash in order to get more support in the form of massages, healing sessions, therapy in multiple forms, and kind attention. Some reading this might disagree with my view. I even question my concern. Really, isn't more support helpful, I ask?

This is how our victim makes life more complicated. They don't need cash to get the kind of attention they wants. Money becomes a sidestep as a good excuse. The attention they want is free, right here, in this moment of realization. This is the move to love, self-love, love your victim.

I realized reflecting on this conversation, my responses to them, my notes, and follow-up actions, that the only place freedom lives is in loving their victim. No one can love their victim but them. When I said their new realizations were important, and yet I did not recommend they sell their property they were stunned. I expressed my concern for the fallout when the real issues in their life had less to do with money and more to do with their relationships, specifically, their unhappy marriage.

Their best moves were to get familiar with their victim, engage and play with their victim, and eventually learn to love their victim. If this process is familiar, you are well aware that once a victim is loved, their energy, vitality, and essence becomes gorgeously integrated into our way of being. Our victim has something important to say and something vital to heal. Listen, learn, live, and love.

From this freed-up place we claim our dignity and right to be here accessing authentic power for healthy change. Our client did claim their dignity loving their victim, took action on the truth of their relationship, and then, from their clear independence and authority, skillfully made decisions about their property. Watch out, world. The healed victim is a force of nature ready to engage life authentically.

A different conversation with a 70-year-old divorcee illustrated another story of "love your victim." Their colorful history began with us just after their divorce and the shocking realization that their opulent lifestyle while married could not be maintained after the divorce. Their primary childhood money message was to marry a rich person. A rich person will take care of you.

Before I continue the story, take a moment to feel into this message.

What do you notice in your body centers?

How does your body respond—maybe close to home, too close?

Whether a man or a woman, the role of hero or victim or villain, scars run deep.

Our client, who received a substantial settlement, was projected to run out of money in three years. That was 20 years ago, and in these two decades they have made much progress. However, the inner wounds of their victim were ripe and alive in a recent conversation. Again, I struggled to love the victim in front of me. (By the way, in case it is not clear, my struggle to love a victim in front of me is really my own struggle to love my victim.) One of my struggles is that victims do not always answer truthfully. Instead of answering they go sideways, avoiding and discussing something else that solidifies their victim position. Again, in a longer than anticipated meeting we found generous attention, encouragement, clarity, questions, and truth telling.

When my colleague saw me after our meeting and I shared the crux of our conversation running an hour over, she said, "Well, you don't look tired." Her question invited me into my body where I recognized vitality and streaming life force. I said I was not tired but alive. I felt the urgency of our client getting the lesson so that they could enjoy the rest of their life sans victim.

Circling back to these questions, after giving more space and attention to the stuck victim, our client was able to answer affirmatively. They had aspirations that brought them joy. They had clarity on what gave them meaning. They gave attention to their true self—which knew by heart that riches did not matter to them. They named their **why**.

In the middle of our work, we practiced belly, heart, and spine to access our safety, connection, and dignity. The worry and fear of their future and their children's future disappeared when they arrived in this moment and gave their victim—all that was "wrong"—pure attention. They loved their victim. That victim will return, yet now they have a direct experience of how to love them, through somatic practice.

Our client, who still struggles to live within their financial comfort, comes to see a few destructive patterns of their own. In an effort to have their children love their victim, they enables unhealthy behaviors with their grown kids. Entangled in trying to grow up, I said, "Focus on your life, and encourage your children to focus on their lives. Using you as a bank when you do not have, and have never had, the resources to bail them out is a repeating pattern that will leave you on the streets." (I did not say these words to instill fear; I came close.)

I did say moving across the country to live with an adult child so that they could afford to rent a nicer place was not a good reason.

I did say their happiness and focusing on what they want for their life is the magnetic pull for their decisions.

I did say their pattern of spending money impulsively to stop the pain of making a decision had to stop.

I did say, once we moved through the victim-speak, their voice tone, energy, and clarity felt strong and grounded with confidence.

I did say their security was not sourced in their finances but right here, in their belly.

And that is when we practiced belly, heart, and spine. When they entered their soma, they relaxed and found clarity to make practice a priority while communicating clearly with their adult child and making moves aligned with their independent aspirations.

Our client reflected more on their failed marriage. They were not happy and felt fake when they lived in big homes, with expensive chattel and designer clothing. They find happiness in their present life, engaging their natural artistic expressions, feeling the salt air on their skin, and being free. Letting go of limiting money beliefs holds hands with loving our victim.

It is as simple as this. Money produces and solidifies victims. Money is a convenient excuse to avoid loving our victim parts. It sounds harsh to point out, you choose victimhood or not. Closer in we can see and feel the immediacy of liberation; the moment we love our victim is the moment the victim finds the Virtuous Flow and loves us right back.

Chapter 30
The Virtues

Great necessities call out great virtues.

—Abigail Adams

You may wonder why I offer a chapter about virtues in this section on fruition, and perhaps why in this book at all. Fruition in a money book is about reaching financial goals, saving well, spending carefully, investing skillfully, and minimizing risk, all of the practical matters of money that enable us to function in life. Right? Well, partially so. You are well aware this book is no ordinary book on money. I am discovering, as we integrate our body with our money journey, the virtues come alive. Abigail Adams's quote points to the necessity of a new way with money. Any new way with money mandates the activation, magnification, and manifestation of virtues. There is no other way.

What are the virtues?

A virtue is a way of being in the world that ignites, sustains, and expands morals, ethics, and goodness. Money longs to be infused with integrity. Many versions of virtues exist, and you may have a favorite. If you like your version, stick with it and feel into these named virtues as we cover this ground. I have no attachment but offer three common references that, understandably, overlap with each other. Then, I distill my sense of virtues in money to

251

contemplate, weave deeper with practice, and discover how the virtues support your development and the world at large.

The most common virtues, I suspect, are the antidotes to the seven deadly sins:

Pride	Humility
Envy	Kindness
Gluttony	Equanimity
Lust	Chastity
Anger	Patience
Greed	Generosity
Sloth	Diligence

Another list of virtues, in this case 10 of them, offered by psychologist and educator Thomas Lickona in his book *Character Matters,* gives us a more contemporary view in service of learning and teaching our children character:[1]

Wisdom;	Positive attitude;
Justice;	Hard work;
Fortitude;	Integrity;
Self-control;	Gratitude;
Love;	Humility.

Wow, such a stunning list of juicy potent-feeling words. As you read them, go slow. Turn off and turn down the pace. Take a breath with each word and allow that word to land closer inside your body.

Where does each word live?
Where does humility, justice, gratitude live?
Where do these words show up most clearly, and what sensations do you notice?
What feelings emerge?
What thoughts emerge?
Do any emotions surface?

Take note in your tour as your body cocreates with you in this moment.

A final list of virtues, offered in the positive psychology field by Martin Seligman, director of the Penn Positive Psychology Center and Zellerbach Family Professor of Psychology at the University of Pennsylvania, and the late Christopher Peterson, former Arthur F. Thurnau Professor of Psychology and Organizational Studies at the University of Michigan, synthesizes the virtues down to six, relating to 24 character strengths:[2]

Wisdom and knowledge;
Courage;
Humanity;
Justice;
Temperance;
Transcendence.

Now bring money closer to the virtues through our Virtuous Flow of Somatic Finance. Let me offer a few morsels to chew, taste, and digest.

- Without humility, **greed** takes hold.
- Patience and courage create generous space to face **scarcity**.
- Diligence and wisdom build skillful energy to stay on the Möbius strip ride.
- **Sufficiency** mirrors equanimity.
- Kindness and humanity open us to the world of "we in **generosity**."

Enjoy the overlap in perspectives as we reflect on human virtues. My wonder reflection is, when we attend to what really matters on our money journey, of course our development of virtues will be a natural outgrowth of the process and practice. Attending to fear, the underbelly of money, releases the fear stuck in any of these blossoming virtues. Simply put, when we give attention to our money sore spots, we become better people. Our character flourishes. We relate to life from a higher ground. All of us prosper. How fascinating.

Let's revisit earlier words about practicing to embodiment found in the moves of "learning to knowing to embodiment." Virtues are a result of embodiment. Do you remember this?

> *Embodiment digests the previous four moves and the qualities of each move: innocence, interest, confidence, humility, and courage. Embodiment breaks your heart. Embodiment tickles subtle spaces.*
>
> *Embodiment is tense and thrilling. Embodiment is tender and fluid.*
>
> *Embodiment shivers and sizzles. Embodiment senses energies, feels feelings, opens to the nano-moments of existence. Embodiment meets each and every situation with eyes and heart and belly wide open—and nothing latches on—because ultimately, there is nothing to latch onto. Embodiment includes everything and everyone. But, again, don't take my words, these words, as truth. Experience for yourself what embodiment looks like and feels like—for you. When your body is welcomed in your existence with intention, invitation, recognition, and realization, your life will never be the same.*
>
> *Allow yourself to be young again as you engage in Somatic Finance practices.*
>
> *What does a beginner's mind and heart and belly mean for you?*

Embodiment means our natural expressions radiate confidence, humility, courage, wisdom—the virtues. Now, on your money journey, you may have clarity on the meaning. More relevant is, What does embodiment feel like to you?

Relating again to the statements presented earlier, I return to the ingredients to make this journey: humility, courage, openness, grace—these are the behaviors, views, and actions moving through the way of the Academic, the way of the Capitalist, the way of the Philanthropist. These come alive with bright energy to abide on the Virtuous Flow of Somatic Finance.

Let's examine closer what we are flowing on, the Möbius strip.

Möbius Strip

There is no "inside" and "outside" on the Möbius strip—the
two apparent sides keep co-creating each other.
—Parker J. Palmer[3]

Parker J. Palmer's book, *A Hidden Wholeness*, rocked my world
when I read it for the first time in 2004.[4] My favorite quotes toggle
with his Möbius strip metaphor daily, igniting my senses. A Möbius
strip is a surface with only one side and only one boundary. The
Möbius strip was discovered in 1858 by the German mathemati-
cians August Ferdinand Möbius and Johann Benedict Listing and
has the mathematical property of being unorientable. It can be created by taking a strip of paper and turning one side halfway and
connecting the ends.

Try making one. Right now. Take a flat sheet of paper and cut a
strip. At one end, turn the strip halfway. Holding both ends, tape the
ends together. Now enjoy the fun part. Trace your finger along the
side of the paper. As you trace the flat surface, you will discover that
there is only one side. The words of Parker J. Palmer come alive.

*"Whatever is inside us continually flows outward to help form, or
deform, the world—and whatever is outside us continually flows
inward to help form or deform our lives.*

*The Möbius strip is like life itself: here, ultimately, there is only
one reality."*
—Parker Palmer.

Palmer continues on the same page, "We all live on the Möbius
strip all the time: there is no place to hide. We are constantly engaged
in a seamless exchange between whatever is 'out there' and whatever is 'in here' co-creating reality, for better or worse."

The Möbius strip illustrates integration. Integration of the landscape, the practices, and the fruition means that each round on the
Virtuous Flow, in our yearning to be whole and embodied, understanding deepens, practices strengthen capacities, and our embodiment reflects virtues blossoming.

Money no longer lives out there. We are right here, full, enriched, capable—centered on truth—moving money as integrity.

Today, now, this moment, not tomorrow, money requires the wisdom of the soul, as Mr. Palmer expresses below. Wisdom of the soul is accessed only through the body. My body feels tight and urgent, as if there is no more time to waste. Have we ever had time to waste? Now my belly aches. It is churning with crud. My eyes sting as they rest on the screen, the cursor blinking.

Is there more to say? Or is the gateway fully open for you?

Joy and grief frequently mix into one, my state right now. My grief of humanity losing its way is held in a mantel of joy; we will make it, one person, one step, one turn on the Möbius strip at a time. I've fallen in love with you on this writing journey. The book is not complete, and I don't know the next step, yet I know you, feel you, and embrace you. Take my hand and let's do this together.

We can thrive amid the complexities of adulthood by deepening our awareness of the endless inner-outer exchanges that share us and our world and of the power we have to make choices about them.

If we are to do so, we need spaces within us and between us that welcome the wisdom of the soul—which knows how to negotiate life on the Möbius strip with agility and grace.

—Parker Palmer[5]

Notes

1. Source: Lickona, Thomas. (2004). *Character Matters: How to Help Our Children Develop Good Judgment, Integrity, and Other Essential Virtues.* New York: Atria. Fair use.

2. Source: Peterson, Christopher and Seligman, Martin. (2004). *Character Strengths and Virtues: A Handbook and Classification.* Washington, D.C. and United Kingdom: American Psychological Association/Oxford University Press. Fair use.

3. Source: Palmer, Parker J. (2004). *A Hidden Wholeness: The Journey Toward an Undivided Life.* New Jersey: John Wiley & Sons. Fair use.

4. Ibid.

5. Ibid.

Chapter 31
Grief, Loss, Betrayal

I don't know where to begin, so let me just start. No one wants to talk about loss, much less be in the depths of it. Yet loss is an integral part of our human condition, and all of our experiences hold some degree of loss, whether we recognize it or not.

Money loss is front and center. We all lose money. Loss of money is woven into life.

But perhaps we don't experience those losses until we grieve, really grieve.

In April of 2019 my father died at the age of 91. He was my first parent to die, and in the beautiful tender awful depths of grief, I wrote these words while feeling pressure that made it hard to breathe and a dense lethargy that made it hard to give my attention.

I loved my father. He was my daddy. Daddies and daughters have a special bond, and I feel grateful for my relationship with my father. I also had no idea how his passing would feel—plummeting into sorrow like I have never known.

Grief like this is a rite of passage into full adulthood. I never knew how much growing up remained in my being. Special little selves linger who emerge from space and take hold when our first parent dies and we are a grown adult. I am speaking of being 50 or older. For those who are in their 50s and your parents are alive: be aware of this special time in adult development. It is not a problem, but it may not be pretty.

Grief hits sideways like Thor's hammer. You know, the Marvel comic Avenger who saves the planet? Having just seen the *End Game* at the theater, the swinging hammer is vivid in my mind. So we are stunned with a wallop and whack, and remain ungrounded, maybe face planted in the dirt, legs sprawled, bruised, and bewildered.

Stay there and don't move. Allow the hurt to be and go with it. Tears and moisture open their gates and flow. They flow their healing caresses for as long as they need to move, and then they flow some more.

For many months prior to my father's death, I cried a loss that had yet to be delivered. I knew he was tired and his remaining days were numbered. Nevertheless, his transition came as a shock wave, and the experience tracked like a train following its route stopping at each station. A fall. A hospital stay. A return to home with hospice. A final breath. A meeting with the funeral home. A meeting with the pastor. Flowers arriving. A memorial. Thank-you notes. Papers and more papers. A meeting with the attorney.

The sealed spaces crack and the ooze seeps through. The hammer hits again and again with silent griefs that have waited patiently in the shadows to show their faces. Your only move is not to move. Pacing becomes your best practice, in every practice.

There are times when a wall hits midday, and my fatigue sends me right to bed. Less than normal nutritious foods slip through my gums. Rarely entered doors of McDonald's and Burger King coax up french fries and hash browns as necessary sustenance. Cocktails served during the week come more frequently. Ice cream has become dinner.

When we slow down in the midst of loss and pause diligently, gratitude takes its seat.

I have never felt such polarities—grief and gratitude—staring directly into each other's eyes and hearts connected with light, love, and eternal truth. One eye cries tears of loss and one eye cries tears of joy.

I am in the rich black velvet of darkness. I will be here as long as I am here. It's the midnight blue-black of the ocean where the whales abide holding all of our grief until it is ours to receive. Generous souls pulsing as their bellies skim the ocean floor. Our tears join the tears of all of those before us in the ocean of life.

You are going to die.

People you love are going to die.

The bodies we temporarily inhabit will become corpses.

Grief and loss open the doors for betrayal, real or imagined, to be seen and forgiveness to cure all ills.

Money loss is every person's destiny. It just is. Some of us lose a lot of money, and some of us lose a little. How fascinating to view money as something different than, say, a tree.

Do we view the falling tree as a loss? Or is a fallen tree hit by lightning simply an act of nature? Or what about red tide causing fish to wash up on the shore dead? Or termites rotting out the siding of a house?

The tighter we grip money as a permanent thing, the farther away we are from our humanity. I am not telling you that the money systems are not going to be what they are. I am saying they reflect what we have become. We are the ones the money world has been waiting for. We are the ones who have the view and force and capacity to change the view and change the world.

Grieving loss is where sustainable change begins and stability moving on the Virtuous Flow becomes possible.

We grieve for the losses our own hands have created.

We recognize our betrayals, and the betrayals of others are the same.

We allow forgiveness to pave the way forward, backward, and six directions.

Would looking at money loss serve you in finding that deeper current of grief?

Are money betrayals tinged with angst aching for forgiveness?

Let me say it again.

You are going to die.

People you love are going to die.

The bodies we temporarily inhabit will become corpses.

Grief and loss open the doors for betrayal, real or imagined, to be seen, felt, fully experienced.

Grief and loss open the roads of forgiveness to pave our way forward.

No surprise, my friends, there is no other way to grieve than through the body, with our body. Healing loss is a somatic practice. Is a loss waiting to be healed in your life, in your lineage?

Chapter 32

Sometimes We Need to Get Angry

Today I have experienced two wild rages of anger, and it's only 9:00 in the morning. The cyclones of fiery energy moved up my core from my open belly, through my chest into my throat, where the taste of metal lingers.

I've worked with a lot of people and their money. Thousands of people. And some of them, many of them, are terrified of their anger, especially when they feel it in their body.

If this includes you, I want you to know that your anger is potent. It is often a truth teller, when we ask what it wants to tell us. And it is necessary. Anger wants your attention. Anger wants to be heard. We live in a world where small and large terrible actions happen in the name of money. The worst moral and physical injustices are done with money as a motivation and an excuse.

In my morning's tumultuous energetic frenzy, I feel certain that anger is a necessary response to many money situations. We need our authentic response to the atrocities materializing in our culture. Pervasive greed that causes great harm is one area. Martin Shkreli immediately comes to mind—his case is currently being seen in the federal courts. For those who are not familiar with his name, he is the fellow who jacked up the price of a life-saving drug used by those who suffer from AIDS. Those afflicted with AIDS rely on this medicine to stay alive. What once cost $13.50 per pill was increased in price by 5,000% to $750 per pill. This CEO, having a monopoly on the drug owned by Turing Pharmaceuticals—meaning there is no other source for this medicine—has those in need by the proverbial short hairs. Sorry for being so crude.

The financial issue this dude faces is his "holy crap" loss in two risky highly leveraged mutual funds that left investors in the hole to the tune of $11 million between 2009 and 2014. To fund his losses in this risky venture, stupidity, and yes, greed, he socked it to the innocent people using the drug produced by the company he is the sole owner of.

To add fuel to the raging fire, he smugly sits and operates with an arrogant (bird-flipping posture) to the system because in his determination, and that of his legal counsel, his actions are well within the law. He is charged with securities fraud, wire fraud, and conspiracy for allegedly cheating investors and what prosecutors define as a Ponzi scheme. He argues that since he repaid all investors for their losses, it is not a Ponzi scheme. It doesn't matter in his view that the source of funds to repay his investors, you guessed it, came from the dollars reaped from his price jacking of life-saving medicine.

So, yes. I am angry. Anger fuels right action.

We need to pay attention to where money flows and from where it flows. We need to pay attention for ourselves and for those who are unable to pay attention—due to lack of capacity—mentally, physically, and emotionally.

Anger in service of the greater good, humanity, what is good, true, and beautiful, amplifies clarity, right action, wisdom, and compassion.

We are called to include money in our hearts.

We are called to attend to the hurts, spurts, and whatever remains in our somatic system, so our bright mind gains access to new ways money, capital, energy, vitality can generate space for all human-kind, plant-kind, animal-kind—all beings who abide here, now.

Financial gain, solely for the purpose of greed—meaning not attending to the greater good—should never be at the expense of life.

Money serves life, not the other way around. Life does not serve money.

Take a moment to pause. Mr. Shkreli's situation is obvious. How many other situations are running rampant that we consider "normal"?

What about cattle, chickens, fish—sources of our sustenance—they are herded, bred, confined, and slaughtered so that we are fed and companies run at profits.

How many believe the high road and sanity looks like a well-dressed professional in a three-piece suit calmly drinking a latte. I'm overriding that movie screen to reveal reality. Sanity honors anger that fuels life, all life. When you get angry about money, stay with it. There is a jewel to discover, a gift to offer, a change to nourish. Do not bypass the opportunity to learn from your wisdom energy.

Part IIC

A New World

Chapter 33

Consumption, Generosity, and Generativity

In the fruition section, we might expect a few conclusions and definitive answers about outcomes. Specifically, you might ask: if I understand the landscape section, and if I engage the somatic practices offered in the Somatic Finance Practice Guidebooks, then what can I expect for my efforts? Surely the results of my labor will be clearly outlined here.

Yes and no.

I have absolutely no idea what specifically will happen for **you** if you understand Somatic Finance and you engage in the practices. I know my genuine motivation for writing this book. I know the experiences of many who have studied Somatic Finance principles with me and somatically practiced to improve their relationship with money.

Somatic Finance is not a path to a specific result. It is a ginormous invitation to develop and to integrate growth using the wisdom of a precious untapped resource (our body) and the challenges of money in the process.

For most who understand these principles and engage in these practices, there are three key openings that nourish their wealthy life, well-being, fulfillment, and happiness.

- Every situation, including money, seems workable. Instead of being contained in fear, doubt, and confusion, there is at least a crack to follow for the situation to change and improve. The way of the **Academic** finds integration and balance with the heart and belly.
- Relationships, beyond money, develop and evolve. I believe it is Ram Dass who said, we remain in a relationship for a reason, a season, or a lifetime. Relationships, like our life, are not static but continue to grow as we do. Being connected without filters purely and wholeheartedly is love expanding. The way of the **Philanthropist** finds integration and balance with the head and the belly.
- Creativity, our unique genius asset, blossoms in new directions. Our driving life force to offer our gifts and be acknowledged for those gifts expands joy, for everyone. The way of the **Capitalist** finds integration and balance with the head and the heart.

As you read these next few paragraphs about consumption, generosity, and generativity, take a breath and hold your biggest view. The writing here takes us well into the "we space" of life.

I trust that you are growing and able to connect to your body.

I trust that you have made strides and progress and you feel sufficient, at least sometimes.

I trust that your aha moments have turned into powerful shifts and new beneficial behaviors.

I trust you are an adult—seeking peers to collaborate with for a better world.

I trust how this book has come to form and that you are benefitting from engaging.

I trust so much more than I did and less than I will tomorrow.

Consumption

As I wrote this book, I discovered another contemporary book about human behavior and the economy, this one called *The Once and Future Worker* by Oren Cass.[1] My continued concern about all such books and teachings delivered about human behavior—even by the smartest, highest IQ, PhDs from our Ivy League schools—is a simple missing link.

We ***think*** pleasure, well-being, and happiness is achieved through an external goodie. Policies, rules, structures, organizations are woven around a restricting idea that if I get this, or if this happens, I will feel better.

Well-being, happiness, and pleasure is *only* known—where?—in our body.

Years ago I was on a webinar offered by a now defunct Integral-affiliated organization. The hosts of the conversation asked a cosmic question about why the spirits/gods/unseen beings would choose to reincarnate to human form. The conversation went on for a while with many esoteric, interesting, mind-stretching answers. My heart tugged. My mind went, huh? The question seemed very stupid to me. And I was far too shy, scared, and insecure to say a word. But these were my thoughts. We reincarnate into this physical form so we can actually feel the glorious pleasures of this precious human form, in our body. Gods, spirits, and other realms do not have visceral feelings in a dense gross form. At least, this seems most true to me. I do not know for sure. I do not have memories of being a light-being, but I do know what my body feels like right now and where the feels are located. I do know how sadness, anger, fear, joy, and sexual energies feel in my body. I know I am lucky to have a body to experience all of these feelings that allow me to connect intimately to life and to all of humanity.

Back to consumption. Oh, how I digress.

Our evolution has taken many ideas about what gives our life meaning and created a path that continues to narrow for the benefit of fewer and fewer people. The book I mentioned above describes how our society has placed values on the following: type of education, efficiency, more of everything, and cognitive intelligence.

Our metrics for growth, good (what are we measuring?), I can't even locate a word, are devoted to consumption, with the belief that if we consume more, we are better off. Some are better off. But those who are left out of societal evolution are scared, angry, and sad. They do not belong anymore, and they are suffering.

In a *New York Times* article, author Oren Cass highlights the fact that our higher education system directly serves only 20% of American students. The remaining 80%: (1) do not graduate from high school, (2) just graduate from high school, (3) drop out of college, or (4) finish college with a degree that is not used in their work.[2]

The jobs that would have been energized by those "different skilled" who did not go to college or dropped out no longer appear in the United States. Efficiency and profit is prioritized over the heart and human. Our beliefs about what is valuable support more consumption and produce a direct hit to the dignity, connection, and safety all of us require to live. Let's continue. We are not finished.

For those utilizing welfare to survive, not only is the message what you have to offer is of no value, but the theme of life is, consume more and you will feel better. Both of these are false.

The article highlights a brilliant question from Oren Cass:

What if people's ability to produce matters more than how much they can consume?

Bingo. We have a winner. I can cry. Yes, tears are pooling.

All of us want the chance to offer what we can—from our own well of creativity, our unique capital. All we want is the chance to share what we have to share for connection. All we want is a pure connection that feels so good to be alive. This is the Capitalist I am talking about. Safe, connected, and dignified with our ability to be in this world, of this world, and valued is all we seek.

Since our focus has been on the value work brings rather than the value of all human capital, divisive rules, policies, and actions sustain suffering. When we tie money to a job (efficiency and growth) rather than the whole human experience, we all fail.

Though I write about education, simply replace the word "education" with health care, insurance, infrastructure, social security—choose your issue—and you have the same condition. We have replicated this pattern in every aspect of our modern world.

Demanding creativity over consumption directs our attention in a new way.

We must get familiar with sufficiency.

We must practice sufficiency.

We must embody sufficiency.

Generosity

We might believe that the pinnacle of Somatic Finance is generosity. It is not. Generosity develops and expands once we embody sufficient sufficiency. ☺ ha ha ha (This is for me and other perfectionists who believe they can never feel scarcity; there may be many moments of feeling scarcity—even when sufficiency is embodied.)

We hone our strength in generosity just like with all muscles, with practice. This is the practice of abiding on the Virtuous Flow. I continue to practice here.

How do I experience the Virtuous Flow when I am abiding? Here are a few ways my life is changing and I am growing.

My self-worth is activated and my spine is ignited with dignity. I recognize the unique gifts only I can bring to the world to be of service and benefit. With this realization, my moral line blazes with devotion. Whatever "is in me" is not just for me, it is for you too. These gifts are not gifts unless they are shared. I enjoy expressing the value I have to bring to the world for the benefit of all of us. I matter. You matter. Every being matters.

Be careful reading these words. They are not *just words*. I feel different in my body. My spine is alive and fiercely saying, "Don't fool yourself with concepts of dignity." If we struggle a smidgeon to value any other human and the rights of all humans—just by being here—our struggle reflects something in us that we do not value. Compassion is our clothing.

My appreciation and joy fuels my heart, as connection is found and experienced in every moment, right now, even this moment you are reading. More and more I trust in my connection to life. My heart sweetens with each breath of this truth. My longing to belong and feel wanted and be seen gives way to a deeper truth that we are always connected. And yet, as I write I still struggle with a few young voices inside me worried that I will not be liked or have friendships. Being accused of a position too far in front of the parade, for someone who loves to play and cocreate, being alone is bone crushing. I trust I am not alone, and I have never been alone.

These too, are not just nice words. My heart is right here pulsing, nodding, prodding with a nudge and a curious question. Gayle, what takes you away from this heart knowing? I offer the same question to you, when you know by heart our inseparable connection, what takes you away?

My ability to recognize fear, release fear, play with fear, and even enjoy fear is a new superpower. My belly rocks and swells and jiggles. I feel safe through the power of my belly and my embodied knowing that I am okay. Our basic fundamental truth is okay-ness. Pure liberation—the continuous current of okay-ness. Loss, in all forms, and particularly money, and the recovery from that loss builds resilience. Resilience teaches us, in each situation, that we are okay. We are still here. How awesome is that?

The simplicity of this truth can easily be lost. Again, the words do not matter. My belly sounds the trumpet, and this tone ripples to every cell of my body. Undeniable.

As these three nutrients feed me, the accumulation and maintenance of material goods is less and less fascinating and more and more taxing. My interest in life abides inside the envelope of my skin. Beauty, space, joy, and wonder look very different today than they did 5, 10, and 20 years ago.

I come from a family of collectors and appreciators of chattel as you know. Nice things became substitutes for safety, connection, and dignity. Today I practice loving all of my experiences without blame. Today I practice kindness and compassion, while feeling the truth of my existence, and without judgment, most of the time. We are all in this together, taking our own steps forward, whatever that may look like for each of us.

Gratitude for all of my good fortune allows me to appreciate where I came from and my responsibilities to this world, not from a place of guilt or the lens of superiority, but seeing clearly lens free.

Abiding on the Virtuous Flow is the muscle that opens our ability to engage generativity.

Generativity

Reading Parker J. Palmer's book *On the Brink of Everything*, I recalled incorrectly the use of the word generativity.[3] In my search to find the word in his writing and the story that demonstrates generativity, I found only the story. It was a weird moment but also, maybe serendipitous. Perhaps we have too few experiences of generativity to read about. Perhaps this is the crack for us to break generativity wide open as a common way of being together. Per Google, generativity is the propensity and willingness to engage in acts that promote the well-being of younger generations as a way of ensuring the long-term survival of the species.

"Generative" is a word that means productive capability. Missing from generative is the motivation. Too much is produced with strong capability sans the heart. And this is the difference in generativity and generative. I believe generativity moves through generosity.

The example of generativity from Palmer's book was his intergenerational mentoring stories through the years—first as a younger man with insightful mentors and then as a growing elder becoming the mentor. In his experience he described the space of cocreation and sharing of wisdom among generations that brought the best of each front and center.

Parker instructs the subtle and not so subtle ways that generativity emerges.

Together we generate energy for personal and societal change that an age segregated society cuts off.

We, young and old, hold the future in our hands. If our common life is to become compassionate, creative and just, it will take an intergenerational effort.

—Palmer, 42

He's suggesting we change the metaphor from passing the baton to young adults to inviting young adults to join the orchestra. (As a reflective practice, substitute "young and old" and "an intergenerational" for male and female/a co-creative, or black bodied and white bodied/a co-creative or domestic and global/international.)

Together we can compose something lovelier and more alive than the current cacophony.

Age and experience have taught me that mentoring is not a one-way street.

It's a mutuality in which two people evoke the potentials in each other.

To borrow a phrase from theologian Nelle Morton, mentoring is about "hearing one another to speech." Equally important mentoring gives us a chance to welcome one another into a relationship that honors our vulnerability and our need for each other.

Mentoring is a gift exchange in which we elders receive as least as much as we give, often more.

—Palmer, 45

When I read Parker J. Palmer's words and feel the experience of generativity, generating good together, my heart swells in music, then she waltzes, and then she takes a long powerful bow. Money generativity is spiraling the focus of our actions with money for all generations and all people. A new emphasis emerges, generativity—generative, generous, and activity—combined.

Money generativity is generational societies flowing on the Virtuous Flow of Somatic Finance. Wow, I had no idea where generativity was going. You see, as we individually embody Somatic

Finance, Somatic Finance embodies us. How secure, connected, and dignified is that?

Consumption is dying. The lies about consumption are revealed each day as we reach an end. Our body tells us we cannot consume any more. Our earth is sounding the extinction of life. This death is paving the road for sufficiency to grace our steps. Generosity takes our hand as we walk together in generativity building a world of generativity. And the music plays.

Notes

1. Source: Cass, Oren. (2018). *The Once and Future Worker: A Vision for the Renewal of Work in America*. New York: Encounter Books. Fair use.

2. Source: Cass, Oren. (2018, December 10). "The Misguided Priorities of Our Educational System." *New York Times*. Fair use.

3. Source: Palmer, Parker J. (2018). *On the Brink of Everything: Grace, Gravity, and Getting Old*. Oakland, CA: Berrett-Koehler Publishers. Fair use.

Chapter 34
Justice and Equity

In these final chapters, you have sufficient knowledge from the landscape and sufficient direct experience with somatic intelligence through your practice to read and receive these points of impact differently, more skilled, and more awake.

Here goes. Fasten your seat belts.

Justice

Money can never provide justice. Name an issue that has reached our legal system and moved through the courts providing a monetary settlement. Money puts a Band-Aid or stitch on a deep wound. Deep wounds are healed from the inside. Deep wounds ache for our heart and belly to unite with the spine of dignity and move to the site of pain. Pulsing bleeding screaming dying injuries can only be met by the salve of the heart and the balm of the belly and the strength of the spine.

A few years ago the courts and media reports gave voice to the aftermath of the Harvey Weinstein scandals. At one point during the #MeToo tsunami explosion, a company offered to purchase Weinstein's company—salvage it—with $90 million of the purchase price to be set aside for the victims. But in the freefall of the explosion, the purchasing company realized there were no assets to be bought. Everything of value was dissolving. Twelve months later the victims aimed to receive justice; the company liability insurance policy for $44 million dictates the amount of justice they would receive. Easy math says $44 million divided by all of the victims equals their monetary justice. But that's not how justice plays out. The board of directors was found innocent of Harvey Weinstein's abuse. The insurance payout was also used for their benefit to pay their legal fees. This is how liability insurance works. It is the reason companies purchase liability insurance, to handle lawsuits.

Stay with me as we look at the reality of monetary justice. Fine brilliant legal minds hold a tight narrow scope on their work in the world. They armor their sight to see only the needs and benefit of their client, even if their client is guilty. This is the beauty and beast of our legal system where every person receives a fair trial and every person is presumed innocent and lawyers work for their client. The $44 million quickly dropped for the benefit of the victims. The attorneys were paid first. Next came the officers and directors of the company who bought the insurance as their protection. Even some creditors were paid too. After the people who the policy prioritizes received theirs, the victims received something. A bankruptcy hearing by a bankruptcy attorney determined the division of the insurance proceeds by looking at the insurance contract terms, the rules, and the measurements of the bankruptcy system.

I do not know the settlement figure the victims received for their pain and suffering, and the number doesn't matter. Justice for their experience can never be healed by money. But they wanted and expected money to do just that, make them feel better and be justified for the pain inflicted on them. In their mind, nothing less than the $90 million will do. The 90-million-dollar illusion sticks in their head from an initial purchase offer that did not materialize. Attorneys might have kept them stuck saying they deserved that higher number. All the while, attorneys earn more fees and the systems play with bright legal minds armored, doing their job. In the end, the victims received something, and the attorney bills were paid.

I know. I am thinking the same thing. This is the best we can do?

The Weinstein case is not the point. It is one of a zillion examples where our mind goes sideways with money and justice. Your perspective and my perspective on abusive behavior in the #MeToo movement and other abuses are not on evaluation here. (But if you are reading, I am sure we both feel nausea in our belly at the mere thought of Weinstein, Crosby, O'Reilly, Brokaw, Lauer, Wynn, the list grows. This is a small handful of names—sorry, just had to go there.)

Money can never be justice to any situation.

We want it to be and it never can be.

Justice, and the longing we crave, resides inside our precious body.

I am not suggesting we eliminate our legal systems. We require a practice of justice. (Please improve the systems.) I am suggesting that we include our body intelligence when we seek justice. If you are employed in the justice systems of our country, if you have control over the policies created to provide justice, if you are given the power by others to sustain the dignity of humans, wake up and honor your client, humanity, all beings. Please do your job. Recognize that no amount of money, large or small, will truly attend to the injury endured by your client, people, and all beings. Make money work better and do more.

Consider how somatic wisdom can be integrated into your field of work.

Money is a Band-Aid or stitch. Period. Do your job.

Equity

Morality has a thread of money righteousness. Pull that thread. Money inequality is just like beauty inequality, athletic inequality, intellect inequality. The rabbit hole will take us on a long, dark, unsatisfying ride.

Disparity with money is our world. How we choose to view that disparity and act are ours to energize.

Stand still.

Look around.

There is always someone who has more and someone who has less.

Comparisons are interesting. Where do they take you?

Ask, how is this comparison helping or hurting?

Where does my mind go when I compare?

What happens in my heart when I compare?

How does my belly respond when I compare?

Here is my spontaneous play. You are invited too.

Bill and Melinda Gates are my object of comparison.

When I compare my money situation to Bill and Melinda Gates (prior to their divorce), I judge their uber wealth and hold high expectations of their actions. I judge their declarations regarding a percentage of wealth they will leave to their children. I judge them to be very intelligent and very lucky to have amassed their wealth. I judge them to be evolutionary and holding a worldview with many perspectives. This is where my mind goes. It judges. That is the job of the mind—to discern. Judging is judging. Sometimes we catch ourselves thinking that judging is right or wrong, good or bad.

When my heart awareness compares my money situation to Bill and Melinda Gates, I notice softening and warmth in my chest. A tender feeling arises with grace. How are we similar? We are. We both give our talent, treasures, and time. No metric of how much is present, except for recognizing this is so. Our hearts beat the same. Our breath expands and contracts. Our way of heart connecting is the same expression. All hearts beat as one and money allows us to drum a sustainable rhythm.

When my belly awareness compares my money situation to Bill and Melinda Gates's, I notice my spine elongating and energy surging in my core, my dan tien (energy center). Solidarity and strength pop. A field of "we can" and "we must" do what is asked of us with what is ours to do. Again, no measurement presides in a comparison of more or less, better or better than. I feel empowered regardless of the Gateses. I feel capable and dignified. I feel whole, blessed, liberated to engage life with conduct fitting for humanity. All bellies sufficiently fed are capable. What do we wait for? What are we comparing?

Try this reflection. Your discoveries might surprise you. I am surprised—funny how practice does that, surprises and delights—by what arose for each query. I allowed my judgments to be just as they were. My heart immediately connected us and all. My belly energized my torso with passion.

Let's try another experiment.

A person with a cardboard sign is standing on the corner of an intersection wearing dirty torn clothes, missing teeth, disheveled hair, and abandoned shoelaces. He is homeless and nameless.

When I compare my money situation to him, my thoughts scramble and pop—feelings of shame followed by thoughts, wow, I feel shame. Feelings of sadness arise and my attention moves to my heart. I wonder how he smells. When did he bathe last? As my heart holds part of my attention (almost saying skip the mental comparison and come to me!), I return to thoughts in question form, who is he, how did he get here, did he serve our country in war, what does his sign say? I want to know more about who he is and his situation. I want to connect with his story. And then I query about money and the judgment of giving money will enable him to buy drugs or alcohol. Am I willing to let him choose? Do I have any food or liquid to offer?

When my heart awareness gets her way, it is almost as if she says, stay here. There is no need to compare in thought. Just hang here and feel connected. Truth emerging from this space is pure. I am reminded of an article written about unhoused people and their most significant suffering is not their lack of material goods on their body, or the lack of food in their belly, but the lack of connection with others. Most often they miss eye contact, hellos, a pleasant query or acknowledgment of being a person. My heart says allow yourself to open, open further. Feel the tender tears of separation. Money may or may not be a part of this scene. My story may include money, but who knows. Maybe this man comes from a family loaded with money and he has simply slipped away, unknown, unfound, unconventional by most standards.

When my belly awareness arises, I notice dignity and my jaw activates electric sensations. My brow line creases. Staying present I notice my jaw, throat, and belly begin to talk. I feel queasy in my belly. (Is it the green smoothie I just made?) My shoulders fall forward and my torso is hunched. Sounds peep from my belly, as I think, this is weird. I said it was an experiment. With my eyes shut, this happens.

It is like my belly wants to merge with my jaw. I have a rising glob from my belly reaching to my throat. I am typing with my eyes shut. Bringing this homeless man to mind and feeling my belly energy. My jaw is a place of anger. Determination, justice, I have more questions than answers and now resting into the okay-ness of being with questions and queasy.

Eyes open once again. That was weird. My arms and hands are stinging with energy too. Again, if you dare, try this experiment with someone who has less monetary wealth than you. See what you discover.

Money disparity is our current human condition. Our wealth exists in the middle. The questions are not where in the middle are we located and what does that mean. The question is, can we let go of the need to compare and let come the inspiration of our integrated Head, Heart, and Belly with a commitment to justice, love, and sufficiency for all?

Justice.

Equity.

A few morsels for your afternoon stroll.

Chapter 35

Generosity: Our Essential Survival Skill

Generosity is not just a nice idea. Generosity is not just a sweet gesture. Generosity isn't just making monetary donations to the World Wildlife Fund, or giving used clothing to Goodwill, or teaching a young underprivileged child how to read. With no disrespect to these altruistic moves, generosity holds a truth and depth far more complex and far more essential to our survival. Indeed, I believe generosity is the essential way of our being that enabled our species of humans to survive through the history of our evolution when many others became extinct.

Let me unpack these ideas.

It was through acts of generosity by Homo sapiens with unrelated Homo sapiens that allowed our species to not only survive but to thrive. All other hominins (humanlike species) died out. Putting on my full disclosure hat, I am not an expert in anthropology, but the research in this area by those who are points to something perfectly stunning and bears merit in embodied generosity.

Not only does being generous make us feel good, it may be the crux of our future survival. Does that get your attention?

Brian Stewart, PhD, assistant professor of anthropology at the University of Michigan, has authored several studies and papers on ecological plasticity.[1] His deep research and findings boil down to generosity. He said until quite recently, we still shared the planet with other humans. While there are similarities in evolutionary patterns and topics that follow, it boils down to an innate ability to see, feel, connect through the heart with another being—generosity in motion—that enables our species to **be here now**. (Another nod to Ram Dass.)

The human ways of being described in the studies are explicit and recognizable in modern-day cognition. The ability to innovate and adapt to diverse climates, habitats, and environments, while coming together in community when in difficult situations, makes sound sense. There is no confusion that innovation and adaptation is a part of the survival of the fittest. Necessary during periods of adaptation billions of years ago was also the ability for humans to gather together. Gathering together allowed for the sharing of information across cultural groups, who used art—a critical part of identity—to help bring different groups together and survive.

> *Homo sapiens may have been able to develop this particular ability by cooperating with other Homo sapiens to whom they weren't related, Stewart says. These non-kin groups would have shared food, communicated over long distances, and had ritual relationships that allowed populations to adapt to local environments quickly.*
>
> *Having a vast trove of cultural information available to do things like make clothing, build shelters, find a spouse—all of the things you need for life beyond simply the diet—was critical for survival of groups in new regions. What was remarkable is how successful we became in so many different habitats as early as we did.[2]*

Through his research in ecological plasticity, Stewart began to answer the question, Why did we manage to survive when all of our closest relatives have died out?

Symbols also helped organize social and economic affairs with one another. Language began through symbols passed down through generations. We were sharing information across social groups from different areas rather than retaining knowledge for ourselves. The sharing of information enabled new solutions to a variety of problems.

Often the size of our brain compared to other hominin species is given credit for our survival. But while the size of our brains may have played a part in our success, it is not the whole story.

It is suggested that our hyper-social cooperative brain is what set us apart. Our distinct social element ignited our creative expression through the use of symbols and art. Isn't this fascinating?

Missing from the research, as much as I can discern, is the understanding our brain develops with the rest of our body, including our heart. Our heart is the seat of connection—the place we recognize another being. Our belly is the source of creation—the place we ignite purposeful innovations. Our brain works with all of the "parts."

Studying evolution and why we are here and other hominids are not, generosity is the crux of our existence. Acts of generosity— social connections with language and symbols and creativity— enabled our survival.

If I have something you need to survive, and you have something I need to survive, unless we enter into *we space* and share— through acts of generosity—we both die. If my culture has something your culture needs to survive, and your culture has something our culture needs to survive, unless we enter into *cultural we space* and share—through acts of generosity—we all die.

Fast-forward 100,000 years.

How is generosity engaged in our modern world today?

Are we practicing generosity that enables our species survival?

Or are we headed toward a slow unconscious greedy extinction?

As these questions penetrate your awareness, your heart, and your belly, take a deep breath. I am somber with you in these queries.

Please note the similarities of the evolutionary story. Money is a predominant symbol in our modern culture. In our moments of reflection, let's wonder about today's symbols of money. Power? Wealth? Security?

What is our use of money? Really?

Abiding on the Virtuous Flow of Somatic Finance, embodying sufficiency and generosity as life weaves in motion—is not just a nice idea. Abiding here may be the future of our survival as human beings, on this planet, right now.

What could be a more apropos ending?

Notes

1. Source: Brian Stewart. https://sites.lsa.umich.edu/brianstewart/publications. Fair use.
2. Source: Brian Stewart. https://news.umich.edu/homo-sapiens-the-global-general-specialist. Fair use.

Chapter 36

The Fruition of the Virtuous Flow

We are here for others. Money is here for all of us.

These words came to me during a period of contemplation about Somatic Finance and thinking about abiding on the Virtuous Flow. I wrote them on a piece of paper. They were rewritten in my notebook of ideas to source inspiration. I source inspiration for you. I am here for you. You are here for you, me, and others who might benefit from the knowledge, understanding, and energy gained from reading, understanding, practicing, and embodying the experience of Somatic Finance.

Money is here for collective human immersion and all life affected by human activity.

Resting in feminine space of curiosity, viewing the Atlantic Ocean and the sparkling bright sun reflecting and dancing on top of the water, I feel fatigue, bewilderment, humor, disbelief—my montage of feelings is complex. Are we aware how much time is invested in money? Of course there is the actual daily (hourly) application of money. Add to that the money mind-state. We invest our energy not only in practical money applications, but we invest our energy— perhaps constantly. Maybe the better question is, When are we *not* thinking about money?

What an interesting question. It is not an original question, but the context here feels fresh.

My answers arise—when I am making love, birthing a baby, devouring a good read, savoring a new flavor, laughing with belly aches, snuggling with my furry felines, gazing into the eyes of friends, practicing with awareness, engaging genius activities, the joys of these experiences are priceless.

Money, as we have discussed, is not a problem. The grip of money causes suffering.

Suffering arises when we fall out of flow and touch scarcity.

My next question, What keeps us flowing on the Virtuous Flow?
Commitment;
Re-commitment;
Choice;
Practice;
Love;
Integrity;
Conduct.

Some of the ingredients—the virtues—presented and explored and practiced. As we near the end of this book, pause for a moment.
What do you recall?
What does your body offer?
Where do energies tingle?
How has your *why* been energized?
Are we clear that we are here for others, and money is here for all of us?
Has that truth been explicit?
I pause again, breathing, abiding in my body with tender grace searching for words and an answer. My fuzziness reflects doubt where trust wants to burst forth.

Money being here for all of us means the promise and potential of abiding on the Virtuous Flow, feeling sufficient and acting with generosity, connects us in ways that we have yet to consistently experience or perhaps even imagine. Maybe this is my doubt.

Have I said enough? (See, even I use the word.)

What else is there to say?

Do you feel my presence and care?

As the tears pool in my eyes, flowing grief and joy for human-ity, popping thoughts of crazy, followed by this is shitty writing, all I long for is resting right here with words and sentences that have been spilling on the page for many years.

May you embody the joy of being here.

May you embody joy for others.

May money continue to flow for all of us.

Chapter 36a
My Last Love Letter to You

We've traveled a wide and deep journey together. My hope is that you have gained what you desired and then some. My hope is that you were surprised, jolted, confused, provoked, scared, overwhelmed, encouraged, fully met, energized, and with each experience you softened to a new expanded space into more of who you really are, while making your money journey an integral part of your life: alive, rich, raw, real, tasty, and satisfying. Notice I did not say safe, calm, secure, managed, in control?

My hope is that money is much less of a mystery and much more humanity.

My hope is that you activated money practices and built new muscles.

My hope is that you open, open further and dive, dive deeper.

My hope is that your realizations optimize for the benefit of others.

My hope is that you are madly in love with your body if you weren't before.

My hope is that your body receives daily appreciation with nourishing food, movement, and meditation.

My hope is that you relate to money and all matters of life from your whole presence—honoring your knowledge, receiving your body wisdom, and offering through the infinite space of love, your heart.

My hope, in one simple phrase, is that you feel peace, joy, love—always.

If just one of the above hopes is manifest for you, that's sufficient. ;)

Oceans of love, my friend,

Gayle

About the Website

Thank you. Thank you. Thank you. You are the best! ☺

Thank you for purchasing and reading *The Body of Money*.

My appreciation is boundless and joyful! And we are just beginning. For you, there are bonus resources, goodies, extra offerings to continue creating sustainable wealth.

Please choose to practice all that you learned by accessing the following additional complementary resources provided for your engagement, development, pleasure, and amusement.

Visit: www.wiley.com/go/colman/thebodyofmoney. Following this link you will access four Practice Guidebooks filled with meaningful resources to learn, practice and grow. Don't miss this important part of your money journey.

Somatic Finance® Practice Instructions Guidebook: a guidebook outlining the structure of the practices and suggested support for your practice engagement.

Somatic Finance® Foundation Practices Guidebook: a guidebook to engage foundation practices as a first step to building a deeper relationship with your body and your body centers. Your way of the Academic, the Philanthropist, and the Capitalist want to be seen, met, and acknowledged somatically. Best option for engagement is to print as a companion practice journal.

Somatic Finance® Focus Practices Guidebook: a guidebook to engage focus practices that shine a light on a specific issue or potential you want to explore, learn, and make progress. Focus practices clarify limiting money beliefs, appreciate them with kind attention, and build new moves and muscles with money. Best option for engagement is to print as a companion practice journal.

Somatic Finance® Integration Practices Guidebook: a guidebook to develop your money mastery and human potential. Integration practices deepen understanding and move toward embodiment—optimizing safety, connection, and dignity and somatically integrating your body centers. Best option for engagement is to print as a companion practice journal.

Acknowledgments

Thank you. Thank you. Thank you. May these words carry the prayer of gratitude I feel for you, the reader, and for all of the people and communities that gave expertise, attention, and wisdom to this work. *The Body of Money* would not be here without you.

I begin with the hundreds of folks I encountered in myriad communities over the last 30 years who touched my heart and soul. I have no doubt our meeting ignited seeds within me laying patiently for Somatic Finance to emerge. Early in my career, The Financial Planning Association, the National Association of Personal Financial Advisors, the CFP Board provided a foundation to build and follow a worthy calling. Bridging the art and heart of our work with the science, I discovered Nazrudin, Integral Theory and Integral Coaching of Canada, Inc., which led to deep-rooted connections with lifelong friends giving and receiving in smaller pods—The Pioneers, The Bitches of Death, various cohorts in play and welcoming the unknown, devoted to human potential and a better world.

Choosing to go only as far with my clients as I go with myself charged my life with a deeper understanding and purpose and the spiritual communities of Dharma Ocean and Pointing Out the Great Way. A deep bow to all of my teachers, sangha sisters and brothers of these traditions—in community we woke up to this precious human birth. To all of my playmates in the Hendricks Institute, a ginormous guffaw laugh, bear hug, and dance to the moon. To the exceptional integrally trained coaches of Integral Coaching of Canada, Inc., my gratitude to walk beside you is immeasurable.

To all of the fearless writers and leaders of the Gateless Writing Community, I swoon with blessings to be with you on and off the page, as vital contributions to create a more just, equitable world live as a touchstone to our work.

To my professional family at Colman Knight, today and since inception, thank you for trusting my vision for better financial planning and opening your heart to deeper truths in our client connections as we grow expertise, competence, and systems in the field of finance. My appreciation for you is boundless.

To the team at Wiley Publishing, thank you for our collaboration, abiding in integrity to do our part in service of this production. In particular, I nod to Kevin Harreld, who saw the merit of my proposal and took it forward.

Certain people earn a dose of specific praise. Thank you, Suzanne Kingsbury, for acknowledging the imperative of my writing your first reading and insisting I stop the letters to get these teachings on the page. Thank you, Becky Karush, for your Gateless attention to details, editing, form, and function and holding generous loving kind-hearted space. Thank you, Stephanie Becker, your infectious energy, along with your wicked brilliant way of the Academic, popped relief and joy in my veins. I'm so happy we giggled wildly playing tennis in our teens. Thank you, Scott Merriam, for being a co-creator from the beginning with generous presence and talent.

And, to my beloved, Rich, thank you for loving and appreciating all of me, enabling my wholeness and my genius to flourish. You are my champion, and wise confidante and none of this would happen without you.

About the Author

Gayle Colman has worked over 35 years as an entrepreneur, financial planner, writer, and coach; her work has been guided by one underlying principle: money is intimately woven into the fabric of our full human experience.

Gayle's career as a financial planner started with a desire to help all people make wise financial decisions. But when she joined the corporate world, she soon realized our humanity was missing. In 1988, Gayle cofounded Colman Knight Advisory Group, LLC, to create a more holistic approach to wealth management, recognizing the complex ways money touches our inner and outer lives.

In the early 1990s, her interest in the psychology of money—the *why* behind our financial choices—led her to the few books on the subject and the Hendricks Institute, where she received in-depth training in body intelligence and interpersonal development to become a Certified Conscious Relationship Coach. Through her study and practice of somatic meditation within the Indo-Tibetan Buddhism tradition, Gayle realized our body wisdom is essential to eliminate embedded money fears and skillfully navigate personal finance. Studying and training in integral theory unified her views and these disciplines. Determined to soften the serious nature of money, Gayle created MoneyMoves® Online Game for friendly money exploration.

Drawing on this work and her experience as a Certified Financial Planner®, a Master Integral Coach®, and a Certified Teacher in Gateless methodology, Gayle developed Somatic Finance® to unite the worlds of money, spirit, and body—empowering people to cultivate the inner truth of sufficiency needed for us to create a better, sustainable world.

Gayle has witnessed powerful results in her own life and with clients and feels the imperative to share as a contribution toward a brighter future. Regardless of money history or current stories, her life's work offers an entirely new way of relating with money and experiencing true wealth. A dedicated practitioner, Gayle relishes her lifelong marriage to Rich and watching her adult children blossom.

Index